FROM AUGUSTUS TO NE

This book presents a narrative of the reigns of the Julio-Claudian emperors, namely Augustus to Nero, with passages in original Latin from Tacitus, Suetonius and Seneca. Their works portray a dark world of murder and debauchery: Augustus with his firm moral policies and adulterous affairs; the depraved Tiberius; the extravagance and madness of Caligula; the ineffective Claudius; and Nero, with his artistic pretensions. The selections are invaluable on an artistic and cultural level, promoting the study of style and rhetoric and exploring human nature, the roles of women and imperialism. This book is essential reading for those students who, having completed an introductory Latin course, are ready to tackle genuine, unsimplified Latin prose. With a comprehensive introduction, detailed notes and an appreciation of each writer which addresses questions of context, analysis and literary criticism, this book will enhance students' understanding and enjoyment of Latin prose.

GARRETT G. FAGAN is Associate Professor of Classics and Ancient Mediterranean Studies and History, Penn State University. He is the author of *Bathing in the Roman World* (1999) and has also written a wide range of articles on the Roman world and pseudo-archaeology.

PAUL MURGATROYD is Professor of Classics at McMaster University. His publications include *The Amatory Elegies of Johannes Secundus* (2000) and *Mythical And Legendary Narrative In Ovid's Fasti* (2005), as well as commentaries on Tibullus and a selection from Ovid's *Ars Amatoria* suitable for undergraduates. He is also a published Latin poet with numerous translations into, and free compositions in, Latin verse.

FROM AUGUSTUS TO NERO

An Intermediate Latin Reader

~

GARRETT G. FAGAN
PAUL MURGATROYD

CAMBRIDGE UNIVERSITY PRESS
Cambridge, New York, Melbourne, Madrid, Cape Town, Singapore,
São Paulo, Delhi, Dubai, Tokyo, Mexico City

Cambridge University Press
The Edinburgh Building, Cambridge CB2 8RU, UK

Published in the United States of America by Cambridge University Press, New York

www.cambridge.org
Information on this title: www.cambridge.org/9780521528047

First published 2006

A catalogue record for this publication is available from the British Library

ISBN 978-0-521-82120-9 Hardback
ISBN 978-0-521-52804-7 Paperback

CONTENTS

~

ILLUSTRATIONS

PREFACE

~

This book is intended primarily as a Latin reader, not as a historical survey of the Julio-Claudian emperors (although readers will pick up much about them in the course of using it). Highlights from Tacitus, Suetonius and Seneca have been chosen which should prove interesting and variously affecting, so that students will want to read on and should actually enjoy translating (this explains why Augustus, who is not such a readily appealing figure in the ancient sources, receives less coverage than his successors). These highlights are also decidedly valuable on several levels – cultural (as a study of human nature, the roles of Roman women, imperialism, corruption, and so on), artistic (especially in the case of Tacitus, a master of style and rhetoric) and academic (as well as being a Latin reader, the book is obviously useful as a supplement to Roman history courses).

The selections are aimed at those who have completed an introductory Latin course and are at the stage of moving on to genuine, unsimplified Latin prose (difficult language has been omitted rather than emended, and the only changes are to names, to avoid confusion – e.g. Caesar is replaced with Tiberius or Germanicus, and so on). The Latin (especially Tacitus) is hard for intermediate students, and we are keen to reach the needs of as wide an audience as possible, so cuts have been made not only within passages but also within sentences (particularly in the earlier selections). In view of this target readership, lots of help is given in the Notes at the start. Later, it is gradually reduced (especially in the Claudius and Nero sections), and students are encouraged to think for themselves more and more. The Notes are mainly intended to assist with basic comprehension (but do also contain some remarks on style and expression), while the Appreciation consists largely of historical comment and literary criticism (to deepen students' perception). For students who need to brush up on the basics, at the end of the Notes on each passage there are initially suggestions for reviewing declensions and conjugations and also the more important constructions (as encountered in the particular passage). The references are to pages in Morwood (abbreviated as: M) and Wheelock (abbreviated as: W) and to sections in the reference grammar at the end of Jones–Sidwell (abbreviated as: RLRG). Those who used a different introductory Latin course should consult the appropriate parts of that for their reviewing.

GGF (the historian) supplied almost all of the Introduction, and the historical background in the Appreciation. PM (the literary critic) conceived the book, made the selections, put together the Notes and Vocabulary, and produced the close readings of the actual passages themselves in the Appreciation. Both would like to thank: two McMaster University graduate students (Lynne White and Audrey McSherry) for valuable help with the bibliographical references; McMaster's Latin 2AA3 classes in 2000 and 2001 (who were taught by PM using a first draft of this book); Dr John Yardley and Dr Evan Haley, who very kindly scrutinized the first draft and suggested various improvements; and at CUP, Dr Michael Sharp for all his support, the anonymous readers for lots of helpful criticism, and Nina Palmer for crucially meticulous copy-editing.

GGF, PM.

INTRODUCTION

~

1 *The Roman Republic*

The Roman Republic (509–31 BC) had no government as we understand the concept today. Rather, it was ruled by a narrow clique of rich families resident in the city of Rome. Members of these families were elected to magistracies by the adult male citizen population (the *populus*) formally gathered into voting assemblies (*comitia*), themselves presided over by a magistrate. A council of elders, the Senate, was comprised mostly of ex-magistrates (exclusively of them after Sulla) and numbered for most of the Republic about 300–500 members. Indeed, it has been estimated that the entire senatorial class represented 0.002 per cent of the Roman Empire's population. The Senate had no formal powers of legislation. Its edicts (*senatus consulta*) were pieces of advice issued to the magistrates and the assemblies as to how they should vote on a given proposal. But the collective social standing, wealth, and experience of the Senate ensured that as time went on, its edicts increasingly passed into law as a matter of course.

It is vital to appreciate that, unlike the United States, no written constitution regulated the relationship between the Senate, the people, and the magistrates. Instead, rather as in Great Britain, the Roman system of governance was the product of long tradition, precedent, and historical compromise. Practice was modulated by accepted codes of behaviour rather than constitutional law. While the Roman aristocracy had a long history of domestic competitiveness, at the end of the second century BC some unscrupulous politicians began to push the boundaries of tradition and precedent, to exploit class differences within Rome's hierarchical society, and to spend greater and greater wealth drawn from the expanded empire on their political struggles with each other. Eventually, they came to use force. As bad precedent piled upon worse, the Roman Republic tore itself apart in a bloody vortex of chaos, rioting, civil war, and vicious political purges. The unarmed Senate and people were sidelined as general fought

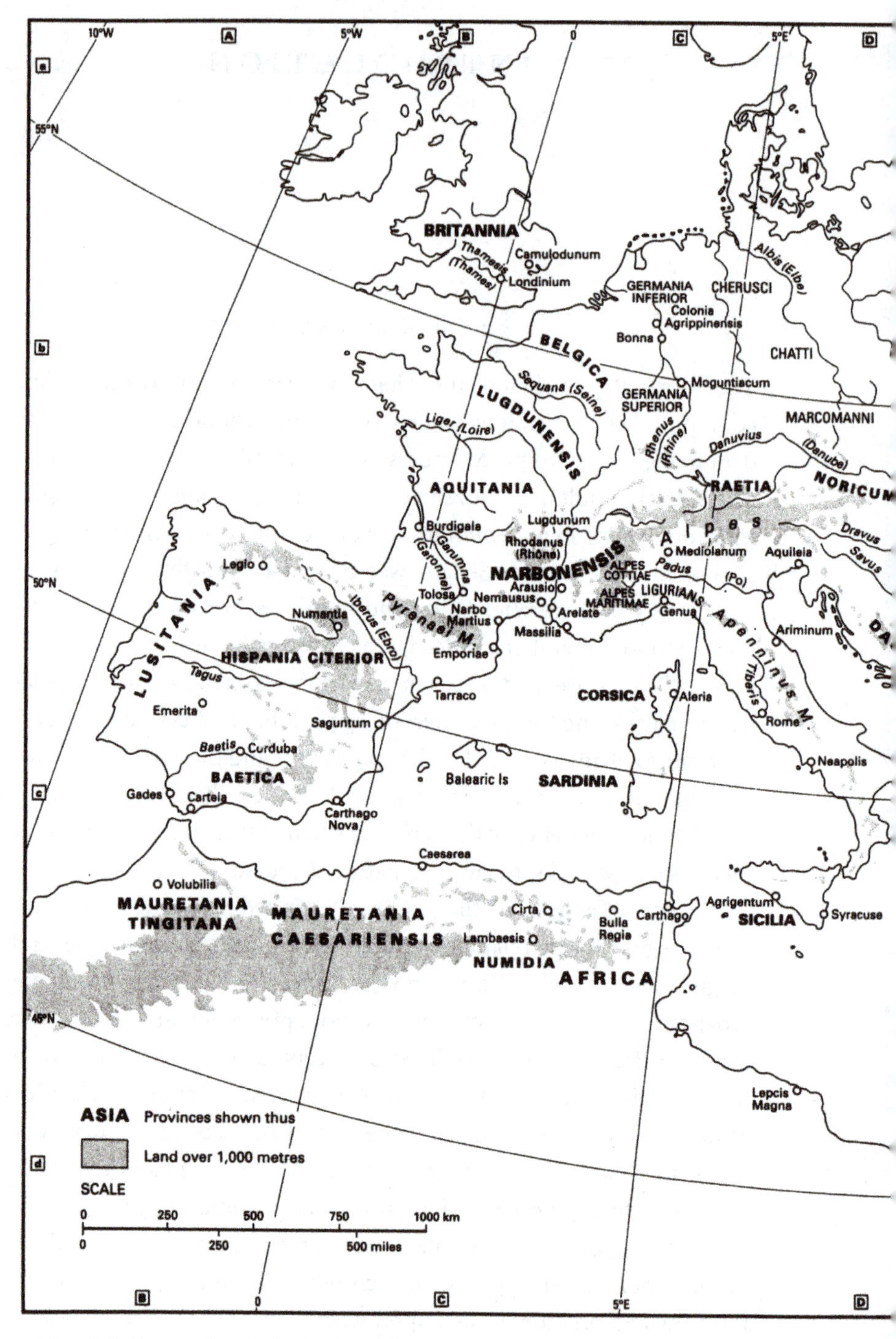

1 Map of the Roman Empire in the time of Augustus and the Julio–Claudian emperors.

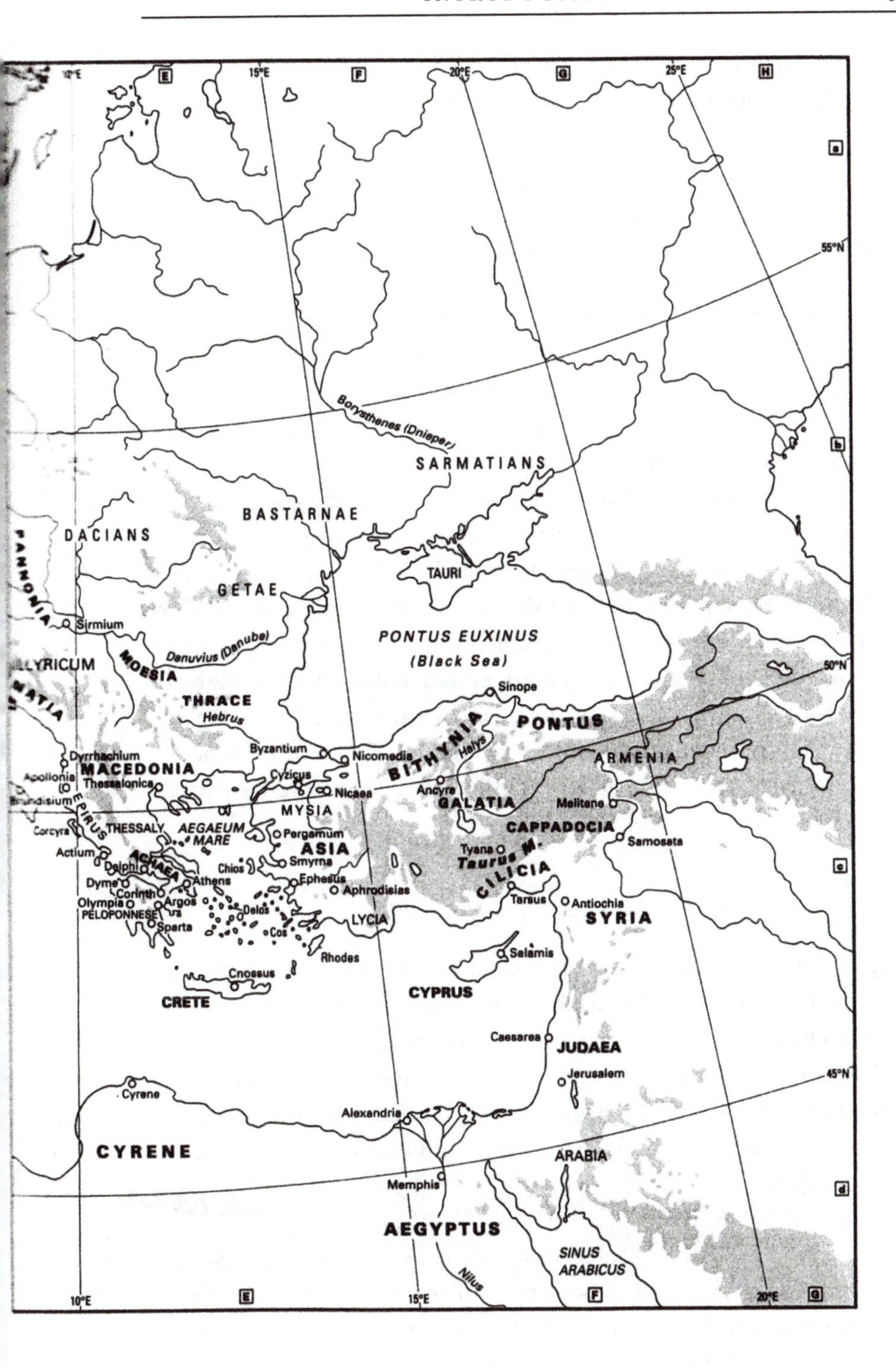
SARMATIANS
BASTARNAE
DACIANS
GETAE
TAURI
PONTUS EUXINUS
(Black Sea)
Borysthenes (Dnieper)
Danuvius (Danube)
MOESIA
THRACE
Hebrus
Sirmium
PANNONIA
ILLYRICUM
DALMATIA
Byzantium
Nicomedia
BITHYNIA
Sinope
PONTUS
Halys
ARMENIA
Dyrrhachium
MACEDONIA
Apollonia
Thessalonica
Brundisium
EPIRUS
Cyzicus
Nicaea
Ancyra
GALATIA
Melitene
MYSIA
Corcyra
THESSALY
AEGAEUM MARE
Pergamum
ASIA
CAPPADOCIA
Samosata
Actium
Chios
Smyrna
Tyana
Taurus M.
CILICIA
Delphi
ACHAEA
Athens
Ephesus
Dyme
Corinth
Argos
Aphrodisias
Tarsus
Antiochia
Olympia
PELOPONNESE
Sparta
Delos
Cos
LYCIA
SYRIA
Rhodes
Salamis
Cnossus
CRETE
CYPRUS
Caesarea
JUDAEA
Jerusalem
Cyrene
Alexandria
CYRENE
ARABIA
Memphis
AEGYPTUS
SINUS ARABICUS
Nilus
10°E
15°E
20°E
25°E
55°N
50°N
45°N

with general to determine the mightiest. (For more, see Beard and Crawford 1999; Lintott 1999.)

2 *The end of the Republic*

In 45 BC, Julius Caesar emerged as the ultimate victor in this contest and set himself up as sole ruler of Rome. Senatorial tradition reviled the concept of kings (in reaction to whom the Republic had been founded in the distant past), but Caesar paid no heed to that tradition and behaved as an open autocrat, complete with purple robes and a golden throne in the Senate House. As is well known, he died at the hands of senatorial assassins on 15 March 44 BC. He left no natural heir.

In his will, however, Caesar adopted as a son his grand nephew, C. Octavius, then in his late teens. Unknown to most, Octavian (or 'Caesar', as he preferred to be called) harboured a ruthless ambition, coupled with considerable powers of leadership and great political acumen. Over the course of the next fourteen years, he manoeuvred and fought against various rivals until, after defeating Mark Antony and Cleopatra at the battle of Actium in 31 BC, he emerged predominant over the entire Roman Empire. In 27 BC, he was named Imperator Caesar Augustus. He had become the first emperor of Rome and reigned for forty-five years. (For more, see Appian, *The Civil Wars*; Syme 1952.)

3 *The nature of the Principate*

Augustus was concerned to prevent civil war and consolidate his own power, while at the same time avoiding the fate of his adoptive father, Julius Caesar. Over the first three decades or so of his rule, he arranged a position for himself in the state as *princeps*, or 'first citizen' (the imperial system is therefore called the 'Principate'). In this role, he could exercise control over all areas of government (command of the armies, appointment of military governors, proposal of legislation, etc.), but the package of powers and privileges that enabled him to do so was voted to him in blocks of five years (later ten) by the Senate and people. Augustus behaved and dressed modestly, lived in a simple house, initiated conservative-looking reforms in society and in religious practices, and consulted the Senate and its magistrates as if they were his peers. He liked to get things done by wielding his towering and intangible influence (*auctoritas*), rather than by constantly exercising his legally conferred powers (*imperium* and *potestas*). He thus did not appear as a raw autocrat like Caesar, but rather seemed to be a super-magistrate and a respecter of Roman traditions. In reality, however, traditional forms were maintained, even as tradition was usurped. His reforms initiated a lasting period of peace and order – the *Pax Augusta.* (For more, see Eder 1990; Lacey 1996.)

4 *Some remarks on Roman society*

Roman society, in all periods, was highly stratified. Legally enforced social distinctions divided the freeborn from the slave (ex-slaves, or 'freedmen', were considered only slightly more respectable than slaves). Among the freeborn, distinction was made between citizen and non-citizen, and the citizens were themselves grouped into 'ranks' (*ordines*) of senators (the most privileged), equestrians (who overlapped with senators in socio-economic terms but did not take part in politics), and the *plebs* (everyone else). In this status-obsessed world, rank was declared by public appearance: influential men could be noted by the size of the entourage of slaves and dependants around them as they moved about in public, by the kinds of (legally regulated) clothes and jewellery they wore, and by the (legally regulated) seats they occupied at public spectacles. In this universe, much got done by wielding influence and pulling rank, and the closer a lesser being could get to a luminary, the more important he became. In this way, the favourite freedmen of emperors could wield greater clout than freeborn senators, bizarre as that may sound (see especially the *Claudius* selections). (For more on Roman society, see Alföldy 1988.)

The Senate's role had also changed drastically. In the days of the Republic, it had been the state's pre-eminent political entity (at least from the mid-third century BC onwards). It had a long and proud tradition behind it, and the mainstay of that tradition was *libertas* – the freedom of political choice that senators enjoyed by virtue of their station. But with the establishment of the Principate that *libertas* evaporated, and the Senate was reduced to little more than a pool of administrators on hand to help a higher power run the Empire. Augustus chose to treat the Senate with due respect, although he did not have to. Later emperors, as we shall see in the selections, felt no such compunction. (For more, see Talbert 1984.)

Unsurprisingly, a strong anti-emperor tradition evolved among senatorial writers of history. Such men could vent their spleen on dead emperors even as they accommodated living incumbents. This facet of our surviving Latin sources must always be borne in mind when trying to assess their accuracy as reporters of events.

5 *Augustus*

(Born 23 September 63 BC; died 19 August AD 14; reigned 31 BC – AD 14.)

Augustus is a figure of immense historical importance for the history of Rome and of Europe. He singlehandedly brought the mayhem of the Late Republic to an end, though not without a degree of ruthlessness, and re-established the state on a firm footing. The Principate (see above, section 3) endured for almost 250 years, the longest period of peace and prosperity in Europe's recorded history. The period is often dubbed the *Pax Augusta* or *Pax Romana*. As his dominance became secure, Augustus presented a tactful and statesmanlike face to the world, a defender of traditional Roman values and practices, and the supreme patron to the people and the empire. He was 'the father of his country,' as his cherished title of 2 BC declared (*pater patriae*). (For more, see Brunt and Moore 1967).

For all its artfulness, however, the Principate was fragile. Rather like the Republic before it, it was based on precedent and acceptable modes of conduct, instead of being founded on constitutional law (despite efforts to make it so, such as the *lex de imperio Vespasiani* of AD 69 or 70; see *ILS* 244). What would happen if someone lacking Augustus' tact and political skill should become *princeps*? For that matter, *who* should become *princeps* when Augustus died, and how should a successor be chosen? This problem of the succession proved to be a fatal weakness at the heart of the Principate. As a sort of super-magistrate, Augustus had no right to name a successor in the manner of an autocrat; at the same time, if the choice were left to the Senate and people (as technically it should be), what would stop some popular general from challenging that choice under arms? That way led back to civil war and the ruination of everything for which Augustus had worked.

Augustus therefore, like any good Roman aristocrat, looked to his own family for potential successors. By a variety of means, both subtle and obvious, he indicated to the Senate and people his favourites, and in a long series, since several of them died. The fact that a chosen favourite (if he survived) eventually shared significant portions of the emperor's

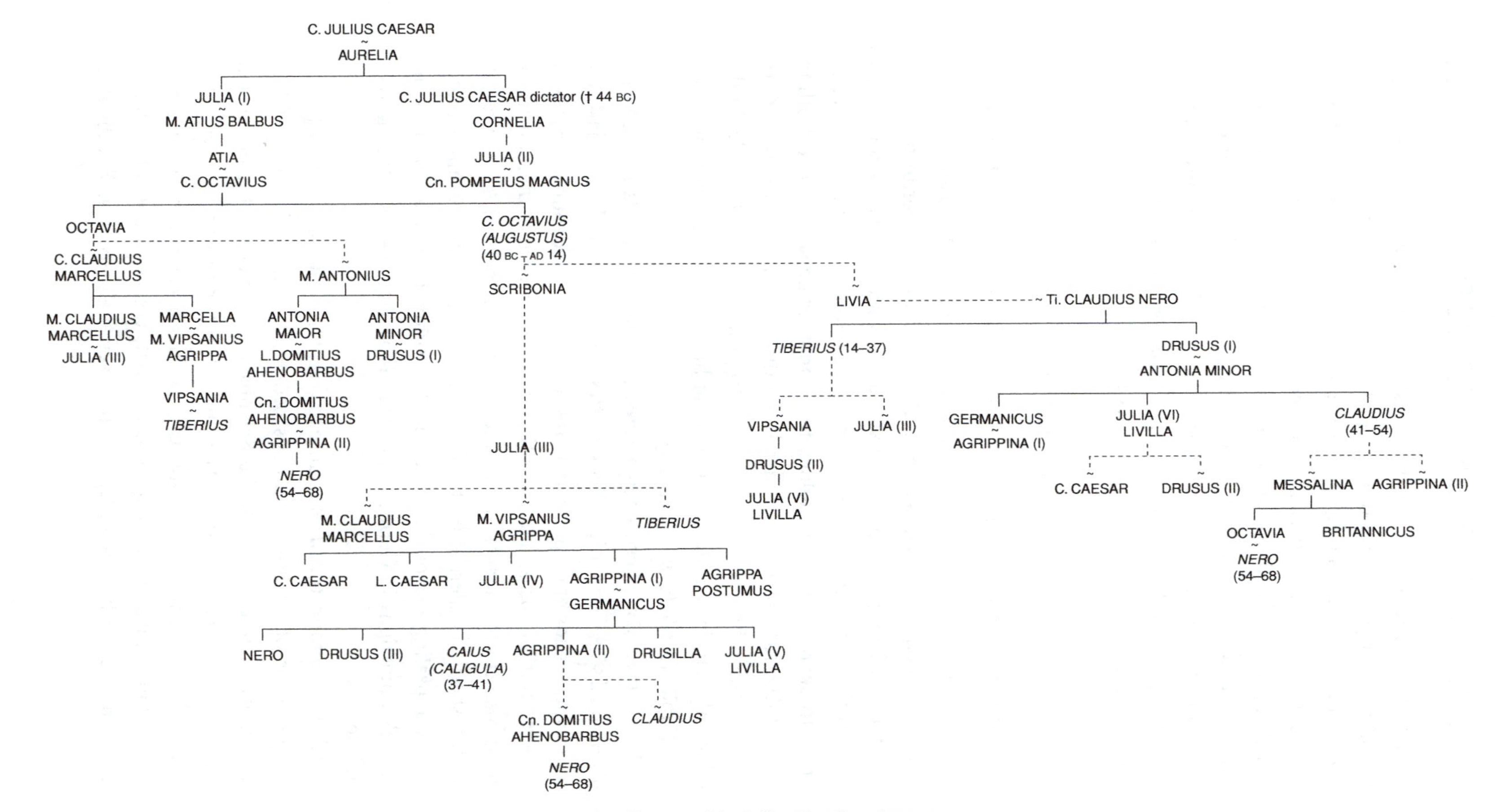

2 Family tree of the Julio-Claudian dynasty.

legal powers ensured that, when Augustus himself died, a quasi-*princeps* was already in place, who only needed confirmation by the Senate and people. But the informality of the Augustan succession scheme bred terrible instability within the imperial house (see *Augustus* passage 5).

Relying on such flimsy arrangements for the succession, the Julio-Claudian dynasty (the family of Augustus) ruled the Roman Empire for fifty-four years after Augustus' death in AD 14. Their rule proved to be something of a rollercoaster ride. (For more on Augustus, see section 3 above and Fagan in *DIR*; Southern 1998.)

6 *Tiberius*

(Born 16 November 42 BC; died 16 March AD 37; reigned AD 14–37.)

Tiberius was a man of a very different disposition to Augustus. Whereas Augustus, as emperor, had been tactful and charming, Tiberius was blunt and dour. He had spent more than half a century waiting in the wings under Augustus' shadow, and in many respects he never escaped from under it. Prone to depression and beholden to his mother Livia until her death in AD 29 (Tiberius missed the funeral), he disengaged from the tedium of administration by abandoning Rome altogether in AD 26 to settle, in the following year, into a life of depravity at his villa on the island of Capri, near Naples (see *Tiberius* passage 13).

The first years of Tiberius' reign were dominated by his relationship with his adopted son, Germanicus. This youth's charm, good looks, and dash as a commander made him a popular figure, in contrast to the sour and reclusive emperor. But Tacitus, an austere critic, offers a nuanced and subtle portrayal of Germanicus that makes him far more than a foil to Tiberius. As a result, readers should be alert to hints of Germanicus' ineptitude or innuendoes of less-appealing personality traits as they study Tacitus' account of the prince's campaigns in Germany in *Tiberius* passages 1–7 (see Pelling 1993 and Ross 1973).

Tiberius' demonstrated reluctance to accept the responsibilities of power left room for other, less scrupulous people to make their moves. Chief among his satellites was L. Aelius Sejanus, commander of the praetorian guard. Between AD 23 and 31, Tiberius fell under this man's spell. That Sejanus became embroiled in dynastic politics is clear from his ultimate demise, but scholars have long debated exactly what he wanted to achieve, and even whether he was guilty of conspiracy at all (see, e.g., Boddington

1963). Sejanus' most likely goal was to become Tiberius' successor. The emperor's absence from Rome after AD 26 greatly strengthened Sejanus' hand; he now controlled access to Tiberius. As Dio puts it (58.5.1), Sejanus appeared the emperor, and Tiberius an island potentate. But on 18 October AD 31, Tiberius denounced his favourite in a letter read to the Senate. Sejanus was summarily executed the same day. The witch-hunt for his followers lasted two years.

Tacitus comments at the opening of AD 23, 'Either Tiberius himself began to behave savagely, or he provided the means for others to do so' (*Ann.* 4.1: *coepit saevire ipse aut saevientibus vires praebere*). This, in fact, could stand as the epitaph for his entire reign. (See further: Levick 1976; Fagan in *DIR*; Seager 1972.)

7 Caligula

(Born 31 August AD 12; died 24 January AD 41; reigned AD 37–41.)

Caligula (Gaius) was the youngest son of Germanicus and Agrippina the Elder, and therefore a direct blood relative of Augustus himself. This parentage and ancestry made him immensely popular – at least, at first. As an infant, he accompanied his parents to the legions' camps in Germany, where he was fitted out in a miniature soldier's outfit. The troops were especially taken with his tiny military sandals and nicknamed him 'Bootikins', *caligula* in Latin – the name by which he is known to posterity. Caligula's childhood was not a happy one. His father died when he was seven, and his mother and brothers suffered under Sejanus' ascendancy. On 16 March AD 37, Caligula was on Capri when Tiberius died. He was quickly hailed as the next emperor, despite having no administrative or military experience. It proved a terrible mistake.

Caligula initially played the role of benevolent ruler. Among other beneficent acts, he had all of Tiberius' private papers about the trials of his relatives burned in the Forum. Those papers undoubtedly contained the names of many informers against his relatives, so this public immolation was an extravagant declaration of amnesty. (According to Dio [59.4.3], however, he kept secret copies and later had anyone implicated executed on the strength of their testimony.)

The honeymoon did not last. What happened to Caligula is still a matter of uncertainty. Some modern scholars ascribe his increasingly bizarre behaviour to some physical ailment (hyperthyroidism, epilepsy), or to a mental illness (mania, depression). But attempts to diagnose a patient 2,000 years dead on the strength of slanted literary testimony are surely doomed to failure. Overall, the issue of Caligula's 'madness' is greatly affected by the view one takes of the sources: if they are basically truthful, then Caligula was clearly deranged (Ferrill 1991); if they are questionable and tainted by exaggeration, then something other than insanity may have been at play (Barrett 1989). Because the pertinent book of Tacitus' *Annals* is lost, we are thrown back on the sensationalistic biography of Suetonius, supplemented by summary accounts in later Greek writers, principally Josephus and Cassius Dio. This situation makes discerning rumour from reality, accusation from action very difficult. Much of Caligula's reported behaviour, while not likely to be complete fabrication, ought to be taken with a grain of salt, since a tradition about him can be shown to have arisen and snowballed following his death (Charlesworth 1933).

Caligula was the first Roman emperor to be assassinated openly, cut down by members of the praetorian guard, acting on personal motives. (For more, see *Fagan* in *DIR*; Hurley 1983).

8 Claudius

(Born 1 August 10 BC; died 13 October AD 54; reigned AD 41–54.)

For much of his life, Claudius was sequestered. On the assumption that his physical disabilities reflected mental incapacity, his elders and peers dismissed him as a fool. Our largely hostile ancient sources are also unanimous in portraying Claudius as a bumbling dupe manipulated easily by his wives and secretaries, comprised of ex-slaves. Since the sources are mostly senatorial in origin, their hostility is understandable. Claudius had been foisted on them by the soldiers of the praetorian guard, and he appears to have operated more in the palace, surrounded by his wives and household, than in the traditional settings of forum and Senate. To Roman senatorial sentiments, such a condition was unconscionably ignominious, and a man who could not control his own household was hardly fit to rule an empire. So his reign is portrayed as a farce.

A cardinal incident in Claudius' reign was the fall of his third wife, Valeria Messalina (see *Claudius* passages 3–16). In the ancient sources, she is portrayed as an out-and-out sex fiend (e.g. Juvenal *Satires* 6.115–32). In modern accounts, however, she is often depicted as a cunning player in court politics, who used sex as a weapon (see Barrett 1996, 93–4; Erhardt 1978; Levick 1990, 55–69). These divergent interpretations of Messalina's character are more than an academic sideshow: they determine how the events surrounding her fall from power are interpreted (see Fagan 2002).

Claudius' next matrimonial union proved even more disastrous than his marriage to Messalina; indeed, it was lethal for him. He married his ambitious niece Agrippina (the Younger), who embarked on an open play for power that was shocking to Roman male sensibilities. Ultimately, Agrippina secured the succession of her son by a previous marriage (the future Nero) and then murdered Claudius (see *Claudius* passages 17–19). Such marital relationships do not, on the face of it, reflect well on Claudius or his ability to control those around him.

Recent scholarship has attempted to rehabilitate Claudius by making him a more active agent in affairs: he was cunning, ambitious, and pursued identifiable policies. Our ancient evidence is too patchy to allow a fair assessment of this interpretation of his reign. From inscriptions, however, we can detect some facets of Claudius' personality. He was bookish and scholarly, and a rambling orator. He sometimes appears 'liberal' in his leanings, extending citizenship to provincials or strengthening the rights of slaves and women. In this light, he does seem the benign ruler. On the other side of the coin, he loved the butchery of the gladiatorial games, reacted violently to any perceived threat to his position, and heard capital court cases behind closed doors in his bedroom. On this perspective, he appears tyrannical. Clearly, Claudius was a far more complex man than either the prevailing ancient or modern views would suggest. (For more, see Fagan in *DIR*; Levick 1990).

9 *Nero*

(Born 15 December AD 37; died 9 June AD 68; reigned AD 54–68.)

As with Caligula, youth and inexperience were the defining features of Nero. When Nero was only sixteen and had no administrative or military experience, his mother Agrippina orchestrated his accession. A powerful and ambitious personality, she initially controlled much of Nero's – and so the state's – business. Tacitus' assessment of Agrippina's influence is memorable (*Ann.* 12.7.5–6): 'From this moment on . . . all obedience was given to a woman, who did not toy with Rome's affairs through lasciviousness, as Messalina had done. An almost masculine dominance was established'. She listened to senatorial debates from behind a curtain and, when an embassy arrived from Armenia, she almost mounted the imperial dais to take up station beside the emperor (Dio 61.3.3–4). The coinage of Nero's early years shows mother and son nose-to-nose, on an equal footing. In coins minted in the provinces, Agrippina often gets one side of the coin entirely to herself. Her influence, however, was not to last. As mother–son relations strained, Nero finally had her murdered in AD 59. In addition to Agrippina, the influence of two powerful courtiers – his tutor L. Annaeus Seneca and the praetorian prefect Sex. Afranius Burrus – is generally considered to have kept Nero's baser impulses somewhat in check. In AD 62, Burrus died and Seneca withdrew. Nero could finally be himself. (See further: Barrett 1996, 143–95; Griffin 1984, 83–118).

The reign rapidly descended into chaos. Nero indulged his penchant for public appearances on stage and in chariot races – both spectacles the preserve of the socially inferior in imperial Rome. Then, in AD 64, disaster struck. Since large sections of Rome comprised makeshift tenements thrown up in unplanned and unregulated circumstances (see, e.g., Cicero *Letters to Atticus* 14.9.1), fire was a constant threat. In AD 64, however, a major conflagration broke out that consumed a large part of the city's centre. Nero chose to replace the ruined regions with a huge palace complex called the Golden House (*Domus Aurea*), which stretched from the Palatine to the Esquiline and was entered from the Forum through a monumental colonnade. Despite the emperor's genuine relief efforts, Nero's construction of the Golden House raised understandable suspicions as to the catastrophe's origins. Some have seen in his behaviour a drive to establish a grander, more absolutist monarchy than had been traditional under the Augustan Principate, and have linked to this desire his philhellenism and stage-appearances (Griffin 1984, 208–20); others think Nero just had an artistic temperament and was largely uninterested in politics (Champlin 2003).

In AD 65, a major conspiracy against Nero was suppressed in Rome, yet in the following year the emperor ill-advisedly left the capital in the hands of an ex-slave while he himself travelled about Greece collecting 1,808 prizes in athletic and artistic festivals (see *Nero* passage 16). As it turned out, Nero's end was encompassed not by senatorial conspirators or praetorian guardsmen but by the troops stationed in the provinces, whose loyalties Nero had done little to secure. A minor revolt in Gaul in March AD 68 led to the Spanish legions renouncing their allegiance to Nero and declaring their general, Galba, emperor. Returning from Greece, Nero panicked and fled Rome, finally committing suicide in a friend's villa with the last words: 'What an artist dies in me!' (*qualis artifex pereo*, Suetonius *Nero* 49.1). (On Nero, in addition to those works already cited, see further: Elsner and Masters 1994; Warmington 1969.)

10 *Emperors and empire*

The focus of our literary sources for the Julio-Claudian period is firmly on the goings-on at court, the palace intrigues, the personalities, the plots and the foibles of individuals. This ought not to obscure wider developments initiated by the move to monarchy. Only a handful of them can be surveyed here.

From the perspective of the provinces, the emperor was a distant entity whose behaviour affected only a miniscule proportion of the empire's population. Most would have lived and died without ever setting eyes on a living emperor. Lacking the apparatus of a modern state – professional police forces, efficient communications, centralized control, etc. – the tyranny of even the worst emperors had a relatively limited impact. And for better or for worse, our sources derive overwhelmingly from those in the firing line, the senators and *equites* resident in Rome itself (see further: Millar 1977).

Another major development in these years was the establishment of a standing imperial army of volunteers, who served for specified periods and looked forward to a pension on retirement. All soldiers swore a personal oath of loyalty to the emperor. This army was stationed by Augustus far away from Rome, guarding the frontiers (except the special detachments of troops in Rome itself). There it was to remain for centuries, save when an emperor exercised his military ambitions (such as Claudius in Britain in AD 43), or on those occasions when dynastic uncertainty caused civil wars that drew contending detachments into the interior. Inscriptions attest that army veterans often retired into local communities, becoming big fish in small provincial ponds. On a sociocultural level, therefore, the imperial army and its veterans represent a major vehicle for the transmission of

Romanness into the provinces. (On soldiers and the army, see, e.g., Alston 1995; Goldsworthy 2003; La Bohec 1994; Pollard 2000; Watson 1969; Webster 1985.)

Compared to the 'Free Republic', provincial administration appears to have been less rapacious and more ordered under the emperors. As the Julio-Claudian period progressed, there was a tendency to replace local 'client kings' (such as Herod of Judaea) with Roman officials sent directly from Rome. Governors, many of them hand-picked by the emperor himself, served several years in their post and now had to answer to a higher authority than their own ambitions. Poor governance reflected badly on the imperial majesty, and might even incur life-threatening suspicions of sedition. The security ensured by a professional army and the order ensured by a (relatively) good administration is reflected in the growing prosperity of local communities, which display an upward curve that peaked in the second century. (See Arnold 1914; Garnsey and Saller 1987; Lintott 1993.)

11 *Tacitus and Suetonius*

Cornelius Tacitus – his *praenomen* is disputed – was born ca. AD 55, probably in southern France (Narbonese Gaul). He enjoyed an illustrious senatorial career and in AD 97 reached the suffect consulship (that is, a substitute consul for a regular *consul ordinarius* who had stepped down). This implies, at the very least, a non-confrontational stance toward the tyrannical rule of Domitian (reigned AD 81–96). His career peaked with the proconsulship of Asia in AD 112–13, and he seems to have died around the year AD 120. (See further Birley 2000).

Tacitus composed three short monographs (*Agricola, Germania, Dialogus de Oratoribus*) before embarking on a major history of the Long Year (AD 69) and the subsequent Flavian Dynasty (AD 70–96), today called the *Histories* (its ancient title is unknown). Only the first four of its original fourteen books survive intact, along with part of the fifth, which takes the story down to AD 70.

In composing the *Histories,* Tacitus felt the need to explain the antecedents to his story. Thus he spent his last years writing his masterpiece, the *Annals* (not the ancient title), which detailed Roman history from the death of Augustus to that of Nero. The *Annals* survives largely intact, with some maddening gaps (e.g., the fall of Sejanus, the entire reign of Caligula, the elevation and first years of Claudius, and the fall of Nero). All the Tacitean selections in this book come from the *Annals*. Drawn from the (now lost) work of prior historians, official documents, and personal interviews, it is a dark and claustrophobic work in which murderous personalities plot and scheme, employing all kinds of subterfuge to conceal their true ambitions and motives. There are few examples of pure virtue in Tacitus' *Annals* (e.g. Octavia in *Nero* passage 20). When assessing the reliability of his detailed account, Tacitus' senatorial attitudes need to be borne in mind – he recognized the necessity of the Principate, but he did not have to like it. (See further Syme 1958; Mellor 1993; Luce and Woodman 1993; Woodman 1998.)

C. Suetonius Tranquillus was a contemporary of Tacitus (born ca. AD 70), and the two shared an acquaintance with Pliny the Younger, who addressed letters to both (e.g., Pliny *Letters* 1.18, 5.10, 6.16, 6.20). There is no direct evidence, however, that Suetonius and Tacitus ever met. Suetonius was of equestrian status and probably hailed from Hippo Regius in Numidia (modern Algeria). He pursued a public career through the equestrian *cursus* and rose to occupy important secretarial positions under Trajan and Hadrian. The latter, however, dismissed him in AD 121–2, which brought his public career to an end. An inscription fom Hippo Regius records his career (*AE* 1953.73).

The age in which Suetonius lived saw a widespread interest in biographies. Roughly contemporary with him are Plutarch's *Parallel Lives* and the later Gospels (the latter are more than straightforward biographies). It is therefore not a surprise that Suetonius wrote biographies, of which his *De Vita Caesarum*, known as *The Twelve Caesars*, survives almost intact (the very beginning of his *Julius* is missing). As an imperial secretary, Suetonius had access to archives long ago denied to the modern scholar (he quotes verbatim, for instance, from letters of Augustus to Livia about Claudius; see Suet. *Claudius* 3–4), which makes it all the more regrettable that he chose to do with them what he did: compose sensational and generalizing sketches under thematic rubrics ('appearance', 'public works', 'relations with family members', etc.). This procedure makes it very difficult to determine the context of specific notices within any given emperor's reign. When Tacitus and other sources are available as a check on Suetonius' presentation, his weaknesses as an historical source are mitigated; but when other sources are lacking (as with the entire reign of Caligula, for instance), the usefulness of Suetonius' account is greatly reduced. (See further: Baldwin 1983; Wallace-Hadrill 1983.)

12 *Genre*

Historiography at Rome had a heritage stretching back to the late third century BC and the (lost) works of Q. Fabius Pictor. Roman historians were usually men of senatorial status who were actively engaged in public life. A dominant form of Roman history-writing was 'yearbooks' (*annales*), wherein the story of Rome unfolded on a year-by-year basis. Tacitus uses this format for his great work – called the *Annals* on no ancient basis – which works very well when the focus is on affairs at Rome. When covering provincial affairs, however, the format shows its weaknesses, particularly for military campaigns conducted over several consecutive years. In such circumstances, it is not unusual for Tacitus to break the annalistic organization in favour of a more focused account spanning several years (see, e.g., Tac. *Ann.* 12.31–40, 14.29–49, 15.1–17). A moralizing Roman bent is certainly present in the pages of Tacitus, but not in the obvious manner one finds in Livy or Sallust, who lecture their readers on moral decline. Instead, Tacitus mostly allows the characters' actions to reveal their moral depravity and adds a level of psychological depth unparalleled in Roman historiography before or after. (See further: Fornara 1983; Woodman 1988.)

The Romans had a tradition of celebrating the achievements (*res gestae*) of prominent citizens and passing public standing (*dignitas*) down family lines (Flower 1996). Biography and autobiography therefore appealed to their tastes and appeared quite early, as leading figures published self-justificatory memoirs (such Caesar's *Commentaries*), or others glorified or vilified their friends and enemies (e.g., Caesar's lost but notoriously vituperative *Anticato* and Tacitus' encomiastic *Agricola*). The biographic genre in Rome therefore overlaps with related genres of literature, such as political or forensic rhetoric, historiography, apologetics, or martyrology. The historical usefulness of Roman biography is not to be denied, so long as its limitations are recognized. Suetonius' *Twelve Caesars* is among the most sensationalistic biographic texts to survive from Rome, especially when compared to his contemporary Plutarch's sober and serious *Parallel Lives*. (See: Geiger 1985; Gentili 1988.)

Satire criticized on moral, social, or aesthetic grounds, attacking and/or ridiculing people's manners, morals, appearance, tastes etc. It could be written in verse alone, or in a mixture of prose and verse (called Menippean satire), as was the work excerpted in passage 20 of the Claudius selections – the *Apocolocyntosis* (for full Latin text, translation and notes, see Eden 1984). Written early in Nero's Principate by Seneca (4 BC–AD 65), it mocks the death and deification of Claudius. The title is formed from the Greek words *apotheosis* ('deification') and *colocynta* ('pumpkin'), and means 'Pumpkinification' – presumably the idea was that instead of being made a god, the buffoon Claudius was turned into a pumpkin.

13 *The style of Tacitus*

An introduction to the main features of the style of Tacitus (a harder author than Suetonius and Seneca) should help students with translation of him. A brief survey seems most appropriate here. (For further discussion, consult Furneaux 1896 vol. I 38ff. and Woodcock 1939 11ff.)

Tacitus' style is highly original, and he tries to be strikingly different and to get readers' attention by avoiding normal and obvious language and constructions. He enlivens and elevates his prose by means of poetic expression (words, senses of words, whole phrases, metaphors, syntax), introducing much from the verse of Virgil in particular. In his constant search for *variatio* (variation) he avoids parallelism, the neat (and predictable) balancing of words, phrases, clauses and sentences found so often in earlier authors, such as Cicero (so, for example, where others would achieve symmetry by employing *ad* meaning 'to' twice, he will use first *ad* and then *in*; also, instead of introducing two reasons by means of *quod* meaning 'because', he will utilize *quod* the first time and then switch to an ablative of cause). Tacitus is also fond of brevity – a terse and at times epigrammatic compression of thought and expression. So he favours short clauses and sentences, and he frequently pares his Latin down by omitting connecting links (like *atque* and *sed*), subjects and objects (when they are clear from context) and verbs, especially parts of *esse* (most often in the third person and in the indicative).

There are a few other common features which are worth bearing in mind. Regular in Tacitus' own period (but not before it) were the local ablative (denoting a place where or whence, without a preposition) and the frequentative subjunctive (denoting the repeated occurrence of an action after words like 'whoever' and 'whenever') in place of the indicative. Tacitus likes to end a sentence with an ablative absolute (rather than with the main clause and the main verb), and he likes to construct ablative absolutes in which the pronoun has to be supplied from a relative clause (e.g. *provisis quae tempus monebat* 'with [those things] that the time warned of having been seen to'). He also has a tendency to slip suddenly into indirect speech, giving people's thoughts, arguments etc., and moving freely between statements, questions and commands. Finally, there is the historic infinitive, which is an infinitive used in place of the imperfect or perfect indicative, generally in the main clause, but sometimes in a subordinate clause. The subject, when actually expressed, is nominative, and we often find a series of historic infinitives (particularly in rapid narrative).

14 *Glossary of technical terms*

The following grammatical and stylistic terms may not be familiar to all students. For further information on them, and on other terminology employed in this book, see Kennedy 1962 and Woodcock 1959.

ablative of attendant circumstances denotes the circumstances under which an action is performed (= 'to the accompaniment of')

ablative of description: a noun and adjective in the ablative are attached to another noun to describe it (*vir nigris capillis* = 'a man with black hair')

ablative of instrument denotes the thing (instrument) with which an action is performed (*gladio caedit hostes* = 'he kills the enemy with a sword')

ablative of manner expresses the manner in which something happens or is done (*magna cura scribit* 'he writes with great care')

ablative of respect specifies that in respect to which a verb or adjective applies (*corde tremit* 'it trembles in respect to its heart')

alliteration: repetition of the same initial letter(s) in closely successive words (e.g. sing a song of sixpence)

anaphora: repetition of words

antithesis: contrast

assonance: repetition of the same or similar vowels (e.g. rabid malice)

asyndeton: the omission of connecting links (such as *atque* and *sed*)

chiasmus: an ABBA arrangement (e.g. ablative, accusative, accusative, ablative; or noun, verb, verb, noun)

cumulative impact: the powerful effect achieved by piling up point after point in a sentence or passage

dative of agent: the dative is sometimes used on its own in place of *a(b)* and the ablative

dative of disadvantage: the person to whose disadvantage something happens or is done is put into the dative (*nobis stulti sumus* 'we are stupid to the disadvantage of ourselves')

dative of purpose: a gerund, noun, or noun plus gerundive can be put into the dative to express purpose (*urbi condendae locum elegerunt* 'they chose a place for founding a city')

deliberative subjunctive is employed when people deliberate about what was to be done, what should be said etc.

emphatic placement: putting a word at the very start or end of a clause, sentence or passage to give it stress

generic relative clause: the subjunctive is used in *qui* clauses which indicate a sort or type of person or thing (*non est is qui hoc dicat* 'he is not the type of person who says this')

genitive of definition expresses that of which a thing consists (*praeda hominum* 'spoil consisting of men')

genitive of quality/description: a noun and adjective in the genitive are attached to another noun to describe it or indicate a distinctive quality (*vir summae virtutis* 'a man of supreme bravery')

genitive of reference is used with adjectives to denote that with respect to which the adjective is applicable (*atrox odii* 'unrelenting in respect of hatred')

homoeoteleuton: rhyme in the endings of closely successive words

hyperbole: exaggeration for rhetorical effect

impersonal expression: the third person singular passive of a verb is used in place of the verb with a personal subject (*curritur* 'it is run' instead of *currunt* 'they run')

jussive subjunctive expresses a command (*fiat lux* 'let there be light')

juxtaposition: the placement of words right next to each other for a particular point (e.g. to bring out the nearness of two juxtaposed characters, to stress the contrast between two juxtaposed colours)

local ablative denotes a place where or whence without a preposition (*muris stant* 'they are standing on the walls')

metaphor: likening A to B by saying that A is B (e.g. 'he is a snake')
onomatopoeia: the employment of a word or words that sound(s) like what is being described
partitive genitive names the whole of which part is being considered (*fortissimus Graecorum* 'the bravest one of the Greeks')
possessive dative is employed in place of a genitive to denote the possessor (*est mihi filia parva* 'I have a little daughter')
potential subjunctive expresses a possibility, what would or might happen/be happening/have happened (*hoc velim* 'I would like this')
predicative dative: the verb *esse* sometimes has as its complement a noun in the dative expressing that which a thing serves as or occasions (*auxilio est* 'he is for a help', i.e. 'he is a source of help')
ring composition/structure occurs when elements at the start are repeated at the end (e.g. words, details or characters at the beginning of a passage are picked up at its conclusion)
sententia: epigrammatic statement, pithy remark
tricolon: a group of three; in a tricolon crescendo, the three members become successively longer (as in 'friends, Romans, and countrymen'); in a tricolon diminuendo, the members become successively shorter

15 *References*

Alföldy, G. (1988), *The Social History of Rome*, revised ed. (Baltimore)
Alston, R. (1995), *Soldier and Society in Roman Egypt: A Social History* (London)
AJP (1999), 'The Senatus Consultum de Cn. Pisone Patre: Text, Translation, Discussion', *American Journal of Philology* 120, Special Edition, 1–162
Arnold, W.T. (1914), *The System of Roman Provincial Administration to the Accession of Constantine the Great*, 3rd edition (Oxford)
Baldwin, B. (1983), *Suetonius* (Amsterdam)
Barrett, A.A. (1989), *Caligula: The Corruption of Power* (New Haven)
(1996), *Agrippina: Sex, Power, and Politics in the Early Empire* (New Haven)
Beacham, R.C. (1999), *Spectacle Entertainments of Early Imperial Rome* (New Haven)
Beard, M. and Crawford, M. (1999), *Rome in the Late Republic*, 2nd edition (London)
Beard, M., North, J. and Price, S. (1998), *Religions Of Rome* (Cambridge)
Birley, A.R. (2000), 'The Life and Death of Cornelius Tacitus', *Historia* 49, 230–147
Boddington, A. (1963), 'Sejanus: Whose Conspiracy?', *American Journal of Philology* 84: 1–16

Brunt, P.A. and Moore, J.M. (1967), *The* Res Gestae Divi Augusti*: The Achievements of the Divine Augustus* (Oxford)
Champlin, E. (2003), *Nero* (Cambridge, MA)
Charlesworth, M.P. (1933), 'The Tradition about Caligula', *Cambridge Historical Journal* 4: 105–19
DIR. De Imperatoribus Romanis*: An Online Encyclopedia of Roman Emperors*, at http://www.roman-emperors.org
Eden, P.T. (1984), *Seneca Apocolocyntosis* (Cambridge)
Eder, W. (1990), 'Augustus and the Power of Tradition: The Augustan Principate as Binding Link between Republic and Empire', in K. Raaflaub and M. Toher (eds.), *Between Republic and Empire: Interpretations of Augustus and His Principate* (Berkeley), 71–122
Elsner, J. and J. Masters, eds. (1994), *Reflections of Nero: Culture, History, and Representation* (Chapel Hill)
Erhardt, C. (1978), 'Messalina and the Succession to Claudius', *Antichthon* 28: 51–77
Fagan, G.G. (2002), 'Messalina's Folly,' *Classical Quarterly* 52: 566–79
Ferrill, A. (1991), *Caligula: Emperor of Rome* (London)
Flower, H.I. (1996), *Ancestor Masks and Aristocratic Power in Roman Culture* (Oxford)
Fornara, C. (1983), *The Nature of History in Greece and Rome* (Berkeley)
Furneaux, H. (1896), *The Annals of Tacitus* (Oxford)
Galinsky, K. (1996), *Augustan Culture* (Princeton)
Garnsey, P. and Saller, R. (1987), *The Roman Empire: Economy, Society, Culture* (Berkeley)
Geiger, J. (1985), *Cornelius Nepos and Ancient Political Biography* (Weisbaden)
Gentili, B. (1988), *History and Biography in Ancient Thought* (Amsterdam)
Goldsworthy, A.K. (2003), *The Complete Roman Army* (London)
Goodyear, F.R.D. (1981), *The Annals of Tacitus Books 1–6*, vol. II (Cambridge)
Griffin, M. (1984), *Nero: The End of a Dynasty* (New Haven)
(1997), 'The Senate's Story', *Journal of Roman Studies* 87: 249–63
Hurley, D.W. (1983), *An Historical and Historiographical Commentary on Suetonius' Life of C. Caligula* (Atlanta)
Jones, P.V. and Sidwell, K.C. (1986), *Reading Latin* (Cambridge)
Kennedy, B.H. (1962), *The Revised Latin Primer* (London)
La Bohec, Y. (1994). *The Imperial Roman Army* (New York)
Lacey, W.K. (1996), *Augustus and the Principate: The Evolution of the System* (Leeds)
Levick, B. (1976), *Tiberius the Politician* (London)
(1990), *Claudius* (London)
Lintott, A.W. (1993), *Imperium Romanum: Politics and Administration* (London)

(1999), *The Constitution of the Roman Republic* (Oxford)
Luce, T.J. and Woodman, A.J. (1993), *Tacitus and the Tacitean Tradition* (Princeton)
Martin, R.H. and Woodman, A.J. (1989), *Tacitus Annals Book IV* (Cambridge)
Mellor, R. (1993), *Tacitus* (London)
Millar, F. (1977), *The Emperor in the Roman World, 31 B.C.–A.D. 337* (London)
Morwood, J. (1999), *A Latin Grammar* (Oxford)
Pelling, C. (1993), 'Tacitus and Germanicus', in T.J. Luce and A.J. Woodman (eds.), *Tacitus and the Tacitean Tradition* (Princeton), 59–85
Pollard, N. (2000), *Soldiers, Cities and Civilians in Roman Syria* (Ann Arbor)
Ross, D. (1973), 'The Tacitean Germanicus', *Yale Classical Studies* 23: 209–27
Seager, R. (1972), *Tiberius* (London)
Southern, P. (1998), *Augustus* (London)
Stewart, A.F. (1977), 'To Entertain an Emperor: Sperlonga, Laokoon and Tiberius at the Dinner-table', *JRS* 67: 76–90
Syme, R. (1952), *The Roman Revolution*, corrected ed. (London)
(1958), *Tacitus*, 2 vols. (Oxford)
Talbert, R.J.A. (1984), *The Senate of Imperial Rome* (Princeton)
Wallace-Hadrill, A. (1983), *Suetonius: The Scholar and his Caesars* (London)
Wardle, D. (1994), *Suetonius' Life of Caligula* (Brussels)
Warmington, B.H. (1969). *Nero: Reality and Legend* (New York)
Watson, G.R. (1969), *The Roman Soldier* (London)
Webster, G. (1985), *The Imperial Roman Army of the First and Second Centuries A.D.*, 3rd edition(Totowa, NJ)
West, D. and Woodman, A. (1979), *Creative Imitation and Latin Literature* (Cambridge)
Wheelock, F.M., revised LaFleur, R.A. (2000), *Wheelock's Latin*, 6th edition (New York)
Woodcock, E.C. (1939), *Tacitus Annals Book XIV* (London)
(1959), *A New Latin Syntax* (London)
Woodman, A.J. (1988), *Rhetoric in Classical Historiography* (London)
(1998), *Tacitus Reviewed* (Oxford)
Woods, D. (2000), 'Caligula's Seashells', *Greece and Rome* 47: 80–7

16 Further reading

Balsdon, J.P.V.D. (1934), *The Emperor Gaius* (Oxford)
Bradley, K.R. (1978), *Suetonius' Life of Nero* (Brussels)
Jones, A.H.M. (1970), *Augustus* (London)
Scramuzza, V.M. (1940), *The Emperor Claudius* (Oxford)

Shotter, D.C.A. (1997), *Nero* (London)

Syme, R. (1974), 'The Crisis of 2 B.C.', *Sitzungsberichte der Bayerische Akadamie der Wissenschaft, München* 7 (1974), 3–34 (= Syme, *Roman Papers*, vol. III (Oxford 1984), 912ff.)

Warmington, B.M. (1977), *Suetonius Nero* (Bristol)

AUGUSTUS

~

3 Coin depicting Augustus.

On Augustus, see section 5 of the Introduction.

1 *Some anecdotes in Suetonius about Augustus' origins, depicting him as the son of a god and foretelling his greatness as an emperor.*

Lego Atiam, cum ad sollemne Apollinis sacrum media nocte venisset, posita in templo lectica, dum ceterae matronae dormirent, obdormisse; draconem repente irrepsisse ad eam pauloque post egressum; illam expergefactam quasi a concubitu mariti purificasse se; et statim in corpore eius exstitisse maculam velut picti draconis nec potuisse umquam exigi, adeo ut mox publicis balineis perpetuo abstinuerit; Augustum natum mense decimo et ob hoc Apollinis filium existimatum. eadem Atia, priusquam pareret, somniavit intestina sua ferri ad sidera explicarique per omnem terrarum et caeli ambitum. somniavit et pater Octavius utero Atiae iubar solis exortum.

[Only words within inverted commas represent actual translations of the latin. The expression 'i.e.' introduces explanation or paraphrase (not actual translation). For any unfamiliar technical terms, see Introduction section 14.]

1 **lego** introduces a long indirect statement – hence the accusatives and infinitives (such as *Atiam...obdormisse*) that follow in this sentence, and the subjunctives in subordinate clauses. Such extended indirect statement is a common feature of Latin prose.

1 **Atiam**: she was Augustus' mother, and the niece of Julius Caesar.

2 **posita...lectica**: ablative absolute.

3 **obdormisse** is the syncopated (shortened) form of the perfect active infinitive of *obdormio* (normally *obdormi(v)isse*).

3 **post** is the adverb (*paulo post* = 'a little later').

4 with **egressum** understand *esse* (it is also an infinitive in indirect statement depending on *lego*).

4 **a concubitu mariti**: 'after intercourse with her husband'.

4 **purificasse** is a syncopated form of *purificavisse* (perfect infinitive of *purifico*). The loss of a syllable from the middle of a verb like this was common.

5 **maculam velut picti draconis**: 'a mark as if consisting of a coloured snake' = 'a mark like a coloured snake' (*picti draconis* is genitive of definition).

6 **potuisse**: perfect infinitive of *possum*.

6 **exigi** is the present infinitive passive of *exigo*.

6 **adeo ut** introduces a result (consecutive) clause – hence the perfect subjunctive *abstinuerit*.

6 **perpetuo** is an adverb.

7–8 **natum...existimatum**: understand *esse* in both cases (these are also infinitives in indirect statement dependent on *lego*). Augustus associated himself closely with Apollo and claimed that the god helped him defeat Antony and Cleopatra at the Battle of Actium.

8 **eadem**: from *idem*.

8 **priusquam pareret**: in Latin of this period, the subjunctive is often found with *priusquam* without any sense of purpose but simply as an alternative for the indicative. *Pareret* is from *pario*.

9 **ferri**: present infinitive passive of *fero* (part of an accusative and infinitive construction after *somniavit*). The dream implies that her son's influence will spread far and wide and that he will even reach heaven (he was deified).

10 **Octavius** was Augustus' father, and the first one to become a senator in his old and wealthy equestrian family.

10 **utero** = *ex utero*. This is a local ablative (a place whence or where expression without a preposition).

11 **exortum**: understand *esse* (in an accusative and infinitive after *somniavit*). The dream suggests Atia giving birth to a figure of great brilliance closely linked to the sun god Apollo.

REVIEW 1st and 2nd declension nouns (M p. 16, W p. 446, RLRG sections H1 and H2) and indirect statement and subordinate clauses in indirect speech (M pp. 82ff., W pp. 164ff., 444, RLRG sections R1 and R4).

2 *Suetonius tells some strange stories about Augustus' childhood, marking him out as somebody extraordinary and superhuman.*

Infans adhuc, repositus vespere in cunas a nutricula loco plano, postera luce non comparuit diuque quaesitus tandem in altissima turri repertus est, iacens contra solis exortum. Cum primum fari coepisset, in avito suburbano obstrepentis forte ranas silere iussit, atque ex eo negantur ibi ranae coaxare. in nemore prandenti ex 5
inproviso aquila panem ei e manu rapuit et, cum altissime evolasset, rursus ex inproviso leniter delapsa reddidit.

Nutrimentorum eius ostenditur adhuc locus in avito suburbano permodicus et cellae penuariae instar, tenetque vicinitatem opinio tamquam et natus ibi sit. huc introire nisi necessario et caste religio 10
est, concepta opinione veteri quasi temere adeuntibus horror quidam et metus obiciatur, sed et mox confirmata. nam cum possessor villae novus seu forte seu temptandi causa cubitum se eo contulisset, evenit ut post paucissimas noctis horas exturbatus inde subita vi et incerta, paene semianimis cum strato simul ante fores 15
inveniretur.

1 **infans adhuc** refers to Augustus while still a child.

2 **postera luce**: i.e. at dawn on the next day.

2 **quaesitus** is the perfect participle passive of *quaero.*

3 **turri** is ablative singular of *turris.*

3 **cum primum**: 'when first' = 'as soon as'.

3 **fari** is the present infinitive of *for.*

4 **obstrepentis** = *obstrepentes* (agreeing with *ranas*). This is an alternative form of the accusative plural in third declension (masculine and feminine) nouns and adjectives.

4 **iussit**: *iubeo* takes an accusative and infinitive.

5 **ex eo negantur ibi ranae coaxare**: 'since then frogs are said not to croak there' = 'they say that since then frogs do not croak there'. *Coaxare* is an unusual (and so striking) verb, and is a good example of onomatopoeia (so the Greek Comedy writer Aristophanes made the chorus of frogs in his play called *The Frogs* sing out *brekekekex coax coax*).

5–6 **prandenti . . . ei**: this dative of disadvantage (denoting the person to whose disadvantage something happens) was common with verbs of depriving like *rapio* (we would say: 'snatched FROM him').

6 **aquila**: the eagle was sacred to Jupiter.

7 **evolasset** = *evolavisset* (syncopated form of the pluperfect subjunctive).

7 **reddidit**: *panem* is the object of this verb as well as of *rapuit.*

8 **Nutrimentorum . . . locus**: i.e. Augustus' nursery.

9 **cellae penuariae instar** = 'like a pantry' (*instar* 'the equivalent of' has the force of an adjective meaning 'like').

9–10 **tenetque . . . ibi sit**: 'and the belief that he was also/even born there possesses the neighbourhood/the neighbours' (i.e. the locals believe that . . .). *tamquam* (like *quasi* in 11 below) is often used by Suetonius with verbs in the subjunctive to express indirect statement, sometimes with and sometimes without a suggestion of doubt about the truthfulness of the statement.

10–11 huc introire . . . religio est: 'there is a religious fear to enter here unless of necessity and in a state of ceremonial purity' (i.e. people are afraid to enter the nursery and will only do so of necessity and after religious purification). *introire* is the present infinitive of *introeo*, while *necessario* and *caste* are adverbs.

11 concepta (and *confirmata* in 12) agree with *opinione veteri* in an ablative absolute construction with a causal sense (= 'because a belief that . . . was formed long ago and, what's more, was soon corroborated'). The adjective *vetus* ('long-standing') functions virtually as an adverb here (= 'long ago').

11–12 quasi . . . obiciatur goes with *opinione* ('a belief that a certain cause of horror and source of dread . . .'). *quasi* introduces a hypothetical situation after *opinione*.

11 adeuntibus is the present participle of *adeo* = 'people entering' (dative with *obiciatur*).

13 temptandi causa: gerund with *causa* ('for the sake of') to express purpose.

13 cubitum: supine in -um to denote purpose.

13 eo is the adverb ('to that place').

14 contulisset governs *se* and is the pluperfect subjunctive of *confero*.

14 evenit ut: 'it came about that . . .' . *ut* introduces a result (consecutive) clause.

15 cum strato simul: 'together with his bedclothes'.

REVIEW **3rd declension nouns (M pp. 16f., W p. 446, RLRG section H3) and the ablative absolute and temporal clauses (M pp. 79f., 118ff., W pp. 155f., 211f., RLRG sections P and T).**

4 Dedication to Gaius and Lucius Caesar, from the portico dedicated to them in the Roman forum in 2 BC, when they were heirs apparent to Augustus.

3 Among his public achievements as emperor, Augustus established widespread peace (while suffering only two serious military defeats), constructed and repaired many buildings to beautify Rome, and did much to promote law and order.

Ianum Quirinum, semel atque iterum a condita urbe ante
memoriam suam clausum, in multo breviore temporis spatio (terra
marique pace parta) ter clusit. graves clades duas accepit – Lollianam
et Varianam (Varianam paene exitiabilem, tribus legionibus cum
duce legatisque et auxiliis omnibus caesis). adeo consternatum 5
ferunt ut per continuos menses barba capilloque summisso caput
interdum foribus illideret vociferans: 'Quintili Vare, legiones redde!'
urbem neque pro maiestate imperii ornatam et inundationibus
incendiisque obnoxiam excoluit adeo ut iure sit gloriatus marmoream
se relinquere quam latericiam accepisset. aedes sacras vetustate 10
conlapsas aut incendio absumptas refecit. grassaturas dispositis per
opportuna loca stationibus inhibuit. leges sanxit de adulteriis, de
pudicitia, de ambitu. ipse ius dixit non diligentia modo summa sed et
lenitate, siquidem manifesti parricidii reum, ne culleo insueretur, ita
fertur interrogasse: 'Certe patrem tuum non occidisti?' 15

1 **Ianum Quirinum** refers to a temple of Janus in Rome with doors at either end which were closed when peace prevailed throughout the empire. This had happened only twice (*semel atque iterum*) before, during the reign of Numa (Rome's second king) and in 235 BC (after the First Punic War).

1 **a condita urbe**: 'since the city having been founded' = 'since the foundation of the city'.

2 **memoriam suam**: i.e. the period of Augustus.

2 **multo** is the adverb ('much').

2–3 **terra marique**: 'on land and sea'.

3 **pace parta**: ablative absolute. *parta* is from *pario.*

3 **Lollianam** (*cladem*) refers to a defeat inflicted by the Germans on Roman troops led by Lollius in 16 BC, during which the standard of the fifth legion was lost to the enemy (a great disgrace).

4 **Varianam** (*cladem*) refers to a much more serious defeat in AD 9, when the general Quintilius Varus and his three legions were trapped in the Teutoburg forest in Germany and almost totally annihilated, with the loss of all their standards. This caused a shock wave throughout the empire.

4–5 **tribus ... caesis**: ablative absolute with a causal force.

5 **consternatum**: understand *esse Augustum* in an accusative and infinitive construction after *ferunt* ('they say').

6 **ut** here introduces a result (consecutive) clause, as it does in line 9 below.

6 **barba ... summisso**: the participle (in an ablative absolute construction) agrees in gender with its nearest noun but also applies to *barba.*

8 **neque ... et**: 'not ... and ...'

9–10 **marmoream ... accepisset**: understand *urbem* in this accusative and infinitive construction ('that the city which he had received built of brick he was leaving behind [at his death] built of marble').

10 **vetustate**: ablative of cause.

11 **refecit** is the perfect indicative of *reficio.*

11 **dispositis**: perfect participle passive of *dispono* in an ablative absolute.

13 **non . . . modo . . . sed et**: 'not only . . . but also'.

13–14 **diligentia . . . lenitate**: ablatives of manner ('with diligence').

14 **manifesti parricidii reum**: i.e. someone who had obviously killed his own father.

14 **ne . . . insueretur**: negative purpose clause.

15 **fertur interrogasse**: 'he is said to have interrogated' (*interrogasse* = *interrogavisse*).

15 **Certe . . . occidisti**: the question is framed in such a way as to elicit an answer in the negative. Those who confessed to such a crime were sewn up in a sack with a dog, a cock, a monkey and a snake and were thrown into a river or the sea, so Augustus is trying to save the man from this particularly horrible form of punishment.

REVIEW **4th and 5th declension nouns (M p. 17, W p. 446, RLRG sections H4 and H5), consecutive/result clauses and purpose clauses (M pp. 96ff., 99ff., W pp. 196f., 189, RLRG sections S2a and S2b), and sequence of tenses (M pp. 86f., W pp. 201 ff., RLRG section L-V c).**

5 Forum of Augustus, Rome. Opened in 2 BC, the forum centred on the Temple of Mars Ultor, vowed by Augustus (then Octavian) in 42 BC as he set out for Greece to confront the conspirators who had assassinated Julius Caesar, his adoptive father.

6 The Hermann Monument in Detmold, Germany (erected 1875) commemorates the *clades Variana* of AD 9, in which three Roman legions under P. Quinctilius Varus were ambushed and annihilated by Arminius, a chief of the Cherusci tribe. In its wake, Roman annexation of Germany east of the Rhine ceased.

Augustus' private life was marked by moderation and frugality (he lived in a modest house on the Palatine, for instance, not a palatial mansion). However, his sexual peccadilloes, as recorded by Suetonius in Passage 4, may have left him open to charges of crass hypocrisy, since in his public pronouncements he championed traditional Roman values of loyalty to the family.

4 *Augustus' adulteries, at a party and elsewhere.*

Adulteria exercuisse ne amici quidem negant, excusantes sane
non libidine sed ratione commissa, quo facilius consilia
adversariorum per cuiusque mulieres exquireret. Marcus Antonius
obiecit feminam consularem e triclinio viro coram in cubiculum
abductam, rursus in convivium rubentibus auriculis, incomptiore 5
capillo reductam; condiciones quaesitas per amicos, qui matres
familias et adultas aetate virgines denudarent atque perspicerent,
tamquam Toranio mangone vendente. postea quoque, ut ferunt, ad
vitiandas virgines promptior, quae sibi undique etiam ab uxore
conquirerentur. 10

1–2 = *ne amici quidem* (*ne... quidem* = 'not even') *negant [Augustum] adulteria exercuisse* (accusative and infinitive in indirect statement after *negant*), *excusantes sane* (= '[although] admittedly pleading in excuse that') *non libidine sed ratione* (ablatives of cause) *[adulteria] commissa [esse]*.

2 quo facilius: *quo* with the comparative adverb introduces a purpose clause.

3 cuiusque: genitive of *quisque.*

4 obiecit: *obicio* here (meaning 'charge, accuse') is followed by an indirect statement, so *esse* should be supplied with *abductam* in 5, *reductam* in 6 and *quaesitas* in 6.

4 viro coram: 'in front of her husband'. More normally, of course, prepositions are placed before their nouns, but such anastrophe (reversal of the normal order) is common enough, especially in poetry. *coram* always follows its noun, unusually for prepositions in prose.

5 rursus: some word for 'and' is missed out before this (as it is before *condiciones* in 6). Such omission of conjunctions (called asyndeton) is common.

5–6 rubentibus... capillo: ablative absolutes (referring to the woman); the (non-existent) present participle of the verb *sum* has to be understood here. The comparative (*incomptiore*) has the force of 'rather' (not 'more').

6 quaesitas with (supplied) *esse* is perfect infinitive passive of *quaero.*

6–7 matres familias: 'matrons' or 'women in charge of households' (i.e. respectable married women).

7 adultas aetate: 'mature with respect to age' = 'grown up'. *aetate* is ablative of respect.

7 denudarent... perspicerent: subjunctives in a subordinate clause in indirect speech.

8 tamquam... vendente: 'as if Toranius the slave-dealer was putting [them] up for sale' (slaves for sale were stripped so that no blemishes or defects could be hidden).

8 ut ferunt: 'as they say'.

8–9 ad... promptior: *erat* or *fuit* is to be understood, and the subject is Augustus (in old age – *postea*). *promptus ad* (+ gerundive) means 'readily inclined to' (do something – in this case to deflower virgins), and the comparative here has just the sense of 'rather' (not 'more'). The alliteration (repetition of initial v) in *vitiandas virgines* draws attention to the words.

9 uxore: i.e. Livia.

10 conquirerentur: subjunctive in a generic relative clause (indicating a sort or type of person).

REVIEW **adjectives (M pp. 19ff., W p. 447, RLRG sections J1 and J2) and generic relative clauses and the gerund and gerundive/future periphrastic (M pp. 100, 108ff., W pp. 269f., 157, 276ff., RLRG sections Q2, N and O).**

The single greatest political problem faced by Augustus and all subsequent emperors was the succession. Uncertainty as to who would be the next emperor opened fault lines within the imperial house, and lent the private actions of princesses distinct political and public significance. Augustus' only natural child, Julia, who was a central figure in Augustus' dynastic manipulations, fell from grace suddenly in 2 BC, as described in passage 5.

7 Mausoleum of Augustus, Rome. Epitaphs of Augustus' nephew and intended successor, Marcellus (died 23 BC) and his sister, Marcellus' mother, Octavia (died 11 BC).

5 *Augustus banishes his daughter Julia for adultery.*

De filia absens ac libello per quaestorem recitato notum senatui fecit, abstinuitque congressu hominum diu prae pudore; etiam de necanda deliberavit. certe cum sub idem tempus una ex consciis

liberta Phoebe suspendio vitam finisset, maluisse se ait Phoebes
patrem fuisse. 5

Relegatae usum vini omnemque delicatiorem cultum ademit
neque adiri a quoquam libero servove nisi se consulto permisit, et
ita ut certior fieret qua is aetate, qua statura, quo colore esset,
etiam quibus corporis notis vel cicatricibus.

Post quinquennium demum ex insula in continentem 10
lenioribusque paulo condicionibus transtulit eam. nam ut omnino
revocaret exorari nullo modo potuit, deprecanti saepe populo
Romano et pertinacius instanti tales filias talesque coniuges
inprecatus.

1–2 **De filia... notum senatui fecit**: 'he informed the senate about his daughter' (*notum facio* + dative means 'I make it known' to someone).

1 **absens ac libello**= 'in his absence and by means of a note...'

3 **necanda**: supply *filia* with this gerundive (= 'the execution of his daughter'). Compare the first Roman consul Brutus, who condemned his sons to death for plotting to restore the royal Tarquins.

3 **sub**: 'at about' = 'at almost'.

3 **consciis** refers to Julia's confidantes (the word is used as a noun).

4 **Phoebes**: genitive singular of *Phoebe* (a Greek name).

6 **Relegatae** (agreeing with an understood *filiae*) is dative of disadvantage with *ademit* (we would say: 'he took away FROM his banished daughter...' = 'after banishing his daughter he deprived her of...'). *ademit* is from *adimo*.

7 **adiri**: present infinitive passive of *adeo* ('he did not allow her to be approached').

7 **quoquam** is ablative singular of *quisquam*.

7 **nisi se consulto**: ablative absolute ('unless himself having been consulted' = 'unless he [i.e. Augustus] had been consulted').

8 **ita ut certior fieret**: 'on condition that he [i.e. Augustus] was informed'. *certior fio* ('I am made more certain') = 'I am informed'.

8–9 **qua... cicatricibus**: there is a series of ablatives of description and indirect questions here ('of what age... the person was').

10 **ex insula in continentem**: Julia was moved from Pandateria (a small island off the west coast of Italy, to which she was originally banished) to Rhegium (on the southernmost tip of mainland Italy).

11–12 **ut omnino revocaret** is an indirect command dependent on *exorari*.

12 **potuit** is perfect indicative of *possum*.

12–14 : i.e. when the Roman people pressed for her return, Augustus prayed that they might be cursed with daughters and wives like Julia ('calling down such daughters and such wives on the Roman people...'). The participles *deprecanti* and *instanti* agree with *populo Romano* (dative).

REVIEW pronouns (M pp. 26ff., W pp. 448f., RLRG section I), indirect commands and indirect questions (M. pp. 89ff., 94f., W pp. 253f., 204, RLRG sections R2 and R3).

After Augustus' death, his successor as emperor (Tiberius, who was Julia's husband) kept her confined to her house and left her destitute, so that she died slowly of malnutrition.

The accounts of Augustus' death preserved in Suetonius and Tacitus (Passages 6 and 7 respectively) reveal much about the very different characters of these two authors and their works. While the overall series of events is largely the same, the tone and focus of their two accounts are quite distinct.

8 Ara Pacis Augustae, Rome (ca. 9 BC): The presentation of the imperial family as a picture of dynastic stability and harmony is rather at odds with the known facts. There is no consensus on who, exactly, the individuals are.

6 Suetonius' version of the death of Augustus: after escorting his stepson (and successor) Tiberius on part of his journey to Illyricum and saying goodbye to him, Augustus (who had been troubled with diarrhoea) falls seriously ill.

In redeundo adgravata valetudine tandem Nolae succubuit, revocatumque ex itinere Tiberium diu secreto sermone detinuit, neque post ulli maiori negotio animum accommodavit.

Supremo die identidem exquirens an iam de se tumultus foris esset, petito speculo, capillum sibi comi ac malas labantes corrigi 5 praecepit, et admissos amicos percontatus est ecquid iis videretur mimum vitae commode transegisse. omnibus deinde dimissis, repente in osculis Liviae et in hac voce defecit: 'Livia, nostri coniugii memor vive ac vale,' sortitus exitum facilem et qualem semper optaverat. 10

Unum omnino ante efflatam animam signum alienatae mentis ostendit, quod subito pavefactus a quadraginta se iuvenibus abripi questus est. id quoque magis praesagium quam mentis deminutio fuit, siquidem totidem milites praetoriani extulerunt eum in publicum. 15

1 **redeundo**: gerund of *redeo*.

1 **adgravata valitudine**: ablative absolute (like *petito speculo* in 5 and *omnibus . . . dimissis* in 7).

1 **Nolae**: locative ('at Nola', an Italian town near Naples).

3 **post**: the adverb ('afterwards').

4 **foris**: the adverb ('outside').

5 **esset**: subjunctive in an indirect question (like *videretur* in 6).

5–6 **malas labantes corrigi praecepit**: he was not strong enough to stop his lower jaw dropping, so he ordered it to be propped up (*corrigi*, like the other present passive infinitive *comi*, depends on *praecepit*).

6 **iis**: dative plural of *is*.

7 **mimum vitae**: translate as 'the comedy of life' (a mime was a dramatic production with a farcical element).

7 **transegisse**: perfect infinitive active of *transigo*, governed by *videretur* ('seemed').

8 **Liviae**: Augustus' wife (and the mother of Tiberius by an earlier husband).

8 **defecit**: perfect indicative of *deficio*.

11 **ante efflatam animam**: i.e. before he breathed his last.

12 **se . . . abripi**: accusative and infinitive in indirect statement after *questus est* (from *queror*).

13 **magis . . . quam**: 'rather . . . than'.

14 **praetoriani**: the praetorian troops were the emperor's bodyguard.

14–15 **extulerunt eum in publicum**: i.e. carried him out (*effero*) to his lying-in-state.

REVIEW **1st conjugation verbs (M pp. 36f., 46f., W pp. 452ff., RLRG sections A–D), causal clauses (M. pp. 126f., W pp. 211f., RLRG section U), and direct commands (M. pp. 88f., W pp. 5, 49, 185, RLRG section L-V (a) 3).**

7 Tacitus' version of the death of Augustus: his wife Livia had Augustus so much under her control that he adopted her son Tiberius as his successor and banished his own grandson Agrippa Postumus (Tiberius' rival for power) to the island of Planasia; later, when Augustus was old and sick, people began to gossip about those who would soon be in charge of them instead.

9 Coin depicting Livia.

Imminentis dominos variis rumoribus differebant: trucem Agrippam et ignominia accensum, non aetate neque rerum experientia tantae moli parem; Tiberium maturum annis, spectatum bello, sed vetere atque insita Claudiae familiae superbia; multaque indicia saevitiae, quamquam premantur, erumpere; accedere 5
matrem muliebri inpotentia: serviendum feminae.

Haec atque talia agitantibus, gravescere valetudo Augusti; et quidam scelus uxoris suspectabant. quippe rumor incesserat paucos ante mensis Augustum, comite uno Fabio Maximo, Planasiam vectum ad visendum Agrippam; multas illic utrimque lacrimas et 10
signa caritatis spemque ex eo fore ut iuvenis penatibus avi redderetur; quod Maximum uxori aperuisse, illam Liviae.

Vixdum ingressus Illyricum, Tiberius properis matris litteris accitur. neque satis compertum est spirantem adhuc Augustum apud urbem Nolam an exanimem reppererit. acribus namque custodiis 15
domum et vias saepserat Livia, laetique interdum nuntii vulgabantur donec, provisis quae tempus monebat, simul excessisse Augustum et rerum potiri Tiberium fama eadem tulit.

Primum facinus novi principatus fuit Postumi Agrippae caedes, quem ignarum inermumque centurio confecit. 20

On Tacitus' style, see Introduction section 13 (lines 1–6 here provide a good example of his brevity).

1 **imminentis** = *imminentes.*

1–6 **trucem . . . feminae:** this is all indirect speech representing the gossip (= '[they said that] Agrippa was . . .').

2 **ignominia:** (ablative) i.e. the disgrace of his banishment.

3 **tantae moli parem:** i.e. up to the great responsibility of running the empire.

4 **vetere atque insita . . . superbia:** ablative of description (= 'possessing the old . . .'). *esse* is to be understood again. *insita* is perfect participle passive of *insero.* The Claudian family (to which Tiberius belonged) had a reputation for arrogance.

5–6 **accedere . . . inpotentia:** 'added [to that] was his mother with her female lack of self-restraint' (another ablative of description), i.e there was also his mother, a woman who knew no self-restraint.

6 **serviendum feminae:** the gerundive expresses obligation and is used impersonally ('it would have to be served to a woman' = 'they would have to be the slaves of a woman', i.e. Livia).

7 **agitantibus:** understand *illis* in an ablative absolute construction.

7 **gravescere:** historic infinitive (used in place of a main verb in the perfect indicative: see Introduction, section 13).

8 **incesserat:** pluperfect indicative of *incedo.*

8–9 **paucos ante mensis:** 'a few months earlier'. *mensis* = *menses.*

9–10 **Augustum . . . Planasiam vectum:** understand *esse* – this is an accusative and infinitive after *rumor* in 8 ('a rumour that Augustus had sailed to Planasia'). The indirect statement continues at 10–12, where *fuisse* has to be supplied with *lacrimas* etc.

9 **comite uno Fabio Maximo:** ablative absolute (understand the (non-existent) present participle of *sum* here).

10 **ad visendum:** 'for the purpose of visiting'.

11–12 **spem . . . redderetur:** 'there was hope that the young man would be restored to the house of his grandfather'. *fore* is the future infinitive of *sum,* and *fore ut* ('it will be the case that') + subjunctive is a way of expressing the future infinitive.

12 **quod:** 'which thing' (= 'this') is the object of *aperuisse.*

12 **illam Liviae:** understand *quod aperuisse* with these words. In grammatically parallel phrases and clauses, it often happens that material in one of them is not expressed in the other but must be supplied from context.

14 **accitur:** historic present (used in place of a perfect or imperfect indicative for variety and vividness).

14–15 **neque satis compertum . . . repperit:** 'and it is not sufficiently ascertained [=it is not known for sure] whether he found Augustus still breathing . . . or dead' (supply *utrum* after *compertum est* in an indirect double question).

17 **provisis quae tempus monebat:** understand *illis* in this ablative absolute (literally: 'with those things that the time/circumstances suggested/warned of having been seen to', i.e. after the necessary steps had been taken).

17 **excessisse:** perfect infinitive active of *excedo.*

18 **fama eadem tulit:** 'one and the same report announced that . . .' (+ two accusatives and infinitives). *Tulit* is perfect indicative active of *fero.*

20 **confecit** is perfect indicative active of *conficio.*

REVIEW **2nd conjugation verbs (M pp. 38f., 48f., W pp. 452ff., RLRG sections A–D) and concessive clauses (M pp. 127f., W pp. 211f., RLRG section V).**

10 Mausoleum of Augustus, Rome. Completed in 28 BC, this was one of Augustus' earliest building projects in Rome. It announced his dynastic intentions, his family's long-term dominance of Roman politics. Augustus was interred here after his own death in AD 14.

11 Coin depicting Agrippa.

AUGUSTUS APPRECIATION

Passages 1–2 Suetonius Augustus 94 and 6

The Romans believed that major events, such as the birth or death of great men, were foreshadowed by various *omina* ('omens') or *prodigia* ('portents') sent by the gods. The *omina imperii* ('omens of power') listed here by Suetonius are typical (see Wardle 1994, 356), and they appear in all his lives of the emperors (e.g. in his *Galba* 4, dreams, miraculous behaviour by animals, and offhand remarks by prior emperors presage Galba's sudden rise to power). These omens for Augustus have parallels in the case of other important individuals. Just as Augustus silenced the frogs, so Hercules silenced the crickets (Diodorus Siculus 4.22.5). The famous Republican general who defeated Hannibal, Scipio Africanus (Aulus Gellius *Attic Nights* 7.1), and the most renowned of all ancient conquerors, Alexander the Great (Plutarch *Alexander* 2–3), were reputedly fathered by snakes (mystical creatures, usually associated with chthonic deities, whose realms they appeared to share). In fact, Suetonius' whole passage is evocative of the stories surrounding Alexander's birth and childhood (Plutarch *Alexander* 2–6); while the haunted nursery item reflects the wider Classical tradition of spooky tales (Pliny *Epistles* 7.27, Apuleius *Metamorphoses* 2.21ff., Philostratus *Life of Apollonius* 4.15f. etc.).

Passage 3 Suetonius Augustus *22, 23, 28, 30, 32–4*

Augustus did, as he claimed, end the civil wars and bring back order. After defeating Antony and Cleopatra in 31 BC, he turned the newly professionalized legions on foreign enemies, finishing the conquest of Spain, pushing Rome's frontiers up to the Danube and beyond the Rhine, and almost annexing large portions of Germany west of the Elbe. This latter drive came to a halt when Varus lost his three legions in an ambush in the Teutoburg Forest (at Kalkreise). To signify a return to stable government and to further his image as a restorer of Roman traditions, Augustus re-established neglected cults in Rome and renewed many temples and other public structures. This successful renovation of the city went hand in hand with a rather less successful attempt at a moral revival, as Augustus introduced a variety of measures designed to nurture traditional virtues such as devotion to family and state. On this moral revival, see further Galinsky 1996, 80ff., 288ff., and for more (in his own words) on Augustus' public achievements in general see his *Res Gestae* (in Brunt–Moore 1967).

Passage 4 Suetonius Augustus *69 and 71.*

Like us, the ancients were interested in the sex lives of public figures, and in his biographies Suetonius routinely includes a chapter or two on this topic. For more on Augustus' reported peccadilloes (with both sexes) see Suet. *Aug.* 68–9. That Augustus had adulterous affairs is quite believable (concubinage was very common among the Roman nobility). Assuming that these tales are true, you may see a clash between Augustus' private behaviour and his public policies in favour of moral rectitude. The clash is probably illusory. In fact, Augustus' social programmes (including the criminalization of adultery) were not concerned with monitoring every nobleman's private life but with increasing the reproductive rate of the aristocracy, to provide Rome with a steady supply of leaders. Similarly, his later banishment of his daughter (and granddaughter) for having extra-marital affairs might strike you as hypocritical, given Augustus' own failings. However, the situations did differ, and there were practical considerations. The liaisons of emperors (and imperial princes) seldom threatened the stability of the state, whereas the love affairs of imperial princesses might well do so (see on passage 5 below).

Passage 5 Suetonius Augustus *65.*

We know little about Julia (born 39 BC). Macrobius (*Saturnalia* 2.5) alludes to her gentleness and wit, but most sources treat her primarily as a cipher in Augustus' dynastic plans. He used formal ties to the immediate imperial family as one means of indicating favour toward potential successors. He adopted people himself and also married Julia to three princes whom he was considering as successors, including Tiberius, who did eventually become the next emperor in AD 14. Julia also provided Augustus with three grandsons, all of whom he adopted as his own sons. So her centrality to the succession is obvious. In assessing Augustus' reaction to the news of her adulteries, we should avoid simplistic assumptions of patriarchy or hypocrisy. The political ramifications of Julia's actions were potentially dire, even if she was not consciously involved in forming a faction within the imperial house (as some scholars have theorized) and was not actually aware of how threatening her actions were. Potential successors gained promotion and favour by direct contact with members of the imperial house (Julia's own marital career demonstrates this). The political consequences of allowing male outsiders into her bed are therefore quite obvious. This is what really angered Augustus, rather than her disappointing behaviour. Suetonius, in his salacious way, concentrates on the morality aspect, but we should not be blind to the dynastic facets.

Passage 6 Suetonius Augustus *98–9.*

When one compares this account with Passage 7 (by Tacitus), it becomes clear that the general situation is the same in both (the worsening of Augustus' health, the setting of Nola for the death, the return of Tiberius, the presence of Livia), but the presentation and interpretation are very different. Suetonius (the biographer) gives us an intimate and clear picture of his subject Augustus, with a quote of his final words. He shows us an Augustus who is brave, at peace, rather philosophical and even a bit light-hearted, amid loving friends and family. The tone is quiet and calm, and the picture is moving (his touching concern for his appearance, his final moments with his wife) and has a miraculous tinge (at 13ff.). Read section 11 of the Introduction (noting differences between biography and history); then translate passage 7 and consider how that version diverges from this one in terms of mood, main thrust and purpose.

Passage 7 Tacitus Annals *1.4–6.*

The historian makes this episode into an early attack on Tiberius' regime and largely effaces Augustus (who is just an obstacle to be removed, under control rather than in control). Tacitus' version is much more sour and sinister than Suetonius'. The death becomes an affair of palace politics, with dark forces at work in the background. Tacitus often uses unsupported gossip as a smear, and here all the rumour and suspicion make the death much murkier. There is gloom about the succession and the whole imperial system, with Augustus a cipher and other characters either unsuitable or malign and murderous. In addition, Livia is far more prominent here. A woman is in control, and she (rather than Tiberius) is the one who acts and orchestrates events, moving with chilling swiftness and ruthless efficiency to bring about and protect the succession of her son and the continuation of her own power. At *Annals* 1.10, Tacitus calls her 'a stern stepmother to the imperial house', implying her involvement in the deaths of the five earlier successors who left the path clear for her son Tiberius to succeed. Cassius Dio (56.30.1–2) even has a story about her killing Augustus by means of poisoned figs. However, the case against her is, at best, unproven. She can be absolved from guilt for the deaths of most the prior successors. Four of them died away from Rome, one on the other side of the empire (in modern Turkey). Unless her unseen hand had an enormous reach, the Black Widow image of Livia (while possessing a certain macabre fascination) probably has little basis in historical reality.

TIBERIUS

~

12 Coin depicting Tiberius.

On Tiberius, see section 6 of the Introduction.

The first passage records an incident in AD 15 from the military campaigns of Tiberius' adopted son and designated heir (Germanicus) which were waged against the German tribes as retribution for the loss of three legions in the Teutoburg Forest in AD 9 (the site of this disaster has recently been discovered).

1 *Germanicus and his army find and bury the remains of the Roman general Varus and the soldiers of his three legions, who had been annihilated by the German chieftain Arminius and his men six years earlier.*

Cupido Germanicum invadit solvendi suprema militibus ducique, permoto ad miserationem omni exercitu ob propinquos, amicos, denique ob casus bellorum et sortem hominum. incedunt maestos locos visuque et memoria deformes. prima Vari castra lato ambitu trium legionum manus ostentabant. dein semiruto vallo, humili

fossa accisae iam reliquiae consedisse intellegebantur. medio campi
albentia ossa, ut fugerant, ut restiterant, disiecta vel aggerata.
adiacebant fragmina telorum equorumque artus, simul truncis
arborum antefixa ora. lucis propinquis barbarae arae, apud quas
tribunos ac centuriones mactaverant. 10

Et cladis eius superstites, pugnam aut vincula elapsi, referebant
hic cecidisse legatos, illic raptas aquilas; primum ubi vulnus Varo
adactum, ubi infelici dextera et suo ictu mortem invenerit; quo
tribunali contionatus Arminius, quot patibula captivis, quae scrobes,
utque aquilis per superbiam inluserit. 15

Igitur, sextum post cladis annum, trium legionum ossa, nullo
noscente alienas reliquias an suorum humo tegeret, aucta in hostem
ira, maesti simul et infensi condebant. primum exstruendo tumulo
caespitem Germanicus posuit, gratissimo munere in defunctos et
praesentibus doloris socius. quod Tiberio haud probatum, seu 20
cuncta Germanici in deterius trahenti, sive exercitum imagine
caesorum insepultorumque tardatum ad proelia et formidolosiorem
hostium credebat, neque imperatorem auguratu praeditum
adtrectare feralia debuisse.

1 **cupido... solvendi suprema**: 'the desire of performing the last things for...' (gerund + neuter accusative plural object) = 'the desire to perform funeral rites for...'

1 **invadit**: historic present (this use of the present for a perfect or imperfect will not be pointed out any more).

2 **permoto... omni exercitu**: ablative absolute.

2 **ob propinquos, amicos** = *ob propinquos et amicos* (asyndeton, as in lines 5–6 with *semiruto vallo, humili fossa*).

4 **visuque et memoria deformes**: i.e. the places were horrible to look at and had horrible associations. These are ablatives of respect. *deformes* is in emphatic position (like *ora* in 9): stress was given to a word by placing it at the very end (or start) of a phrase, clause or sentence.

4 **prima Vari castra**: it seems that this was the camp pitched by all three of Varus' legions after the first day's fighting with the Germans, and that subsequently the Romans marched on from there but were severely mauled by the enemy, and the survivors tried to make a stand in a second camp behind its hastily and imperfectly constructed fortification of rampart and ditch.

4 **lato ambitu**: ablative of description or means.

5 **manus**: 'handiwork'.

5–6 **semiruto vallo, humili fossa**: local ablatives (i.e. the preposition *in* is omitted, as often in Tacitus).

6 **accisae** is from *accido* ('cut up').

6 **consedisse intellegebantur**: i.e. Germanicus and his men could deduce that the survivors had taken up position there.

6 **medio campi**: 'in the middle of the plain' (*medio* is another local ablative). There seems to be an echo here of Virgil *Aeneid* 12.36 (*campique... ossibus albent*), i.e. a typically poetic feature in Tacitus' prose narrative.

7 **ossa... aggerata**: supply *sunt* with *disiecta vel aggerata*. The bones were scattered (*disicio*) as (i.e. where) men had fled, and were piled up as (i.e. where) men had made a stand (*resisto*).

8–9 **truncis... ora**: understand *erant*. These were probably skulls of Roman soldiers who had been sacrificed (*ora* is from *os oris*).

9 **lucis propinquis**: understand *erant* with this local ablative.

11 **superstites** is used as a noun here ('survivors of...').

11 **pugnam... elapsi**: these are men who escaped from the battlefield or were captured but subsequently rescued or ransomed.

11 **referebant** introduces reported speech – first accusatives and infinitives (supply *esse* with *raptas* in 12) and then indirect questions (understand *sit* with *adactum* in 13 and with *contionatus* in 14, and *fuerint* with *quot patibula captivis, quae scrobes* in 14; these perfect subjunctives after *referebant* are unusual – the pluperfect would be far more usual).

12 **cecidisse**: from *cado*.

12 **primum**: agrees with *vulnus*.

13 **adactum... invenerit**: *adactum* is from *adigo*. In the *ubi* clause the idea is that Varus killed himself with a blow from his own unhappy hand.

13–14 **quo tribunali**: local ablative.

14 **scrobes**: pits in which to bury captives alive or torture them when partly buried.

15 **utque**: 'and how'.

15 **per superbiam**: 'with arrogance' = 'arrogantly'.

16 **sextum post cladis annum**: 'after the sixth year of the disaster' = 'six years after the disaster'.

16 **ossa** (from *os ossis*) is object of *condebant* in 18.

16–17 **nullo noscente** (ablative absolute, like *aucta... ira*) introduces an indirect double question (supply *utrum* = 'whether' before *alienas reliquias*).

17 **suorum** (used as a noun) = '[the remains] of his own ones' (i.e. friends and/or relatives).

17 **aucta** is from *augeo*.

17 **hostem**: singular for plural. We often find *hostis* for *hostes*, *Romanus* for *Romani* etc. in historical narrative.

18 **exstruendo tumulo**: dative of purpose (see Introduction section 14).

19 **munere in defunctos**: 'by way of a tribute to the dead' (ablative of instrument).

20 **praesentibus doloris socius**: i.e. sharing in the grief of those present at the scene.

20 **quod Tiberio haud probatum**: understand *est*. *quod* ('which thing') refers to Germanicus' act, and *Tiberio* is dative of the agent.

20–1 **seu... trahenti** = 'either [because] interpreting all things [= actions] of Germanicus unfavourably'. *trahere in deterius* means literally 'to ascribe to/transform into something worse'. With typical *variatio* (see Introduction section 13) Tacitus abandons this participial construction in the following *sive* clause.

21–3 **sive... credebat**: *sive* = *sive quod* ('or because he imagined that the army had been... and was...'). Supply *esse* with *tardatum* and with *formidolosiorem*. *ad proelia* means 'for/with a view to fighting'. *imagine* means 'vision', and *caesorum* is the perfect participle passive of *caedo*.

23–4 **neque... debuisse**: further indirect statement dependent on *credebat*. As well as being a general, Germanicus also held the position of augur (a priest), and contact with corpses and objects connected with the dead caused ritual pollution for such priests.

REVIEW **3rd conjugation verbs (M pp. 40f., 50f., W pp. 452ff., RLRG sections A–D) and (no example in this passage) fear clauses (M pp. 102f., W p. 285, RLRG section S 2e).**

13 Bust of Germanicus (15 BC–AD 19). His popularity was much resented by the older Emperor Tiberius, according to Suetonius and Tacitus, who implicate the emperor in his (probably natural) death.

14 Kalkreise, Germany. Site of archaeological discoveries that are generally identified with the *clades Variana* battlefield (or at least a good portion of it). This may have been the place visited by Germanicus and his troops in AD 15.

Germanicus continued campaigning in Germany in AD 16, in a combined seaborne and land advance. East of the Visurgis (the River Weser), the Romans engaged a large force of Germans under Arminius (Hermann), chief architect of the Roman defeat in AD 9.

2 *On the eve of the battle of Idistaviso, Germanicus learns of the massing of German tribes (led by Arminius, Inguiomerus and other chiefs). But Roman morale is high (the troops revere their general and are outraged by a German attempt to get them to desert).*

Germanicus transgressus Visurgim indicio perfugae cognoscit delectum ab Arminio locum pugnae, convenisse et alias nationes ausurosque nocturnam castrorum oppugnationem. habita indici fides, et cernebantur ignes, suggressique propius speculatores audiri fremitum equorum immensique et inconditi agminis murmur attulere. 5

Igitur propinquo summae rei discrimine explorandos militum animos ratus, nocte coepta, contectus umeros ferina pelle, Germanicus adit castrorum vias, adsistit tabernaculis fruiturque fama

sui, cum hic nobilitatem ducis, decorem alius, plurimi patientiam, 10
comitatem laudibus ferrent. inter quae unus hostium, Latinae
linguae sciens, acto ad vallum equo, voce magna coniuges et agros, si
quis transfugisset, Arminii nomine pollicetur. intendit ea contumelia
legionum iras: veniret dies, daretur pugna; sumpturum militem
Germanorum agros, tracturum coniuges. tertia ferme vigilia 15
adsultatum est castris, sine coniectu teli, postquam crebras pro
munimentis cohortes et nihil remissum sensere.

2–3 **delectum... ausurosque**: understand *esse* with both words. These two infinitives (like *convenisse*) are part of the indirect speech after *cognoscit. ausurosque* (from *audeo*) refers to all the Germans together. *Et* in 2 means 'also', 'as well'.

3 **habita indici fides**: supply *est* ('trust was put in the informant', i.e. he was believed).

4 **ignes**: i.e. fires of the Germans.

6 **attulere** = *attulerunt*, from *affero* ('brought news that...').

7 **propinquo summae rei discrimine**: ablative absolute (understand the non-existent present participle of *sum*). Literally: 'with the decisive stage of the critical situation being imminent').

7 **explorandos**: understand *esse* with this gerundive of obligation ('to be investigated'), in an accusative and infinitive construction with *ratus* (from *reor*).

8 **contectus umeros**: the perfect participle has an active meaning here ('having covered his shoulders') in imitation of the Greek middle voice (which had generally the same form as the passive but possessed an active force and denoted the doing of something for oneself). Germanicus is disguising himself as one of the tribesmen who served as auxiliaries (support troops) in his army. Others would explain this as a normal perfect participle passive with an accusative of respect.

9 **adit** is from *adeo*.

9–10 **fama sui**: 'his own popularity' (*fama* is ablative with *fruiturque*, and *sui* is genitive of *se*).

10 **cum**: 'when'.

10 **hic... alius... plurimi** ('one man... another... most men') are all subjects of *laudibus ferrent* ('raised up in praise' = 'praised') in 11. Note the variation in the placement of the subjects and in the number of the objects.

10–11 **patientiam, comitatem** = *patientiam et comitatem*.

11 **inter quae**: 'among which things', i.e. while all this was going on (the relative pronoun is often used to connect sentences like this).

12 **acto** is from *ago*.

12–13 **coniuges... transfugisset**: i.e. he promised German wives and land for any Romans who deserted. As often happens with conditions in indirect speech, the pluperfect subjunctive represents a future perfect indicative in the original direct speech.

14 **veniret... pugna**: '[just] let the daylight come, let battle be granted' (there is indirect speech in 13–14, representing the Romans' response).

14 **militem**: singular for plural, referring to the Roman soldiers, who intend to seize German land and wives as booty.

15 **tracturum** is from *traho*.

15 **tertia ferme vigilia**: ablative of time, i.e. at about midnight (the Romans divided the hours of darkness into four 'watches', i.e. periods for keeping watch).

16 **adsultatum est castris**: impersonal expression (= 'an attack was made on the camp'), for which, see Introduction section 14.

17 **sensere** (= *senserunt*) has as its subject the Germans attacking the camp.

REVIEW **4th conjugation verbs (M pp. 42f., 52f., W pp. 452ff., RLRG sections A–D) and conditional clauses (M pp. 114ff., W pp. 228ff., RLRG section S 2c).**

Tacitus has the two commanders give speeches to rouse the spirits of their troops. Germanicus tells the Romans to strike at the unprotected faces of the poorly armed barbarians, who look formidable and are good for a short charge but cannot stand getting hurt. Arminius claims that the enemy are demoralized cowards and urges his men to fight to the death rather than become slaves of greedy and arrogant Rome. His words inflame the Germans and get them shouting for battle.

3 *Most of the German forces are drawn up on a plain and in the outskirts of a forest, while the Cherusci (the tribe led by Arminius) occupy adjoining hills, ready to sweep down on the Roman army, which now attacks and wins a splendid victory.*

Pedestris acies infertur, et praemissus eques postremos ac latera impulit. mirumque dictu, hostium qui silvam tenuerant in aperta, qui campis adstiterant in silvam ruebant. medii inter hos Cherusci collibus detrudebantur, inter quos insignis Arminius manu, voce, vulnere sustentabat pugnam. incubueratque sagittariis, illa rupturus, ni Raetorum Vindelicorumque et Gallicae cohortes signa obiecissent. nisu tamen corporis et impetu equi pervasit, oblitus faciem suo cruore, ne nosceretur. quidam adgnitum a Chaucis inter auxilia Romana agentibus emissumque tradiderunt. virtus seu fraus eadem Inguiomero effugium dedit. ceteri passim trucidati.

Et plerosque tranare Visurgim conantis iniecta tela aut vis fluminis, postremo moles ruentium et incidentes ripae operuere. quidam, turpi fuga in summa arborum nisi ramisque se occultantes, admotis sagittariis per ludibrium figebantur, alios prorutae arbores adflixere.

Magna ea victoria neque cruenta nobis fuit. quinta ab hora diei ad noctem caesi hostes decem milia passuum cadaveribus atque armis opplevere, repertis inter spolia eorum catenis quas in Romanos portaverant.

1 **praemissus eques**: singular for plural. The Roman cavalry dislodge the German rear and flanks, driving them from the woods onto the plain, while the Roman infantry drive the Germans on the plain into the woods.

2 **impulit**: 'dislodged' (from *impello*).

2 **mirumque dictu**: literally 'and marvellous in respect of telling' = 'remarkable to relate' (*dictu* is the supine of *dico*, explained by some scholars as the ablative form of the supine).

2 **hostium** (of the enemy driven in flight) goes with both *qui* clauses ('those of the enemy who had occupied the forest [rushed] into the open, [and] those of the enemy who . . . ').

4 **collibus**: local ablative (*de* or *e* has been omitted).

4–5 **manu, voce, vulnere**: i.e. by striking out, shouting and showing his wound. There is vigour in this tricolon (group of three, a common grouping in Latin prose) with asyndeton.

5–6 **illa rupturus . . . obiecissent**: 'likely to make a breakthrough . . . ', i.e. and he would have made a breakthrough by that route if Roman auxiliaries had not barred the way, forming up with standards (*signa*) in his path. The future participle *rupturus* (from *rumpo*) takes the place of the apodosis and stands for *et rupisset*.

7 **oblitus** (from *oblino*) is again a perfect participle with an active force in imitation of the Greek middle voice.

8 **ne nosceretur**: negative purpose clause.

8–9 **quidam . . . tradiderunt**: 'some have related that he was recognized by . . . ' The Chauci were Germans serving (*agentibus*) as auxiliaries in the Roman army.

11 **iniecta** is from *inicio*.

11 **conantis** = *conantes* (which governs *tranare*).

12 **moles ruentium**: i.e. the mass of fugitives rushing to the river.

12 **operuere** = *operuerunt*.

13 **turpi** (at the head of its clause) is stressed by its position.

13 **in . . . nisi**: 'having struggled (*nitor*) into the topmost things of trees' = 'having climbed with difficulty to the tops of trees'.

14 **per ludibrium**: 'with derision', 'amid mockery'.

15 **adflixere** = *adflixerunt*.

18 **opplevere** = *oppleverunt* (this form of the perfect will not be pointed out any more).

18 **repertis . . . catenis**: Tacitus is fond of tacking on an extra bit of information in the form of an ablative absolute at the end of a sentence.

18 **spolia eorum** = 'spoils taken from them'.

18 **in Romanos**: 'for the Romans' (i.e. to be used on the Romans).

REVIEW **3rd/4th conjugation verbs in – io (M pp. 44f., 54f., W pp. 452ff., RLRG sections A–D) and supines (M p. 97, W pp. 264f., RLRG section A7) and expressions of time and place (M pp. 71ff., W pp. 255ff., RLRG Lc, f, and g).**

4 *After another victory over the Germans, the Romans return to winter quarters. Some go overland, but the majority sail down the river Ems to the North Sea, where they are caught in a great storm.*

Atro nubium globo effusa grando, simul variis undique procellis
incerti fluctus prospectum adimere, regimen inpedire; milesque
pavidus et casuum maris ignarus, dum turbat nautas vel
intempestive iuvat, officia prudentium corrumpebat. omne dehinc
caelum et mare omne in austrum cessit, qui rapuit disiecitque 5
naves in aperta Oceani aut insulas saxis abruptis vel per occulta vada
infestas. quibus paulum aegreque vitatis, postquam mutabat aestus
eodemque quo ventus ferebat, non adhaerere ancoris, non exhaurire

inrumpentis undas poterant. equi, iumenta, sarcinae, etiam arma praecipitantur, quo levarentur alvei manantes per latera. 10

Illa clades novitate et magnitudine excessit, hostilibus circum litoribus aut ita vasto profundo ut credatur novissimum ac sine terris mare. pars navium haustae sunt, plures apud insulas longius sitas eiectae; milesque, nullo illic hominum cultu, fame absumptus, nisi quos corpora equorum eodem elisa toleraverant. sola Germanici 15 triremis Chaucorum terram adpulit. quem per omnes illos dies noctesque apud scopulos et prominentis oras, cum se tanti exitii reum clamitaret, vix cohibuere amici quominus eodem mari oppeteret.

1 **globo effusa**: understand *est* ('was poured from a mass').

1 **variis undique procellis** (causal ablative) goes with *incerti.*

2 **adimere . . . inpedire**: historic infinitives, with asyndeton.

2 **milesque**: singular for plural.

4 **officia prudentium corrumpebat**: i.e. they hampered the work of the experts (*prudentium* is used as a noun here and refers to the sailors).

4–5 **omne . . . cessit**: the gales from all directions now gave way to the south wind, which swept powerfully across all the sky and sea. *cessit* is from *cedo.*

6 **aperta Oceani:** 'the open things [i.e. parts] of Oceanus' = 'the open sea'.

6 **saxis abruptis**: ablative of description, with *insulas.*

6 **per**: 'on account of'.

7 **quibus** refers to the islands of 6.

7 **mutabat** is intransitive here (= 'altered direction').

8 **eodemque quo ventus ferebat**: 'and led to the same place to which the wind [led]' = 'and ran in the same direction as the wind'.

9 **inrumpentis** = *inrumpentes* (this accusative form will not be pointed out any more).

10 **quo**: 'so that thereby' (introducing a purpose clause). In Latin prior to Tacitus, *quo* was normally so used when the purpose clause contained a comparative word.

10 **manantes per latera**: 'leaking through the sides' (i.e. at the joints of the timbers along the sides of the ships).

11 **novitate . . . excessit**: 'exceeded [others] in novelty and magnitude' (i.e. was absolutely unprecedented and greater than all others).

11–12 **hostilibus . . . profundo**: ablative absolutes, with the non-existent present participle of *sum* understood. *profundum* is a noun here, meaning 'sea'.

12–13 **ut credatur . . . mare**: understand *esse* ('that it was believed to be the last and landless sea', i.e. the ultimate sea on earth with no land in it or beyond it). The reference will be to Oceanus, the huge sea or river which was supposed to flow around the land masses of the earth.

13 **pars . . . haustae sunt**: although *pars* is grammatically singular, it denotes plurality and is equivalent to *aliae* ('some') – hence the plural verb.

14 **eiectae** = *eiectae sunt.* Henceforth (e.g. later in this line), when you see something which looks like a participle but does not make sense as a participle, remember that you might have to supply *sunt* or *est* or some other part of *esse.*

14 **nullo . . . cultu**: ablative absolute (the islands were uninhabited, so there was nobody with food to beg or steal from).

14–15 nisi quos = *nisi illi quos* ('except for those whom . . .').

15 eodem elisa: 'ejected to the same place' = 'washed up on the same shore'.

16 quem (referring to Germanicus) is the object of *cohibuere . . . quominus* ('prevented him from . . .'). The conjunction *quominus* commonly introduces a clause after a verb of preventing or refraining.

17 prominentis oras: i.e. headlands, promontories.

18 reum: understand *esse* in an accusative and infinitive construction.

18 clamitaret: *clamito* is the frequentative form of *clamo* (denoting repeated shouts).

18–19 eodem mari oppeteret: i.e. drowning himself in the same sea (local ablative).

REVIEW **irregular verbs (M pp. 57ff., W pp. 457ff., RLRG section E) and *cum* and *dum* clauses (M pp. 122f., 124f., W pp. 208f., 219, RLRG section T b, c, d, e).**

5 The survivors of the storm are reassembled. The Germans start to think of taking advantage of the disaster, so Germanicus launches a vigorous onslaught against them. He is close to a final and complete victory when he is summoned back to Rome.

15 Coin depicting Germanicus.

Tandem, relabente aestu et secundante vento, claudae naves raro remigio aut intentis vestibus, et quaedam a validioribus tractae, revertere. quas raptim refectas misit ut scrutarentur insulas. collecti ea cura plerique; multos Angrivarii nuper in fidem accepti redemptos ab interioribus reddidere; quidam in Britanniam rapti et remissi a regulis. miracula narrabant (vim turbinum et inauditas volucris, monstra maris, ambiguas hominum et beluarum formas), visa sive ex metu credita.

Sed fama classis amissae ut Germanos ad spem belli ita Germanicum ad coercendum erexit. Pergit introrsus, populatur,

excindit non ausum congredi hostem aut, sicubi restiterat, statim pulsum nec umquam magis (ut ex captivis cognitum est) paventem. quippe invictos et nullis casibus superabiles Romanos praedicabant, qui, perdita classe, amissis armis, post constrata equorum virorumque corporibus litora, eadem virtute, pari ferocia et velut 15
aucto numero inrupissent.

Reductus inde in hiberna miles, laetus quod adversa maris expeditione prospera pensavisset. addidit munificentiam Germanicus, quantum quis damni professus erat exsolvendo. nec dubium habebatur labare hostes petendaeque pacis consilia sumere 20
et, si proxima aestas adiceretur, posse bellum patrari.

Sed crebris epistulis Tiberius monebat rediret ad decretum triumphum; satis iam eventuum, satis casuum; prospera illi et magna proelia; eorum quoque meminisset, quae venti et fluctus (nulla ducis culpa) gravia et saeva damna intulissent; se novies ab Augusto in 25
Germaniam missum plura consilio quam vi perfecisse.

1 **relabente ... vento**: i.e. when the tide turned and the wind changed direction with it.

2 **raro ... vestibus**: i.e. by means of their few remaining oars or makeshift sails. *intentis* is from *intendo*.

3 **quas** refers to the *naves* of 1–2 (this use of the relative to connect sentences will no longer be pointed out).

3 **collecti**: from *colligo*.

4 **nuper in fidem accepti**: 'recently accepted into trust' = 'recent subjects [of Rome]'.

5 **interioribus**: 'those further on', 'more remote peoples'.

5 **remissi**: from *remitto*.

7 **ambiguas ... formas**: i.e. forms that were half-human and half-beast.

7–8 **visa ... credita**: agree with *miracula* in 6. There is some typically Tacitean characterization here (such is human nature).

9 **ut ... ita**: these are adverbs linking parallel ideas ('just as the rumour of the loss of the fleet [roused] the Germans to ... so it roused Germanicus to ... ').

11 **hostem** is singular for plural, and *non ausum* (from *audeo*), *pulsum* (from *pello*) and *paventem* all agree with *hostem*. Most of the enemy did not dare to face Germanicus, and the few who did oppose (*resisto*) him were immediately defeated.

12 **ut**: 'as'.

14–15 **post ... litora** = 'after the shores had been covered with ... '

15 **eadem virtute, pari ferocia**: ablatives of manner, to be taken with *inrupissent*.

15–16 **velut aucto numero**: i.e. it even seemed as if there were more Romans than before. *Aucto* is from *augeo*.

17 **miles** refers to the Roman soldiers.

17 **adversa maris**: 'the troubles of [i.e. at] sea' refers to the storm and shipwrecks, while *expeditione prospera* denotes the Romans' subsequent attack on the Germans.

19 **quantum ... exsolvendo**: 'by paying for how much of loss anyone had claimed' (i.e. compensating the men for whatever losses they claimed). Tacitus often uses the ablative of the gerund as equivalent to a present participle agreeing with the subject. *damni* is a partitive genitive (naming the whole of

which part is being considered). Such a genitive is often used after neuter adjectives and pronouns instead of an adjective in agreement (e.g. *multum auri* 'much of gold' in place of *multum aurum* 'much gold').

19–20 nec dubium habebatur: 'nor was it regarded as doubtful that...' (= 'it seemed certain that...').

20 petendaeque... sumere: i.e. began to plan for/talk about suing for peace.

21 si... adiceretur: i.e. if they had another summer there fighting. The imperfect subjunctive represents a future indicative in the original direct statement.

22 monebat introduces indirect speech in 22–6 ('that he should return...; [there had been] now enough of successes...; [there had been] victorious and important battles for him [i.e. Germanicus]; he [i.e. Germanicus] should also remember those things which...; he himself [i.e. Tiberius], sent nine times..., had accomplished more by diplomacy than by...'). *Moneo* often takes *ut* and the subjunctive but can also take the subjunctive alone (*rediret*). The subjunctive *meminisset* represents a command in the original direct speech, while *intulissent* (from *infero*) is subjunctive in a subordinate clause in indirect speech.

22–3 decretum triumphum: Germanicus had earlier been awarded a triumph (a victory-parade in Rome) for his successes in Germany. *Decretum* comes from *decerno*.

24–5 nulla ducis culpa: 'through no fault/wrongdoing of the general' (i.e. Germanicus). This is a causal ablative.

25 gravia et saeva damna: in apposition to *eorum quae venti et fluctus intulissent* ('those things which winds and waves had inflicted – serious and severe losses').

Tacitus goes on to say that when Germanicus asked for just one more year to finish his work in Germany, Tiberius offered him a second consulate (to be occupied personally at Rome) and added that if the war had to continue, Germanicus should let his brother win distinction in it. Germanicus acquiesced, although he knew that jealousy was the real reason why Tiberius was denying him glory already within his grasp.

Having celebrated his triumph over Germany in AD 17, Germanicus was dispatched to a prestigious Eastern command in the following year. In AD 19, however, he died suddenly and in suspicious circumstances at Antioch in Syria.

6 Germanicus' death arouses universal mourning. After he is cremated, although she has been warned of the great danger she faces from enemies in Rome (including Tiberius), his sorrowing widow Agrippina takes his ashes by sea back to Italy.

Extinguitur ingenti luctu provinciae et circumiacentium
populorum. indoluere exterae nationes regesque: tanta illi comitas in
socios, mansuetudo in hostes. funus per laudes ac memoriam
virtutum eius celebre fuit. et erant qui formam, aetatem, genus
mortis Magni Alexandri fatis adaequarent. 5

At Agrippina, quamquam defessa luctu et corpore aegro, ascendit classem cum cineribus Germanici et liberis, miserantibus cunctis quod femina nobilitate princeps, pulcherrimo modo matrimonio, tunc feralis reliquias sinu ferret, anxia sui. nihil intermissa navigatione hiberni maris, Agrippina Corcyram insulam advehitur. illic paucos dies componendo animo insumit, violenta luctu et nescia tolerandi. 10

Interim, adventu eius audito, intimus quisque amicorum et plerique militares multique etiam ignoti vicinis e municipiis ruere ad oppidum Brundisium, quod naviganti celerrimum erat. atque ubi primum ex alto visa classis, complentur non modo portus et proxima mari sed moenia ac tecta maerentium turba. classis paulatim successit, non alacri (ut adsolet) remigio, sed cunctis ad tristitiam compositis. postquam duobus cum liberis, feralem urnam tenens, egressa navi defixit oculos, idem omnium gemitus; neque discerneres proximos, alienos, virorum feminarumve planctus. 15 20

1 **ingenti luctu**: ablative of attendant circumstances ('amid/to the very great grief of...').

1 **provinciae**: i.e. Syria.

2 **illi**: understand *fuerat* with this possessive dative (= 'his').

4–5 **formam, aetatem, genus mortis**: note the tricolon crescendo.

5 **Magni Alexandri**: Alexander the Great (356–323 BC), King of Macedon (in Greece), was a figure of great glamour and one of the most famous generals in the ancient world. He invaded the huge Persian Empire and swept all before him, conquering much of the known world, until his death in Babylon. He was often employed for purposes of comparison (e.g. at Velleius Paterculus 2.41, Lucan 10.20ff.). Like Germanicus, he was a handsome young man who died in the east amid suspicious circumstances.

5 **adaequarent**: subjunctive in a generic relative clause ('there were those who likened...').

6 **corpore aegro**: ablative of description.

8 **pulcherrimo modo matrimonio**: ablative of description (= 'who had recently enjoyed a most glorious marriage').

9 **anxia sui**: *sui* is genitive of respect, from *se* ('anxious in respect of herself' = 'apprehensive for herself').

9–10 **nihil...maris**: *nihil* is adverbial in this ablative absolute (literally: 'with her sailing of [i.e. on] the wintry sea having been not at all discontinued', i.e. without a pause in her journey across the wintry sea). Voyages were especially dangerous in winter.

11 **componendo animo** is dative with *insumit* (= 'for the calming of her mind').

11 **nescia tolerandi**: 'ignorant of enduring' = 'not knowing how to endure'.

12 **intimus quisque amicorum**: 'each most close one of friends' = 'all their closest friends' (*quisque* is often used with a superlative to denote 'all the most –').

13 **ruere** could = *ruerunt* or be a historic infinitive.

14 **quod...erat**: 'which to someone sailing [from Corcyra] was the quickest [place to reach]', i.e. which was the nearest Italian port. Corcyra = modern Corfu.

14–15 **ubi primum**: 'when first' = 'as soon as'.

15 **ex alto**: 'out at sea' (*altum* here is the noun meaning 'the deep').

15–16 **non modo...sed**: 'not only...but also'.

16 proxima mari: 'things [i.e. areas] closest to the sea', i.e. the shores.

16 maerentium turba: *turba* is ablative (with *complentur*), and the participle acts as a noun here (= 'mourners').

17 ut adsolet: 'as is customary'.

17–18 cunctis ad tristitiam compositis: 'with everything modified to convey sadness'.

19 navi: ablative of *navis*, with *egressa*.

19 idem omnium gemitus: i.e. all the onlookers made the same groaning sound.

19–20 neque discerneres: here, as often, the imperfect potential subjunctive denotes what could have happened in the past ('and you couldn't have distinguished between close relatives, strangers [or] ...').

7 Germanicus' ashes are borne in a solemn procession from Brundisium to Rome, where they are consigned to the mausoleum of Augustus.

Miserat duas praetorias cohortes Tiberius. tribunorum
centurionumque umeris cineres portabantur. atque ubi colonias
transgrederentur, atrata plebes, trabeati equites odores aliaque
funerum sollemnia cremabant. in urbe consules et senatus ac magna
pars populi viam complevere, flentes; aberat adulatio, gnaris 5
omnibus laetam Tiberio Germanici mortem male dissimulari.

Dies quo reliquiae tumulo Augusti inferebantur modo per
silentium vastus, modo ploratibus inquies. illic miles, magistratus,
populus concidisse rem publicam, nihil spei reliquum clamitabant.
nihil tamen Tiberium magis penetravit quam studia hominum 10
accensa in Agrippinam, cum decus patriae, solum Augusti sanguinem,
unicum antiquitatis specimen appellarent.

3 transgrederentur: the subjunctive is frequentative (denoting repeated occurrence of an action).

3 atrata plebes, trabeati equites: the people wore black in mourning, the members of the equestrian order wore the *trabea* (the dress uniform for ritual occasions) out of respect.

3–4 odores ... cremabant: it was customary to burn perfumes and other offerings at funerals.

4 urbe: i.e. Rome.

5–6 gnaris ... dissimulari: *gnaris omnibus* (ablative absolute, with causal force) is followed by indirect statement ('that the death of Germanicus [being] pleasurable to Tiberius was being scarcely concealed', i.e. that Tiberius could scarcely conceal his pleasure at Germanicus' death).

7 quo: ablative of time.

7–8 modo ... modo: 'now ... now' = 'at one point ... at another point'. Understand *erat* as the main verb here.

9 nihil spei reliquum clamitabant: supply *esse*. *Spei* is partitive genitive with *nihil*. Note the frequentative form of the verb.

10–11 studia ... Agrippinam: 'people's enthusiasm for Agrippina'.

11–12 cum ... appellarent: 'as they called [her] the glory of the fatherland, the only [real] descendant of Augustus [and] the peerless/sole embodiment of ancient conduct [i.e. ancient Roman standards and virtues]'.

Tacitus adds that some complained that Tiberius (who refused to appear in public) had not organized for Germanicus a funeral in Rome with the proper pageantry; to repress the comments of the crowd, Tiberius issued a statement saying how much he valued their great grief for Germanicus but urging them to observe a proper moderation and show fortitude; they should return to their ordinary occupations and (as the Megalesian Games were imminent) to their pleasures as well.

Years later, Agrippina finally paid for her enmity with the emperor.

8 *After mentioning that some suspected that Tiberius had been behind Germanicus' death (by poisoning), Suetonius now describes the emperor's maltreatment of Agrippina (over several years), which confirmed this suspicion.*

Suspicionem confirmavit ipse postea coniuge ac liberis Germanici
crudelem in modum afflictis. nurum Agrippinam, post mariti mortem
liberius quiddam questam, manu apprehendit, Graecoque versu, 'Si
non dominaris,' inquit, 'filiola, iniuriam te accipere existimas?' nec
ullo mox sermone dignatus est. quondam inter cenam porrecta a 5
se poma gustare non ausam etiam vocare desiit, simulans veneni se
crimine accersi. novissime calumniatus modo ad statuam Augusti
modo ad exercitus confugere velle, Pandatariam relegavit,
conviciantique oculum per centurionem verberibus excussit. rursus
mori inedia destinanti per vim ore diducto infulciri cibum iussit. 10
perseverantem atque ita absumptam criminosissime insectatus, cum
diem natalem eius inter nefastos referendum suasisset, imputavit
quod non laqueo strangulatam in Gemonias abiecerit.

2 **crudelem in modum:** 'in a cruel manner', 'cruelly'.

2 **nurum:** Germanicus was Tiberius' adopted son.

3 **liberius quiddam questam:** 'having complained of something rather/too boldly/frankly' (*questam* is from *queror*).

3 **Graecoque versu:** i.e. a line of Greek verse whose meaning is given here in Latin.

4 **iniuriam te accipere:** 'that you are suffering a wrong' = 'that you are being wronged'.

4–5 **nec... est:** *nec ullo mox* = *et mox nullo*; with *dignatus* est supply *eam*.

5–6 **porrecta... gustare:** *porrecta* agrees with *poma*, which is the object of *gustare*. *se* refers to Tiberius.

6 **non ausam** governs *gustare poma* and agrees with an understood *eam*, which is the object of *etiam vocare desiit* ('he actually stopped inviting her after she had once not dared to taste...').

7–8 **calumniatus... velle:** 'having brought false accusations that she wanted/intended to flee for refuge now... [and] now...' (*velle* is from *volo*).

8 **Pandatariam:** a small island (so the preposition *ad* is not required).

9 conviciantique . . . excussit: i.e. when she angrily abused him for banishing her, he had a centurion beat/flog her, and in the course of the beating/flogging she lost an eye. The sense of *per* is 'by means of' (Tiberius' responsibility is brought out by making him the subject of the verb). *convicianti* refers to Agrippina and is either dative of possession (= 'the eye of her uttering abuse') or dative of disadvantage ('to the disadvantage of her uttering abuse').

10 mori . . . iussit: i.e. when she decided to starve herself to death (*mori* is the present infinitive of *morior*, and *inedia* is ablative of means), Tiberius had her fed forcibly.

11 perseverantem . . . insectatus: i.e. having violently slandered Agrippina when she managed to starve herself to death.

11–12 cum . . . suasisset: 'after he had urged [the senate] that . . . '

12 inter nefastos referendum = *inter dies nefastos referendum esse*. The gerundive expresses obligation ('should be counted'). The *dies nefasti* were ill-omened days (e.g. anniversaries of national disasters) on which public business could not be transacted.

13 Gemonias: the bodies of criminals were exposed on the Gemonian Steps (on the Capitoline Hill in Rome) prior to being thrown into the River Tiber.

16 Mausoleum of Augustus, Rome. Epitaph of Agrippina Maior, wife of Germanicus, mother of Caligula, and bane of Tiberius.

The death of Germanicus is Tacitus' cue to introduce us to the machinations of L. Aelius Sejanus. Cunning, ruthless, and sycophantic, he was a consummate manipulator who, between AD *23 and 31 manoeuvred himself into position as Tiberius' successor. But for Sejanus to get there, people had to die.*

9 A sketch of Sejanus, the commander of the praetorian guard (the emperor's bodyguard), who insinuates himself into the favour of Tiberius, cleverly strengthening his own power-base in Rome.

17 The Temple of Castor and Pollux in the Roman forum, Rome. Originally dedicated in 484 BC, the temple we see today was restored by Tiberius and dedicated in AD 6.

Mox Tiberium variis artibus devinxit, adeo ut sibi uni incautum intectumque efficeret, non tam sollertia quam deum ira in rem Romanam. corpus illi laborum tolerans, animus audax; sui obtegens, in alios criminator; palam compositus pudor, intus summa apiscendi libido, eiusque causa modo largitio et luxus, saepius industria ac vigilantia. 5

Vim praefecturae (modicam antea) intendit, dispersas per urbem cohortis una in castra conducendo, ut simul imperia acciperent, numeroque et robore fiducia ipsis, in ceteros metus oreretur.

inrepere paulatim militaris animos adeundo, appellando; simul centuriones ac tribunos ipse deligere. neque senatorio ambitu abstinebat, Tiberio ita prono ut socium laborum non modo in sermonibus sed apud patres et populum celebraret. 10

1 **sibi uni:** 'to himself [i.e. Sejanus] alone'.

2–3 **non tam . . . Romanam:** 'not so much thanks to his cleverness as thanks to the anger of the gods towards Rome'. *sollertia* and *ira* are ablatives, while *deum* is an archaic form of the genitive plural (of *deus*), often used by Tacitus (and poets) but uncommon in other prose authors (apart from Livy, who was fond of poeticisms).

3 **illi:** understand *erat* (= 'he had'). *illi erat* or just *erat* must be supplied in all the other clauses at 3–6 too. Those lines provide a good example of Tacitean brevity and antithesis (= contrast, between body and mind, etc.).

4 **in alios:** 'with regard to others'.

4 **criminator:** Tacitus is in general fond of agent nouns ending in *-tor* (and *-sor*), but this particular one is rare and so emphatic.

4 **palam . . . intus:** 'outwardly . . . inwardly', 'on the surface . . . inside'.

4 **summa:** neuter accusative plural ('supreme/highest things'), object of *apiscendi* (= 'a longing to secure supremacy').

5 **eiusque causa modo . . . saepius:** *causa* is ablative ('and as a result of that sometimes . . . more often').

7 **urbem** = *Romam.*

8 **cohortis** (object of *conducendo*) refers to cohorts of the praetorian guard.

8 **conducendo:** the instrumental use of the ablative of the gerund is virtually equivalent to a present participle agreeing with the subject of the main verb.

8 **ut simul imperia acciperent:** 'so that they might [all] receive their orders simultaneously'.

9 **numeroque et robore:** ablatives of cause.

9 **fiducia . . . oreretur:** '[so that] confidence/courage for them themselves [i.e. the praetorian cohorts] and a threat towards others would arise', i.e. so they would become confident in themselves and intimidate others. *oreretur* is imperfect subjunctive of *orior.*

10–11 **inrepere . . . deligere:** historic infinitives, with Sejanus as their subject.

10 **adeundo:** gerund of *adeo.*

12 **Tiberio . . . prono:** ablative absolute.

12–13 **ut . . . celebraret:** 'that he praised him as . . . not only in conversations but also in speeches to the Senate and people'.

10 *Sejanus strengthens his position further by poisoning Tiberius' son Drusus, after seducing the young man's wife (Livilla). Tiberius is strangely unmoved by his son's illness and death.*

Ceterum plena Caesarum domus, iuvenis filius, nepotes adulti moram cupitis adferebant. Placuit a Druso incipere, in quem recenti ira ferebatur. nam Drusus, impatiens aemuli, orto forte iurgio, intenderat Seiano manus et os verberaverat. igitur promptissimum visum ad uxorem eius Livillam convertere. hanc, ut amore incensus, 5
adulterio pellexit et ad coniugii spem, consortium regni et necem

mariti impulit. atque illa (cui avunculus Augustus, socer Tiberius, ex Druso liberi) se ac maiores et posteros municipali adultero foedabat. pellit domo Seianus uxorem Apicatam, ex qua tres liberos genuerat, ne paelici suspectaretur. 10

Drusus querebatur incolumi filio adiutorem imperii alium vocari. neque raro neque apud paucos talia iaciebat, et secreta quoque eius, corrupta uxore, prodebantur. igitur Seianus deligit venenum quo paulatim inrepente fortuitus morbus adsimularetur. id Druso datum per Lygdum spadonem. ceterum Tiberius per omnis valetudinis 15 eius dies (nullo metu an ut firmitudinem animi ostentaret), etiam defuncto necdum sepulto, curiam ingressus est. effusum in lacrimas senatum oratione erexit: vix propinquorum adloquia tolerari, vix diem aspici a plerisque lugentium; se tamen fortiora solacia e complexu rei publicae petivisse. 20

1 **plena Caesarum domus**: 'the well-stocked household of the Caesars' = 'the large imperial family' (i.e. there were lots of rivals and potential successors to Tiberius).

1 **iuvenis** ('young') is the adjective here. Tiberius' son Drusus was by now in his mid-thirties.

2 **cupitis**: 'to the desired things' = 'to his desires'.

2 **placuit**: 'it seemed good [to Sejanus] to . . . ' = 'Sejanus decided to . . . '

2–3 **in quem . . . ferebatur**: 'against whom he was led/he moved because of . . . '

3 **impatiens aemuli**: Drusus saw Sejanus as a rival for power.

3 **orto forte iurgio**: *orto* comes from *orior*, and *forte* is the adverb.

4 **intenderat Seiano manus**: i.e. had raised his hands to Sejanus.

4–5 **promptissimum visum**: 'it seemed [to Sejanus] most practical to . . . ' *visum (est)* is from *videor*.

5 **ut**: 'as if'.

6 **adulterio**: ablative of instrument.

6 **coniugii spem, consortium regni**: i.e. hope of getting married to Sejanus and becoming empress after he took over as emperor.

7 **impulit**: from *impello*.

7 **cui**: understand *erat* with this possessive dative (= 'who had').

8 **municipali adultero**: 'with a small-town adulterer' = 'by having an affair with a small-town romeo'.

10 **genuerat**: from *gigno*.

10 **ne paelici suspectaretur**: *paelici* is dative of agent. Sejanus did not want his mistress Livilla to have suspicions about his feelings for her, so he got rid of his wife.

11 **incolumi filio**: ablative absolute (i.e. while Tiberius' son Drusus was alive and well).

12 **neque . . . paucos**: i.e. often and in the presence of many.

12 **secreta quoque eius**: i.e. Drusus' remarks in secret too.

13 **corrupta**: from *corrumpo*.

13–14 **quo . . . adsimularetur**: a purpose clause ('so that by means of which [=it] gradually creeping in a chance illness might be feigned', i.e. he chose a slow-acting poison so that it would not be obvious that Drusus had been poisoned and it would seem that he just happened to fall ill).

15 **Lygdum**: he was a beloved and trusted slave of Drusus.

15 **omnis** is not genitive singular.

16 nullo . . . ostentaret: i.e. either because Tiberius did not fear that Drusus would die or in order to . . .

16–17 etiam defuncto necdum sepulto = 'even when he [Drusus] was dead and not yet buried'. *necdum* = *et nondum*.

19 a plerisque lugentium: these words go with both *tolerari* and *aspici*, in indirect statement picking up from *oratione* (he said that most mourners can hardly bear the condolences of their relatives and can hardly look on the light of day).

20 complexu rei publicae: i.e. throwing himself into affairs of state. The state is here suggestively personified (treated as a person).

Sejanus first set about ruining Agrippina's friends and associates by using the 'treason' law (lex maiestatis). One such associate, brought to trial in AD 25, was the historian Cremutius Cordus.

11 *Cremutius Cordus is charged with treason, makes an able but futile defence at his trial in the Senate, and commits suicide.*

Cremutius Cordus postulatur novo ac tunc primum audito crimine,
quod editis annalibus laudatoque Bruto Cassium 'Romanorum
ultimum' dixisset. accusabant Seiani clientes. id perniciabile reo, et
Tiberius truci vultu defensionem accipiens, quam Cremutius in hunc
modum exorsus est: 'Verba mea, patres conscripti, arguuntur: adeo 5
factorum innocens sum. sed neque haec in principem aut principis
parentem, quos lex maiestatis amplectitur: Brutum et Cassium
laudavisse dicor, quorum res gestas cum plurimi composuerint, nemo
sine honore memoravit. Livius Pompeium tantis laudibus tulit ut
"Pompeianum" eum Augustus appellaret; neque id amicitiae eorum 10
offecit. num, armatis Cassio et Bruto ac Philippenses campos
obtinentibus, belli civilis causa populum per contiones incendo?
suum cuique decus posteritas rependit; nec deerunt, si damnatio
ingruit, qui non modo Cassii et Bruti sed etiam mei meminerint.'

Egressus dein senatu vitam abstinentia finivit. libros cremandos 15
censuere patres; sed manserunt, occultati et editi. punitis ingeniis
gliscit auctoritas, neque aliud externi reges aut qui eadem saevitia
usi sunt nisi dedecus sibi atque illis gloriam peperere.

1–2 postulatur . . . crimine, quod: 'was prosecuted on the . . . charge that . . .'

2 editis is from *edo* (like *editi* in 16).

2–3 laudatoque . . . dixisset: Brutus and Cassius were two of the men who killed the dictator Julius Caesar in 44 BC. Praise of Brutus could be taken as approval of the practice of assassination of men in positions of supreme power in general and of the murder of an ancestor of Tiberius in particular, while calling Cassius 'the last of the Romans' implied that Cordus' contemporaries (including Tiberius) were not real Romans.

3 Seiani clientes: these were two senators. A 'client' was somebody who attached himself to a man of greater influence or political power (the *patronus*), supporting him and showing loyalty and respect to him, in return for which the *patronus* bestowed on his 'client' various favours (money, assistance, protection etc.).

3–4 id perniciabile reo, et . . . accipiens: 'That [was] ruinous for the defendant, and [so was] Tiberius . . .'

4–5 in hunc modum: 'in this manner', 'as follows'. From Herodotus onwards, ancient historians freely invented speeches for major (and sometimes minor) characters, to provide a psychological portrait, to present differing points of view, issues, policies etc.

5–6 verba . . . innocens sum: i.e. he had not actually done anything wrong, so the accusation was brought against his writings (*verba* in emphatic position). *patres conscripti* = 'senators'.

6 neque haec in principem: with *haec* (picking up *verba*) understand *composui* ('I did not even write those against [i.e. aimed at] the emperor').

8 laudavisse dicor: 'I am said to have praised'.

8 res gestas ('exploits') is object of both *composuerint* and *memoravit* in 9.

9–10 The famous historian Livy (64 BC – AD 17) was a friend of the Emperor Augustus and wrote a history of Rome in which he praised the soldier and statesman Pompey, the opponent in the civil war of Julius Caesar (who was the great-uncle of Augustus and adopted him). For that, Augustus called Livy a supporter of Pompey, but did not let it spoil their friendship.

9 tulit: 'elevated' (from *fero*).

11–12 num . . . incendo: i.e. it is not as if Cassius and Brutus were still alive and ready to fight at Philippi (where they were defeated in battle by Augustus and Antony in 42 BC in the civil war) and Cordus was giving public speeches to incite the people to civil war.

12 causa: ablative.

13 suum cuique decus: 'To each man his own distinction'. *cuique* is dative of *quisque*.

14 meminerint: subjunctive in a generic relative clause (after *nec deerunt . . . qui* = 'there will not be lacking (*desum*) men who remember . . .').

15 libros cremandos: supply *esse*, in an accusative and infinitive construction after *censuere*. The books were those written by Cordus.

16 patres: 'the senators'.

16–17 punitis ingeniis gliscit auctoritas = 'when men of genius are punished their standing grows' (*ingeniis* is possessive dative: 'the standing for [= of] men of genius . . .'). *glisco* (always preferred to *cresco*) is a favourite verb of Tacitus. Elsewhere, it occurs mainly in verse and Livy (who has much poetic vocabulary). This is a typically Tacitean *sententia*.

17–18 neque aliud . . . peperere: 'and foreign kings or [those] who . . . have not brought about anything other than (*nisi*) disgrace for themselves and honour for them [i.e. the men of genius whom they punished]'. *peperere* is the third person plural of the perfect indicative of *pario*.

18 Massive substructures of the imperial residences on the Palatine Hill. Much of what is visible here belongs to the *Domus Tiberiana*, credited to Tiberius but actually built by Nero.

As time went on, the depressive Tiberius grew less and less interested in the mundanities of administration. Now in AD *26, with Sejanus' active encouragement, Tiberius left Rome for the pleasant resorts of southern Italy. He was never to return to the city.*

12 *Sejanus encourages Tiberius to leave Rome (so that he can increase his own power), and the emperor does eventually depart, going first to Campania (an area in Italy south of Rome) and then to the beautiful island of Capri (near Naples).*

Seianus multa providebat: sua in manu aditus litterarumque magna ex parte se arbitrum fore, cum per milites commearent; mox Tiberium, vergente iam senecta, secretoque loci mollitum, munia imperii facilius tramissurum. igitur paulatim negotia urbis, populi adcursus, multitudinem adfluentium increpat, extollens laudibus (5) quietem et solitudinem.

Tandem Tiberius in Campaniam, specie dedicandi templa, sed certus procul urbe degere. causam abscessus quamquam ad Seiani artes rettuli, plerumque permoveor num ad ipsum referri verius sit, saevitiam ac libidinem locis occultantem. erant qui crederent in senectute corporis quoque habitum pudori fuisse. quippe illi praegracilis et incurva proceritas, nudus capillo vertex, ulcerosa facies ac plerumque medicaminibus interstincta. traditur etiam matris inpotentia extrusum, quam dominationis sociam aspernabatur neque depellere poterat. 10 15

Ac forte illis diebus oblatum Tiberio periculum praebuit materiem cur amicitiae constantiaeque Seiani magis fideret. vescebantur in villa, nativo in specu. eius os lapsis repente saxis obruit quosdam ministros. hinc fuga eorum qui convivium celebrabant. Seianus genu utroque et manibus super Tiberium suspensus opposuit sese incidentibus. 20

Tiberius, dedicatis per Campaniam templis, quamquam edicto monuisset ne quis quietem eius inrumperet, perosus tamen municipia omniaque in continenti sita, Capreas se in insulam abdidit. solitudinem eius placuisse maxime crediderim. caeli temperies hieme mitis; aestas, aperto circum pelago, peramoena; prospectabatque pulcherrimum sinum. 25

1 **Multa providebat**: 'foresaw many things [i.e. advantages]'. This is followed by indirect statement at 1–4, listing the advantages.

1 **sua in manu aditus**: 'access [to Tiberius] would be in his [Sejanus'] hands'.

2 **magna ex parte... fore**: 'would be... to a large extent' (*fore* is the future infinitive of *sum*).

2 **per milites**: letters to the emperor were conveyed by members of the praetorian guard (commanded by Sejanus).

3 **secretoque loci**: 'and by the seclusion of the place' (i.e. the place to which Tiberius would move from Rome).

7 **tandem Tiberius**: understand a verb meaning 'went'.

7 **specie**: 'under the pretext of...'

8 **certus... degere**: *certus* + infinitive = determined to do something, and *procul* is used as a preposition here ('far from').

8 **causam abscessus**: these words belong inside the following *quamquam* clause.

9 **rettuli**: from *refero* ('ascribe').

9 **plerumque permoveor... sit**: 'I am often inclined [to wonder] whether it might be more sound/consistent with fact for it [the *causam abscessus*] to be ascribed to the man himself'.

10 **locis**: i.e. the places he visited when he left Rome.

10 **crederent**: subjunctive in a generic relative clause.

11 **pudori**: predicative dative ('was a source of shame [to him]' = 'made him ashamed').

11 **quippe illi**: supply *erat.*

12–13 the unusual expression here (the unique *praegracilis* and *nudus capillo*, the as yet rare *ulcerosus* and *interstinguo*) brings out the singularity of Tiberius' appearance and highlights the points being made.

12 **nudus capillo**: i.e. bald.

13–14 **traditur... extrusum**: understand *esse* ('It is also related that he was driven out by...'). His mother was Livia.

14 **sociam aspernabatur**: 'he rejected as a sharer of...'

15 neque: 'but... not'

16 oblatum Tiberio periculum: 'a danger put in the way of Tiberius' = 'a danger encountered by Tiberius' (*oblatum* is from *offero*).

18 nativo in specu: the villa's dining-room was fashionably situated in a natural cave (for an interesting article on it and its decoration see Stewart 1977).

18 os lapsis: *os* refers to the cave's mouth, and *lapsis* is from *labor.*

19 ministros are servants (not vicars!).

19 hinc fuga: supply *fuit.*

19–20 genu... et manibus... suspensus: these are ablatives of instrument, and *suspensus* is from *suspendo.*

21 incidentibus: understand *saxis* (= 'the rock-fall').

23 monuisset ne quis... inrumperet: 'he had warned that not anyone should...' = 'he had issued a warning that nobody should invade his [= Tiberius'] privacy'.

24 continenti: i.e. mainland Italy.

24 Capreas in insulam: 'into [= on] the isle of Capri'.

25 crediderim: potential subjunctive ('I would suppose that...'); the perfect tense has the same sense as the present tense.

25 caeli temperies = 'the climatic conditions'.

26 aestas: i.e. summer on the island, the island in summer.

26 aperto circum pelago: ablative absolute.

27 prospectabatque: the island is the subject of this verb.

19 Villa Jovis, Capri: this is the palace occupied by Tiberius during his self-imposed exile from Rome, AD 26–37.

As with Augustus (see Augustus, *Passage 4), lurid speculations surrounded the sexual activities of emperors, and the voluntarily exiled Tiberius in his luxurious island hide-out presented a juicy target indeed. In fact, none of the following charges can be verified.*

13 *Sex and savagery – Tiberius on Capri.*

Excogitavit sedem arcanarum libidinum, in quam undique
conquisiti puellarum et exoletorum greges invicem incestarent coram
ipso, ut aspectu deficientis libidines excitaret. cubicula tabellis ac
sigillis lascivissimarum figurarum adornavit librisque Elephantidis
instruxit, ne cui exemplar imperatae schemae deesset. in silvis 5
quoque passim Venerios locos commentus est prostantisque per
antra ex utriusque sexus pube, Paniscorum et Nympharum habitu.
fertur etiam in sacrificando quondam captus facie ministri acerram
praeferentis nequisse abstinere quin, vixdum re divina peracta,
seductum constupraret simulque fratrem eius tibicinem; atque 10
utrique mox, quod mutuo flagitium exprobrarant, crura fregisse.

1–2 **in quam... incestarent:** a relative clause expressing purpose ('so that groups of..., having been brought together from all over into which [centre], might defile reciprocally (*invicem*) = defile one another').

3 **deficientis libidines:** i.e. the passion of the aged emperor.

4 **Elephantidis:** Elephantis was a (female) Greek erotic author.

5 **ne... deesset:** 'so that a model/illustration of a sexual position prescribed [by Tiberius] might not be lacking to anyone [of those who performed for the emperor]'. *cui* is dative of *quis*, and *deesset* comes from *desum.*

6 **commentus est** (from *comminiscor*) governs both *venerios locos* and *prostantisque... ex utriusque sexus pube* (= 'people from the adult population of both sexes standing [as prostitutes] for hire...').

7 **Paniscorum et Nympharum habitu:** i.e. dressed as little Pans and Nymphs (male and female divinities of the countryside renowned for promiscuity). *habitu* is ablative of description.

8 **fertur:** 'He is said'.

9–10 **nequisse... constupraret:** 'to have been unable to restrain himself from... raping him [i.e. the assistant] having been taken aside' (= 'from taking him aside and raping him'). Here, as often, *quin* introduces a clause after a verb of refraining in the negative.

9 **re divina:** 'the religious activity' = 'the ceremony'.

11 **mutuo** is the adverb ('to each other').

11 **exprobrarant** = *exprobraverant* (syncopated form).

11 **utrique... crura fregisse:** this is still indirect statement depending on *fertur. utrique* is possessive dative of *uterque* (= 'the legs of them both').

In AD 31, Sejanus fell from grace with bewildering suddenness. With no warning, all who had pinned their hopes for success on Sejanus' closeness with the emperor now found that alliance a basis for accusation, arrest, or execution. Many fled or killed themselves. The purge lasted three years, claiming the lives of dozens of prominent citizens. Passage 14 relates its last, brutal phase in AD 33.

14 *Tiberius now orders the execution of the surviving children of Sejanus and all those held in custody on a charge of complicity with Sejanus.*

Placitum ut in reliquos Seiani liberos adverteretur, vanescente
quamquam plebis ira ac plerisque per priora supplicia lenitis. igitur
portantur in carcerem, filius imminentium intellegens, puella adeo
nescia ut crebro interrogaret quod ob delictum et quo traheretur;
neque facturam ultra, et posse se puerili verbere moneri. tradunt 5
temporis eius auctores, quia triumvirali supplicio adfici virginem
inauditum habebatur, a carnifice laqueum iuxta compressam. exim,
oblisis faucibus, corpora in Gemonias abiecta.

Tiberius cunctos, qui carcere attinebantur accusati societatis cum
Seiano, necari iubet. iacuit immensa strages, omnis sexus, omnis 10
aetas, inlustres, ignobiles, dispersi aut aggerati. neque propinquis aut
amicis adsistere, inlacrimare, ne visere quidem diutius dabatur; sed
circumiecti custodes et in maerorem cuiusque intenti corpora
putrefacta adsectabantur, dum in Tiberim traherentur, ubi fluitantia
aut ripis adpulsa non cremare quisquam, non contingere. 15

1 **placitum ut . . . adverteretur:** 'it was pleasing [= it was decided] that punishment should be inflicted on . . .' (impersonal expression).

1 **reliquos Seiani liberos:** it seems that the eldest of the three children died along with Sejanus, leaving a son and young daughter.

2 **quamquam** here qualifies the ablative absolute and is not a conjunction introducing a concessive clause.

2 **plebis ira:** when Sejanus fell from power, the Roman people angrily attacked his supporters in the streets.

4 **quod ob delictum et quo:** 'on account of what offence and to which place'.

5 **neque facturam ultra:** supply *se* and *esse* = [she said that] 'she would not do it [whatever she had done that was wrong] any more'.

5 **tradunt:** 'relate', followed by accusative and infinitive (*compressam* = *compressam esse*) in indirect statement.

6–7 **adfici . . . habebatur:** 'it was considered unheard of for a virgin to be visited with [= be subjected to] . . .'

7 **laqueum iuxta:** 'beside the noose' (which would shortly be used to strangle her).

10–11 omnis sexus, omnis aetas: i.e. people of both sexes and all ages. Note the emphatic anaphora here and below in 15.

11–12 neque propinquis aut amicis . . . dabatur: 'Nor was it allowed [= nor was permission granted] to relatives or friends to . . . '

12 ne . . . quidem: 'not even'.

13 in . . . intenti: i.e. looking at everybody to see how much sorrow they were showing. *Cuiusque* is genitive of *quisque.*

14 ubi fluitantia: 'where floating' = 'and as they floated there'.

15 non cremare quisquam, non contingere: the infinitives are historic. *non quisquam* (understand *quisquam* with the second *non* too) = 'nobody' (literally 'not anyone').

Submerged in his depression and paranoia, Tiberius made no solid arrangements for the succession in his final years. This situation allowed a nefarious alliance between Sejanus' replacement as the praetorian commander, Macro, and Agrippina's sole surviving son, Gaius (Caligula), to flourish. According to Tacitus in passage 15, this alliance ultimately proved fatal for Tiberius.

15 *The death of Tiberius and succession of Gaius (Caligula) as emperor thanks to Macro (commander of the praetorian guard).*

Iam Tiberium corpus, iam vires, nondum dissimulatio deserebat:
idem animi rigor; sermone ac vultu intentus quaesita comitate
manifestam defectionem tegebat. eum adpropinquare supremis tali
modo compertum. erat medicus, nomine Charicles. is, velut propria
ad negotia digrediens et per speciem officii manum complexus, 5
pulsum venarum attigit. neque fefellit: nam Tiberius instaurari
epulas iubet discumbitque ultra solitum, quasi honori abeuntis amici
tribueret. Charicles tamen labi spiritum nec ultra biduum duraturum
Macroni firmavit. inde cuncta conloquiis inter praesentes, nuntiis
apud legatos et exercitus festinabantur. 10

Septimum decimum kal. Aprilis, interclusa anima, creditus est
mortalitatem explevisse. et multo gratantum concursu ad capienda
imperii primordia Gaius egrediebatur, cum repente adfertur redire
Tiberio vocem ac visus, vocarique qui cibum adferrent. pavor hinc in
omnes; et ceteri passim dispergi, se quisque maestum aut nescium 15
fingere; Gaius in silentium fixus a summa spe novissima expectabat.
Macro intrepidus opprimi senem iniectu multae vestis iubet. sic
Tiberius finivit octavo et septuagesimo aetatis anno.

1 **corpus**: 'constitution'.

2 **idem animi rigor**: supply *illi erat* (= 'he had').

2 **sermone ac vultu intentus**: 'energetic in word and look' (ablatives of respect).

2 **quaesita comitate**: 'with a contrived/forced affability'.

3 **tegebat**: 'he tried to conceal' (the imperfect tense often expresses something attempted).

4 **compertum**: 'it was discovered that he . . . ' (impersonal expression).

4 **Charicles**: Tacitus frequently adds authority to his narratives by naming minor characters like this.

5 **per speciem officii**: i.e. under the cover of a gesture of respect.

5 **complexus**: from *complector*.

6–8 **nam Tiberius . . . tribueret**: Tiberius prolonged the banquet that his friend Charicles was leaving and made him stay on a bit longer at it, ostensibly in his honour but actually for another reason (possibly to conceal his irritation at Charicles' trick, possibly to show that there was nothing wrong with him).

6 **fefellit**: from *fallo*.

7 **ultra solitum**: 'beyond what was customary', i.e. longer than he usually did.

7 **abeuntis**: genitive singular of the present participle of *abeo*.

8 **tribueret**: supply *id* (referring to the act of starting up the banquet again).

8 **labi spiritum**: 'that [Tiberius'] life was slipping away'.

9–10 **cuncta . . . festinabantur**: i.e. all the arrangements for the succession of Caligula were hurriedly seen to by means of discussions with people who were present at the villa where Tiberius was and by means of messages in the case of (*apud*) those who were absent.

11 **septimum decimum kal. Aprilis**: 'on the 16th of March'.

11 **interclusa anima**: apparently a natural cessation of breathing.

12 **multo . . . concursu**: ablative of attendant circumstances. *gratantum* is genitive plural of the present participle of *grator*.

12–13 **ad . . . primordia**: i.e. in order to begin his reign.

13 **adfertur**: 'it was reported that . . . '

14 **qui cibum adferrent**: the subjunctive expresses purpose ('people to bring [him] food').

14–15 **pavor hinc in omnes**: supply a verb such as *venit*.

16 **in silentium fixus**: 'frozen into silence'.

TIBERIUS APPRECIATION

Passage 1 Tacitus Annals *1.61–2.*

On Tacitus' portrayal and employment of Germanicus, see Introduction section 6. Put baldly, here Germanicus buries the remains of Varus' men and Tiberius disapproves. Tacitus tries to build up this bare incident into a memorable and significant episode.

He produces a sensational and emotive account. This is an atmospheric passage, filled with pathos and horror. The focus narrows effectively from the general (at 3f.) to the particular, especially at 5–10 with the scenes of devastation and barbarism, where the horses' limbs and the skulls are telling (almost surreal) details. The reminiscences at 11ff. add to the sadness and outrage, and are a realistic touch (although ancient historians often created and embellished material: see especially West–Woodman 1979, 143ff.).

Tacitus also lets his liking for Germanicus and distaste for Tiberius colour his account (and influence the reader's reaction). The savagery and dangerousness of the Germans and Arminius here bring out the value of the subsequent victory over them. Tacitus also takes us through the march, discoveries, recollections and burial with Germanicus' army so that we share in the whole experience and identify with them. From the start (2f.) he depicts this as an act of compassion and *pietas* (dutifulness to relatives, friends and countrymen). At 17–20, he represents the burial as good for morale, something that drew troops and general together and a *gratissimum munus.* Tiberius' disapproval, suddenly and baldly introduced at 20 after all the foregoing, seems mean-spirited (especially next to the caring Germanicus). Then, at 21ff., Tacitus engages in some favourite techniques – speculating about motives (Tiberius' are in marked contrast to those assigned to the army at 2f.) and offering alternative explanations, one of which is sinister (put first at 21 for stress, and carefully followed by one which Tacitus has recently undermined).

Passage 2 Tacitus Annals *2.12–13.*

This was one of the few pitched battles fought in Germany by Germanicus which Tacitus describes, and it was his great victory, so passages 2 and 3 really celebrate it in a stirring narrative. Tacitus begins by building anticipation and tension at 2ff. (especially the large numbers of the Germans), and then shows us what a careful commander Germanicus is (the twofold reconnaissance) and how loved he is by his men (9ff.). Roman morale is seen to be high (13ff.) and Roman discipline is tight (16f.), raising expectations further.

Before moving on to the actual fighting, note that ancient battle accounts are often unreliable (especially when, like Tacitus, the author had little experience of combat) and notoriously formulaic (battle lines are drawn up; commanders on both sides give speeches; the fighting is described; one side breaks and is slaughtered). The formula no doubt reflects reality to an extent, but some details here are found elsewhere (e.g. the tactic of striking at the enemy's faces also occurs in an entirely different context at Appian *Civil Wars* 2.78) and so look like optional items that can be inserted to lend credence to an account of any battle.

Passage 3 Tacitus Annals *2.17–18.*

When the battle begins, the Romans are almost instantly victorious. But so that the victory is not devalued, Tacitus is careful to depict Arminius as a formidable foe (yet also stresses that he was wounded by alluding to his wound twice). Then comes the slaughter of the enemy. Tacitus dwells on this at length and highlights it with some grimly graphic touches (at 11ff. and 17f.), emphasizing the enormous losses of the Germans in contrast to the Romans. He also tries to distinguish this engagement from the general ruck of battles by some memorable touches, such as Arminius covering his face with blood, the Germans up the trees shot down amid mockery, and the chains brought for the Romans. Other details should give you real pause for thought. How likely is it that out of this enormous horde of Germans only two escaped alive (Arminius, who was wounded, and Inguiomerus)? And how believable is the (highly emotive) picture of ten whole miles absolutely filled with corpses and weapons (a clear instance of hyperbole)?

Passage 4 Tacitus Annals *2.23–4.*

For the treatment of Germanicus here, see Introduction section 6. The first paragraph (describing the storm) contains lots of detail, danger and drama, and the presentation of separate stages in order makes for clarity. In particular (after *atro*, with its connotations of ill omen, death, mourning, terror, malevolence), the first sentence packs in various details, suggesting their swift succession and producing pace and excitement. In this paragraph, suggestively nature occupies most of the lines and is in control. In the sombre second paragraph (depicting the storm's actual impact), remoteness and isolation are stressed, and there is much destruction, death and despair, with survivors memorably reduced to eating horses; 16ff. effectively zoom in on Germanicus grieving in a hard and desolate landscape. We may be meant to think of Achilles grieving on the shore at Homer *Iliad* 1. 348ff. There may also be throughout Tacitus' account deliberate echoes of tempests in epic and tragedy to bring out the epic and tragic nature of the storm here, and in particular Germanicus may be depicted as a second Aeneas (cf. Virgil *Aeneid* 1.81ff.), with his fleet widely scattered by a great storm, deeply concerned at that, and only later reunited with his men (see further Goodyear 1981 243ff.).

Passage 5 Tacitus Annals *2.24–6.*

The recovery begins gradually, as some vessels limp back, but then after Germanicus' rapid response in 3 more and more men return. The momentum increases in the second paragraph, as Germanicus promptly launches a vigorous expedition and wins instant successes. Suddenly everything seems to have been turned around, and all the earlier mishaps actually result in the enemy's total demoralization. The third paragraph looks like the end of the episode, on a note of joy and optimism, but then comes a sting in the tail as Tiberius suddenly intrudes, crushing all the high hopes out of jealousy. He appears negative and grudging (after the Romans' recovery, victory and confidence) and a cautious, mean and grey figure (beside the generous, colourful and dashing Germanicus). As in passage 1, we find the late appearance of Tiberius for a sour and damping effect, the unflattering contrast with Germanicus, and the negative speculation about the emperor's motivation. In contrast to Tacitus, most modern scholars feel that Germanicus had not really distinguished himself and the subjugation of all Germany, if actually possible, would have been costly. So they see Tiberius, as a man with personal experience of fighting there (25f.), being diplomatic (24f.), not wanting to hurt Germanicus' reputation by replacing him, and trying to get him to leave so the German campaign could be ended.

Passage 6 Tacitus Annals *2.72–3, 75, 3.1.*

This dismal episode is dexterously employed for a variety of purposes. There is further glorification of Germanicus in the widespread grief and especially in 2–5 (although the Germans might have disputed the claim there of his clemency, and modern scholars reject the comparison of Germanicus, who conquered nothing, to Alexander the Great, who conquered large parts of the known world – Tacitus does not make the comparison himself, but he does not disown it either). This passage also does much to develop the character of Agrippina and to create admiration and sympathy for her (prior to her persecution and death). What are the various qualities ascribed to her here, and what are the various ways in which pathos is built up? Tacitus tries to make his lines on her come alive so that they will have impact. In particular, 12ff. show a cinematic technique: he begins with a crowd scene, as large numbers come streaming into Brundisium from all around, and then at 15f. he pans from the harbour to the shore, walls and roofs; next comes the slow motion arrival of the fleet; at 19f. there is a zoom-in on the children, urn and Agrippina (the tragic remains of the Germanicus family); finally, there is the effective sound of the universal groan.

Passage 7 Tacitus Annals *3.2–4, 6.*

In Passage 6, Agrippina demonstrated a *pietas* (dutifulness to family) which the emperor is here depicted as singularly lacking (Germanicus was his adopted son), and there is much else here that reflects badly on Tiberius. His scarcely concealed pleasure at the death, his glaring absence from the public eye, his resentment of Agrippina (implied at 10f.), and his grudging of the proper pageantry look particularly bad in the context of the general mourning, and the comments of people at 11f. are most unflattering to him. Tacitus ends on a note of foreboding (especially after Agrippina's apprehension at 6.9), conjuring up a bleak and ominous picture of the emperor cooped up and brooding in his palace while the crowd roars outside.

Agrippina and others suspected that Tiberius (jealous of his adopted son's popularity and keen to facilitate the succession of his natural son Drusus) was involved in Germanicus' death. However, no convincing evidence for this has surfaced, and the assassination of such an admired figure would have been very risky. The recent discovery in Spain of an inscription bearing The Senatorial Decree concerning Cn. Piso Senior casts new light on Germanicus' death, the official investigation of it, and Tacitus' manipulation of his sources. For text, translation and discussion, see Griffin 1997 and AJP.

Passage 8 Suetonius Tiberius 52–3.

When exactly Agrippina's relationship with Tiberius soured – had it ever been otherwise? – is not known. Certainly, the death of Germanicus and the inflammatory role played in the events surrounding it by Cn. Calpurnius Piso (a close friend of Tiberius') ensured that Agrippina and Tiberius would be driven further apart. When she spread rumours of the emperor's involvement in her husband's death, the enmity was intensified. The intrusion into this already strained situation of the manipulative Sejanus (see Passage 9) brought matters to a head. Agrippina's relegation to a small island represents a tragic and ignominious end for a granddaughter of Augustus, an intelligent and proud woman (aware of her place in the world and not afraid to proclaim it) who produced six children in the course of a very happy marriage. See further Barrett 1996, 13–39.

Passage 9 Tacitus Annals 4. 1–2.

On Sejanus and his involvement in dynastic politics, see Introduction section 6. We may relish this scandalous story, but Tacitus' tone is one of stern disapproval. This is evident in the allusion to divine anger at 2f., which briefly conjures up a society so evil that enraged deities punish it and invests this episode with gravity (like a tragedy, such as Euripides' *Hippolytus* or Aeschylus' *Persae*, it exhibits the working out of divine wrath and retribution; Sejanus is a tool of heaven, like the destructive Fury Allecto in Virgil *Aeneid* 7.323ff.). Tacitus' sinister and formidable Sejanus is a powerful creation, thanks to both direct and indirect characterization. With the former method (openly attributing specific traits) the sketch at 3–6 depicts him as ominously possessed of many, varied accomplishments and recalls Sallust's description at *Catilina* 5 of Catiline (who tried to seize supreme power in 63 BC), suggesting that Sejanus was, like Catiline, corrupt, power-mad and of great danger to Rome (for the similarities between the sketches, see Martin-Woodman 1989, 84f.). Elsewhere in this passage and the next one, the characterization is indirect, as Sejanus is shown by his actions to be extremely ambitious, ruthless in the pursuit of his ambition, calculating, insidious, cunning etc. (look for more traits yourself).

Passage 10 Tacitus Annals *4.3, 7, 8.*

In passages 9 and 10 we are shown a wide-ranging and well thought-out campaign. The first objective, Tiberius, was taken in 9.1 (where the brevity of *mox... devinxit* implies speed and slickness in the remarkable feat of winning the confidence of this notoriously guarded emperor). Next, at 9.7ff., Sejanus shrewdly secured his power-base, by massing the praetorians into one threatening and easily employed force, and by ensuring their support, from the highest to the lowest. Then, at 9.11f., he turned his attention to the Senate. In passage 10, he finally moves against the imperial family and begins with Drusus, the first obstacle to himself as the successor. Exploitative in connection with Drusus' wife and heartless towards his own, he efficiently infiltrates Drusus' household by means of some well-chosen targets, before craftily and callously engineering his death. And, of course, Tiberius does not emerge well from this. He is completely taken in by the criminal Sejanus, and (especially in contrast with the Senate) at 15ff. he shows a rather repellent concern for appearances in connection with the death of his own son.

Passage 11 Tacitus Annals *4. 34–5.*

According to Tacitus, Sejanus' *modus operandi* was to convince Tiberius that enemies (especially Agrippina) were plotting against him and then remove them, to protect the emperor. He destroyed first Agrippina's friends (they were indicted and committed suicide or fled into exile) and then Agrippina herself (in AD 33) and two of her three sons (not Caligula), one of whom was imprisoned in the cellars of the palace and starved to death (he was last seen eating the stuffing out of his mattress). Sejanus' main mechanism for ruining the emperor's supposed enemies was the courts. The vague charge of *maiestas* (*minuta populi Romani*), 'lessening the majesty of the Roman people', had long been on the books and was reserved for cases of what we would today call treasonable behaviour. Under Tiberius, its application was broadened to encompass any perceived attack or criticism of the regime. For example, in AD 25 A. Cremutius Cordus was charged under the *maiestas* law for having included in his history praise for the Republican heroes

Brutus and Cassius (both of whom had been dead for nearly seventy years); facing conviction, Cordus committed suicide (see *Annals* 1.72, 4.34–5 and Levick 1976, 180ff.). One insidious feature of the law, aside from its flexibility, was that it rewarded successful accusers with portions of the property belonging to the convicted. Predictably, this led to a rash of *maiestas* cases. For Sejanus' purposes, *maiestas* was almost custom-made to allow him to remove obstacles to his advancement while simultaneously posing as the emperor's ever-vigilant protector.

Passage 12 Tacitus Annals *4.41, 57, 59, 67.*

On Tiberius' move to Capri, see Introduction section 6. Here, we are shown the extraordinary situation of a Roman emperor turning his back on Rome and Italy, and the government in the hands of two evil and repugnant figures. First Sejanus, the master manipulator of persons and events, appears at 1–6 as callously calculating, shrewd (4–6 were well aimed: see 23 and 25) and insidious (*paulatim* in 4: according to Tacitus, he worked on Tiberius for almost a year) and at 19ff. as a quick-thinking and brave opportunist (although in fact he may have acted instinctively out of genuine friendship and loyalty). The second figure is Tiberius, and his move from Rome is marked out as something remarkable by the space devoted to his motivation. At 8ff., Tacitus seems to weigh judiciously the various possible reasons; but none of them reflects favourably on the emperor, and he does not allow for less negative causes, such as a desire to escape in-fighting in the court or conspiracies (as suggested by some modern historians). In addition to Tiberius' typical dissimulation (7f.) and distaste for his own people (23f.), there is at 11ff. the bleak sketch of a body as warped and ugly as its owner's mind and at 25ff. the description of a beautiful and gentle setting for a hideous old man engaged in repulsive and savage acts (see line 10 and passage 13).

Passage 13 Suetonius Tiberius *43–4.*

Tiberius' life in the 'House of Jupiter' on Capri is not well attested. The fact that he was accompanied by astrologers, scholars, and close senatorial confidants suggests that he spent some time in cerebral rather than physical pleasures. But the ancient sources depict a dark and brooding tyrant indulging in perversity and savagery. Suetonius at *Tib.* 60 and 62 has several such tales: e.g. the mangled bodies of suspected enemies were hurled from the cliffs to waiting marines, who battered them with oars and boat-hooks to make sure they were dead; and Tiberius would trick men into drinking lots of wine and then tie up their private parts (compare also Tacitus *Annals* 6.6 on the emperor's inner torment).

Whether such stories are true or not, there can be little doubt that Tiberius disengaged more and more from administering the empire during his stay on Capri (as is adequately demonstrated by the fact that he made no real arrangements for the succession after his death).

Passage 14 Tacitus Annals *5.9, 6.19.*

This passage is made up of two concise and telling accounts of persecutions after the fall of Sejanus (on which, see the Introduction section 6). The first one brings out the viciousness of the emperor (in contrast to most other people: 1f.) by means of pathos in particular. It is sad enough that Sejanus' son is taken to prison knowing what is going to happen to him, but the daughter's bewildered ignorance is even sadder (underlining her childish innocence), and her remarks in line 5 highlight the extremity of the action taken against mere children. That is rapidly followed by the unforgettable brutality of the rape of the girl, with the grimly graphic *laqueum iuxta*. The second account is more lurid, and stresses Tiberius' savagery mainly by means of (extensive) horror. What instances of horror do you see there (note that the absence of a funeral was especially appalling to an ancient), and can you spot any possible exaggeration for effect?

Passage 15 Tacitus Annals *6.50.*

This rather low-key and detached account reflects badly on the emperor and the characters with whom he surrounded himself. One senses no sympathy for him here; instead, there may well be some malicious satisfaction. This is a brutal end for a brutal man, and Tiberius dies as another engineers the succession in the same way that Augustus died as Livia ensured that Tiberius himself succeeded (compare *Augustus* Passage 7). Dour and dissimulating even now, he is seen to have aroused no feelings for himself in his courtiers, and to have built up a court that is as dissembling (4f., 15f.), callous, and murderous as himself, for which he here reaps his reward. Caligula (the next emperor) betrays the emperor and his own grandfather, and his cowardice and indecision are highlighted at 17f. by the contrast with the undaunted man of action Macro. He is even worse than Caligula: as prime mover in the whole business, he keeps a close eye on Tiberius' health, moves quickly to secure the succession of his choice and will not even wait for a natural demise but acts with chilling efficiency at 17f. There is a black irony in all this (the commander of the praetorian guard was supposed to protect the emperor), and there is also dark humour at 13ff., as the corpse suddenly recovers and the rats hurriedly desert (too soon, in fact).

CALIGULA (GAIUS)

~

20 Coin depicting Caligula.

On Gaius (better known as Caligula), see section 7 of the Introduction.

1 *At nineteen, Caligula is summoned by his grandfather Tiberius to join him at Capri, and there he avoids being drawn into court intrigue, while indulging his natural viciousness.*

Undevicensimo aetatis anno accitus est Capreas a Tiberio. hic
omnibus insidiis temptatus elicientium cogentiumque se ad querelas,
nullam umquam occasionem dedit, quae ipse pateretur incredibili
dissimulatione transmittens, tantique in avum obsequii ut non
immerito sit dictum nec servum meliorem ullum nec deteriorem 5
dominum fuisse. naturam tamen saevam atque probrosam ne tunc
quidem inhibere poterat, quin animadversionibus cupidissime
interesset et ganeas atque lupanaria (capillamento celatus et veste
longa) noctibus obiret. ferum eius ingenium sagacissimus senex ita
prorsus perspexerat ut aliquotiens praedicaret exitio suo 10
omniumque Gaium vivere et se natricem populo Romano,
Phaethontem orbi terrarum educare.

2 elicientium . . . querelas: 'of those enticing and forcing him to complaints', i.e. of courtiers enticing and forcing Caligula to complain about Tiberius.

3 occasionem: i.e. an opportunity to make use of complaints by him.

3 quae ipse pateretur: as part of the maltreatment of Caligula, we hear elsewhere of taunts about his sexual tastes.

4 tantique . . . obsequii: genitive of quality/description (= 'and possessed of such great . . . ').

5 sit dictum: (impersonal) 'it was said' (of Caligula).

9 senex: i.e. Tiberius.

10–11 exitio suo omniumque: dative of purpose (i.e. for the destruction of Tiberius and of all men).

12 Phaethontem: accusative. Phaethon was the young and immature son of the sun-god. He foolishly persuaded his father to let him ride his fiery chariot, but soon proved unable to control the spirited horses and set the earth on fire by driving too close to it (and was on the point of totally destroying it when Jupiter saved it by hurling a thunderbolt at Phaethon and killing him).

When Caligula came to power in AD 37, there was widespread rejoicing for two reasons: the sour Tiberius was finally dead; his successor was the son of the very popular Germanicus.

2 *After noting that Caligula very probably killed Tiberius in his villa at Misenum, Suetonius now describes the universal joy as he succeeds Tiberius as emperor.*

Sic imperium adeptus, populum Romanum (vel dicam hominum
genus) voti compotem fecit, exoptatissimus princeps maximae parti
provincialium ac militum (quod infantem plerique cognoverant) et
universae plebi urbanae (ob memoriam Germanici patris
miserationemque prope afflictae domus). itaque ut a Miseno movit, 5
quamvis lugentis habitu et funus Tiberi prosequens, tamen inter
altaria et victimas ardentisque taedas densissimo et laetissimo
obviorum agmine incessit, 'sidus' et 'pullum' et 'pupum' et 'alumnum'
appellantium. ingressoque urbem statim consensu senatus et
irrumpentis in curiam turbae ius arbitriumque omnium rerum illi 10
permissum est, tanta publica laetitia ut tribus proximis mensibus
supra centum sexaginta milia victimarum caesa tradantur.

1 adeptus is from *adipiscor.*

1–2 vel . . . genus: 'or I might say the human race'.

2 voti compotem fecit: i.e. he fulfilled the prayers (that he would become emperor) of the Roman people/human race.

3 infantem = *eum infantem* ('him as an infant').

5 prope afflictae domus: Caligula's brothers had died, as well as his mother and father.

5 ut: 'when'.

6 quamvis here qualifies *lugentis . . . prosequens* (it does not introduce a concessive clause).

6 lugentis habitu: 'in the dress of one mourning' (i.e. wearing dark clothes).

6–7 inter altaria et victimas: i.e. people on his route sacrificed to the gods in thanks for his accession.
7–8 densissimo . . . agmine: ablative of attendant circumstances ('accompanied by a very . . .').
8 'sidus' . . . 'alumnum': these are pet names that those who met Caligula called him.
9 ingressoque: dative, agreeing with *illi* in 10.
11 tanta publica laetitia: ablative of attendant circumstances ('amid such great . . .').
12 caesa: supply *esse* (again the sacrifices are in thanksgiving).

Incest was abhorrent to ancient Romans, and accusations of it were a regular part of the rhetorical tradition of vituperatio (political abuse). Therefore, to find that Caligula is alleged to have perpetrated this perversion comes as little surprise.

3 *Suetonius states that Caligula regularly committed incest with his three sisters, and of them loved Drusilla best (being devastated at her death); of his wives, he was most attached to the fourth (Caesonia), who bore him a girl who took after her father all too much.*

Cum omnibus sororibus suis consuetudinem stupri fecit. ex iis
Drusillam vitiasse virginem praetextatus adhuc creditur atque etiam
in concubitu eius quondam deprehensus ab avia. mox Longino
consulari conlocatam abduxit et in modum iustae uxoris propalam
habuit; heredem quoque bonorum atque imperii aeger instituit. 5
Eadem defuncta, iustitium indixit in quo risisse, lavisse, cenasse cum
parentibus aut coniuge liberisve capital fuit. nec umquam postea
nisi per numen Drusillae deieravit. reliquas sorores nec cupiditate
tanta nec dignatione dilexit, ut quas saepe exoletis suis prostraverit.
Caesoniam neque facie insigni neque aetate integra, sed luxuriae 10
ac lasciviae perditae, et ardentius et constantius amavit, ut saepe
chlamyde peltaque et galea ornatam militibus ostenderit, amicis
etiam nudam. uxorio nomine non prius dignatus est quam enixam.
infantem autem (Drusillam appellatam) per omnium dearum templa
circumferens Minervae gremio imposuit, alendamque et 15
instituendam commendavit. nec ullo firmiore indicio sui seminis esse
credebat quam feritatis, quae illi quoque tanta iam tunc erat ut
infestis digitis ora et oculos simul ludentium infantium incesseret.

2 Drusillam . . . virginem: 'Drusilla [when she was] a virgin'.
2 vitiasse = *vitiavisse.*
2 praetextatus adhuc: the *toga praetexta* (a toga with a purple border) was worn by well-born children until they were considered to have become adults (some time between thirteen and seventeen). Caligula was about four years older than Drusilla.
3 deprehensus = *deprehensus esse* (going with *creditur*).

4–5 **in modum . . . habuit:** 'openly treated [her] after the fashion of [=as] his lawful wife'.
5 **aeger** = 'when he was ill' (he appointed her as his heir).
6 **eadem:** refers to Drusilla.
6 **cenasse** = *cenavisse.*
7–8 **nec umquam . . . nisi per:** 'and not ever if not by' = 'and only ever by'.
8 **numen Drusillae:** i.e. Drusilla was declared a goddess.
9 **tanta:** goes with *dignitate* as well as with *cupiditate.*
9 **ut quas** = 'obviously, for he often prostituted them to . . . '
10–11 **neque facie . . . perditae:** Caesonia's characteristics are designated firstly by ablatives of description and then by genitives of quality/description (= 'possessed of . . . ' with both constructions).
12 **ostenderit:** the rule about sequence of tenses does not apply in consecutive (result) clauses, and a perfect subjunctive after a main verb in secondary sequence is common (to stress a historical fact).
13 **uxorio . . . enixam:** 'he did not consider her worthy of the title of wife before [= until] she had given birth' (to a child of his). *enixam* is from *enitor.*
14–16 The idea seems to be that such a special child (and the daughter of someone with divine pretensions himself) deserved to be brought up by a goddess, and Minerva was the one chosen to do the job, so he deposited the baby in the lap of a statue of Minerva.
15–16 **alendamque . . . commendavit:** 'and he entrusted her [Drusilla] to be nurtured and instructed [by Minerva]'. The gerundives express obligation.
16–17 **nec ullo . . . feritatis:** 'and he believed her to be of his seed/parentage through no more reliable evidence than [the evidence] of her ferocity' = 'and the evidence that convinced him above all that she was his daughter was her ferocity'.
17 **illi quoque** refers to Drusilla as well as Caligula.
17 **iam tunc:** 'already then' (i.e. even as an infant).
18 **simul:** i.e. with her.

One of the features of Caligula's reign and character that stands out in the sources is his brutality. It ought to be remembered, however, that Augustus and Tiberius had also displayed cruel streaks, as would Claudius. The exact extent to which Caligula can be singled out for opprobrium on this front remains uncertain.

4 *Suetonius recounts various crimes committed by Caligula that illustrate his innate savagery.*

Saevitiam ingenii per haec maxime ostendit. multos honesti
ordinis, deformatos prius stigmatum notis, ad metalla aut ad bestias
condemnavit aut bestiarum more quadripedes cavea coercuit aut
medios serra dissecuit, nec omnes gravibus ex causis. parentes
supplicio filiorum interesse cogebat; quorum uni valetudinem 5
excusanti lecticam misit, alium a spectaculo poenae epulis statim
adhibuit atque omni comitate ad hilaritatem et iocos provocavit.
curatorem munerum ac venationum per continuos dies in conspectu
suo catenis verberatum non prius occidit quam offensus putrefacti

cerebri odore. equitem Romanum obiectum feris, cum se 10
innocentem proclamasset, reduxit abscisaque lingua rursus induxit.

Revocatum quendam a vetere exilio sciscitatus quidnam ibi facere consuesset, respondente eo per adulationem 'Deos semper oravi ut periret Tiberius et tu imperares', opinans sibi quoque exsules suos mortem imprecari, misit circum insulas qui universos 15
contrucidarent. cum discerpi senatorem concupisset, subornavit qui repente hostem publicum appellantes invaderent, graphiisque confossum lacerandum ceteris traderent. nec ante satiatus est quam membra et artus et viscera hominis tracta per vicos atque ante se congesta vidisset. 20

1 **saevitiam:** note the emphatic placement of this word (and that of *parentes* in 4 and several other significant words in this passage).

2 **metalla:** work in the mines was very hard, so this was one of the worst punishments.

2 **ad bestias:** i.e. they were thrown to wild animals in the arena.

3 **bestiarum more:** 'like wild animals' (which were kept in cages before being let loose in the arena).

4 **medios serra dissecuit:** i.e. he sawed them in half.

4 **nec omnes:** i.e. and he did not do this to all of them as a result of...

5 **quorum** refers to *parentes.*

6 **a:** 'after'.

7 We are told elsewhere that the father pretended to be cheerful to save another son of his from being executed.

9 **non prius occidit quam:** 'did not execute before' = 'only executed when'.

11 **proclamasset** = *proclamavisset.*

11 **rursus induxit:** i.e. he had him taken back into the arena.

12–16 Caligula asked a man recalled from a lengthy exile what he used to do during it, and when the man said flatteringly that he had prayed for Tiberius' death and Caligula's accession, Caligula decided that the people he himself had sent into exile on islands must be praying for his death, so he sent men to butcher them all (the subjunctive *contrucidarent* in 16 expresses purpose). In this involved sentence, two of the participles (*sciscitatus* and *opinans*) agree with the subject of the main verb (Caligula), *revocatum* goes with *quendam* (from *quidam*), and *respondente eo* is an ablative absolute, while *consuesset* in 13 = *consuevisset.*

16 **concupisset** = *concupivisset.*

16–17 **qui... invaderent:** 'men to suddenly attack him, calling him a public enemy' (the subjunctive here denotes purpose, like *traderent* in 18).

18 **lacerandum ceteris traderent:** 'to hand him over to the other [senators] to be mangled' (the gerundive expresses obligation).

18 **nec ante... quam:** 'and not before' = 'and not until'.

5 Some examples of how the monstrous things that Caligula did were aggravated by the terrible and cruelly humorous things that he said.

Immanissima facta augebat atrocitate verborum. monenti aviae, 'Memento,' ait, 'omnia mihi et in omnis licere.' trucidaturus fratrem, quem metu venenorum praemuniri medicamentis suspicabatur, 'Antidotum,' inquit, 'adversus Gaium?' relegatis sororibus non solum insulas habere se sed etiam gladios minabatur. non in quemquam (5) nisi crebris et minutis ictibus animadverti passus est, perpetuo notoque iam praecepto 'Ita feri ut se mori sentiat'. tragicum illud subinde iactabat 'Oderint, dum metuant.' infensus turbae faventi adversus studium suum exclamavit, 'Utinam populus Romanus unum cervicem haberet!' queri etiam palam de condicione temporum (10) suorum solebat, quod nullis calamitatibus publicis insignirentur; atque identidem exercituum caedes, famem, pestilentiam, incendia, hiatum aliquem terrae optabat. convivio effusus subito in cachinnos, consulibus (qui iuxta cubabant) quidnam rideret quaerentibus, 'Quid,' inquit, 'nisi uno meo nutu iugulari utrumque vestrum statim (15) posse?' cum, assistens simulacro Iovis, Apellen tragoedum consuluisset uter illi maior videretur, cunctantem flagellis discidit, conlaudans subinde vocem quasi etiam in gemitu praedulcem. quotiens uxoris vel amiculae collum exoscularetur, addebat: 'Tam bona cervix, simulac iussero, demetur.' quin et subinde iactabat (20) exquisiturum se vel fidiculis de Caesonia sua cur eam tantopere diligeret.

2 **memento**: second person singular of the imperative of *memini*. Caligula is telling her to bear in mind that he can do anything he likes to anyone he wants.

3 **metu**: ablative of cause.

3 **praemuniri**: the passive is here used in a reflexive sense (= 'was protecting himself in advance').

5 **gladios**: i.e. he was threatening to execute his sisters (not Drusilla, the other two), not just banish them to an island.

5–6 **non ... passus est**: 'He did not allow it to be executed [= execution to be inflicted] on anyone if not by means of ...' = 'he only allowed people to be executed by means of ...' *Passus est* is from *patior*.

6–7 **perpetuo ... praecepto**: ablative absolute (supply 'being').

7 **feri**: second person singular imperative of *ferio*. The quotation gives Caligula's command (to his executioners).

7 **tragicum illud** = 'the well-known line from tragedy' (from the play *Atreus* by the tragedian Accius).

8 **oderint, dum metuant**: *oderint* is jussive subjunctive ('let them hate [me]'), and *dum* means 'provided that'.

8–9 turbae . . . suum: i.e. the crowd (at Rome) angered him by not supporting whom he supported, either at a chariot-race (where his favourite was the Green team) or at a gladiatorial show (where he favoured the type of gladiator known as Thracian).

9–10 unum cervicem: so that he could kill them all at once.

13 hiatum . . . terrae: due to an earthquake.

13 convivio: 'At a dinner-party'.

14–16 quid . . . posse: 'he said, "At what [am I laughing] if not that at a single nod from me both of you . . ."' *Vestrum* is genitive of *vos.*

17 consuluisset: 'consulted' = 'asked'.

20 iussero: future perfect of *iubeo.*

20 quin et: 'And furthermore'.

21–2 exquisiturum . . . diligeret: i.e. that he would even torture Caesonia to find out why he loved her so much (as if she had given him a love potion or something).

6 His extravagance (in connection with bathing, food, pleasure boats, and building) was so great that he quickly ran through an immense fortune and had to resort to selling off some gladiators of his at a huge price through trickery and opening a brothel in the palace.

21 When Lake Nemi near Rome was drained in 1928–30, two Roman ships, 200 ft long and 60 ft wide, were found. Their luxurious decoration (mosaic floors, bronze fittings) suggested that they were pleasure barges. They dated to the early first century AD but were destroyed toward the end of World War II.

Sumptibus omnium prodigorum ingenia superavit, commentus novum balnearum usum, portentosissima genera ciborum atque cenarum, ut calidis frigidisque unguentis lavaretur, pretiosissima margarita aceto liquefacta sorberet, convivis ex auro panes et obsonia apponeret. fabricavit et Liburnicas, gemmatis puppibus, 5 versicoloribus velis, magna thermarum et porticuum et tricliniorum laxitate, magnaque etiam vitium et pomiferarum arborum varietate, quibus discumbens inter choros ac symphonias litora Campaniae peragraret. in extructionibus praetoriorum atque villarum nihil tam efficere concupiscebat quam quod posse effici negaretur. et iactae 10 itaque moles infesto ac profundo mari et excisae rupes durissimi silicis et campi montibus aggere aequati et complanata fossuris montium iuga. immensas opes non toto vertente anno absumpsit.

Exhaustus igitur atque egens ad rapinas convertit animum. nota res est, Saturnino inter subsellia dormitante, monitum a Gaio 15 praeconem ne praetorium virum crebro capitis motu nutantem sibi praeteriret, nec licendi finem factum quoad tredecim gladiatores sestertium nonagies addicerentur. lupanar in Palatio constituit, distinctisque et instructis pro loci dignitate compluribus cellis, in quibus matronae ingenuique starent, misit circum fora et basilicas 20 nomenculatores ad invitandos iuvenes senesque. novissime contrectandae pecuniae cupidine incensus, saepe super immensos aureorum acervos nudis pedibus spatiatus et toto corpore aliquamdiu volutatus est.

1 **prodigorum:** masculine (used as a noun).

1 **ingenia:** 'ingenuity'.

2 **novum balnearum usum:** 'a new bathing experience' (explained in the next line). This is an aptly novel expression.

3 **ut** introduces a consecutive (result) clause.

4 **ex auro** ('made from gold') goes with *panes* and *obsonia.*

5–7 The ablatives are descriptive. *magna thermarum . . . laxitate* ('with great spaciousness of hot baths . . . ') = 'with very spacious hot baths . . . ' *vitium* comes from *vitis.* The ships' lavishness is brought out by the lush and elegant style (e.g. the balanced arrangement of the ablative plurals, the parallelism between *magna . . . laxitate* and *magna . . . varietate* (with genitives enclosed), and the homoeoteleuton).

8 **quibus** ('on which') refers to *Liburnicas* and introduces a relative clause expressing purpose.

9–10 **tam . . . quam . . . negaretur:** 'as much as the kind of thing that was denied to be able to be achieved' (i.e. was said to be impossible). *negaretur* is subjunctive in a generic relative clause.

11 **moles:** not small furry animals, but pilings (masses of rubble) on which expensive villas were built extending out into the sea.

12 **aggere . . . fossuris:** ablatives of means.

13 **non toto vertente anno:** i.e. in less than a year.

14–18 Saturninus the ex-praetor (a praetor was a high-ranking official at Rome) was nodding off to sleep during an auction of Caligula's gladiators, so the emperor warned the auctioneer not to overlook Saturninus' nods, which were taken as bids, until the man had run up an enormous bid of 9 million sesterces (*sestertium nonagies*).

15–17 monitum . . . factum: supply *esse* with each of these, in reported statement after *nota res est* (= 'it is well known that . . . ').

17 licendi: gerund of *liceor*.

19 cellis: the small rooms in which prostitutes did their business.

20 starent: 'stand to solicit custom' (the subjunctive expresses purpose).

22 contrecto: (used of amorous caresses and intercourse) *cupido* and *incendo* have erotic associations and (together with the physical contact) suggest a perverted sexual relationship with money.

The ancient belief in physiognomy dictated that an evil personality had to be housed in an abnormal body. Suetonius' description of Caligula, therefore, should not be accepted at face value.

7 Suetonius describes Caligula's physical peculiarities (about which he was extremely sensitive) and his mental aberrations (including sleeplessness, nightmares, and an abnormal fondness for his horse).

Statura fuit eminenti, colore expallido, corpore enormi, gracilitate
maxima cervicis et crurum, oculis et temporibus concavis, fronte lata
et torva, capillo raro at circa verticem nullo, hirsutus cetera. quare,
transeunte eo, prospicere ex superiore parte aut omnino quacumque
de causa capram nominare criminosum et exitiale habebatur. 5
vultum natura horridum ac taetrum etiam ex industria efferabat,
componens ad speculum in omnem terrorem ac formidinem.

Creditur potionatus a Caesonia uxore amatorio medicamento quod
in furorem verterit. incitabatur insomnio maxime; neque enim plus
quam tribus nocturnis horis quiescebat, ac ne iis quidem placida 10
quiete, sed pavida miris imaginibus. ideoque magna parte noctis
(vigiliae cubandique taedio) nunc toro residens, nunc per longissimas
porticus vagus, invocare identidem atque expectare lucem consuerat.
Incitato equo (praeter equile marmoreum et praesepe eburneum
praeterque purpurea tegumenta ac monilia e gemmis) domum 15
etiam et familiam et supellectilem dedit, quo lautius nomine eius
invitati acciperentur; consulatum quoque traditur destinasse.

1–3 The ablatives are ablatives of description.

2 **temporibus:** 'temples'.

3 **torva:** i.e. frowning.

3 **capillo . . . nullo:** 'with a little hair [on his head] but none around the crown [of his head]'. This was why to look out from a higher place as he passed by was treated as a crime punishable by death (4–5).

3 **hirsutus cetera:** i.e. his body was hairy (like a goat). This was why to mention a goat for any reason at all was treated as a crime (4–5).

7 **componens . . . formidinem:** 'modifying [it] before a mirror into every conceivable intimidation and dreadfulness' = 'practising all kinds of intimidating and dreadful expressions before a mirror'.

8 **potionatus:** supply *fuisse*. Caesonia would have given him the love potion to ensure that he stayed faithful to her, but it was supposed to have turned him mad instead.

10–11 **ne iis . . . imaginibus:** 'not even during them [did he sleep] in a peaceful sleep but [in a sleep that was] fearful because of extraordinary visions' (seen in nightmares).

12 **vigiliae . . . taedio:** the ablative is causal (i.e. because he was weary of lying awake in bed for so long).

13 **consuerat** = *consueverat.*

14 **Incitato:** the name Incitatus means 'swift'.

15 **monilia e gemmis:** 'collars of precious stones'.

16–17 **quo lautius . . . acciperentur:** 'in order that those invited [to dinner] in his [i.e. Incitatus'] name might be entertained more sumptuously'.

17 **consulatum . . . destinasse:** there was a story that he intended to make his horse consul. *destinasse* = *destinavisse.*

One of the more obvious manifestations of Caligula's supposed madness, according to the sources, is his German campaign of AD *39.*

8 Suetonius describes how, for no real reason, Caligula mounted a German campaign, which proved to be a complete farce.

Militiam semel attigit, neque ex destinato, sed cum ad visendum
nemus flumenque Clitumni processisset, admonitus de supplendo
numero Batavorum quos circa se habuit, expeditionis Germanicae
impetum cepit. legionibus et auxiliis undique excitis, dilectibus
ubique acerbissime actis, contracto et omnis generis commeatu, 5
iter ingressus est, confecitque modo festinanter et rapide, interdum
adeo segniter delicateque ut octaphoro veheretur atque a
propinquarum urbium plebe verri sibi vias et conspergi propter
pulverem exigeret.

2–3 **admonitus . . . habuit:** presumably the oracle near the river Clitumnus (about 100 miles north of Rome) reminded him to bring the imperial bodyguard of Batavi (from Germany) back up to their full strength.

3–4 **expeditionis . . . cepit:** 'he got the impulse for an expedition to Germany'.

5 **ubique . . . actis:** *ubique* is the adverb, and *actis* is from *ago.*

6 modo . . . interdum: 'at one point . . . sometimes . . . '

8 propinquarum: 'near' (to his route), i.e. cities which he was passing close to and possibly ones through which he would shortly pass.

9 *Suetonius recounts how Caligula claimed ridiculously that on this campaign he faced great dangers and won magnificent victories.*

Adminio Britannorum regis filio (qui pulsus a patre cum exigua manu transfugerat) in deditionem recepto, quasi universa tradita insula, magnificas Romam litteras misit. mox, deficiente belli materia, paucos de custodia Germanos traici occulique trans Rhenum iussit ac sibi post prandium quam tumultuosissime adesse hostem nuntiari. (5) Quo facto, proripuit se cum parte equitum praetorianorum in proximam silvam; reversus eorum qui secuti non essent timiditatem corripuit. rursus obsides quosdam abductos e ludo clamque praemissos, deserto repente convivio, cum equitatu insecutus veluti profugos ac reprehensos in catenis reduxit, in hoc quoque mimo (10) intemperans. atque inter haec absentem senatum populumque gravissimo obiurgavit edicto quod, Gaio proeliante et tantis discriminibus obiecto, convivia, circum et theatra celebrarent.

Postremo, quasi perpetraturus bellum, derecta acie in litore Oceani ac ballistis machinisque dispositis, repente ut conchas (15) legerent imperavit, 'spolia Oceani' vocans; et in indicium victoriae altissimam turrem excitavit, ex qua (ut Pharo) noctibus ad regendos navium cursus ignes emicarent.

1–2 Adminio . . . in deditionem recepto: i.e. after the surrender of Adminius had been accepted.

1 pulsus: from *pello.*

3 insula: i.e. Britain.

3 magnificas Romam litteras: in the word order *Romam* is suggestively engulfed by *magnificas litteras.*

3 belli materia: i.e. people to fight and/or an occasion for fighting.

5 quam . . . nuntiari: 'it to be announced with as much confusion/alarm as possible that the enemy was upon [them]'.

7 proximam silvam: this is where he pretended the enemy was.

9 insecutus = *insecutus est.*

11 populumque: i.e. the people of Rome.

13 obiecto: 'exposed to'.

14–15 Caligula drew up his battle-line and siege equipment probably on the French coast of the English Channel (here denoted by *Oceanus*), as if about to attack Oceanus.

16 'spolia Oceani' vocans: 'calling them [the sea shells] spoils of [= taken from] Oceanus' (as though Oceanus had been conquered and plundered).

16 in indicium victoriae: i.e. as a memorial to his victory.

17 **ut Pharo:** 'as on Pharos' or 'as from the lighthouse at Pharos' (Pharos was an island lying off Alexandria, a city in Egypt, and its lighthouse was very famous in the ancient world).
18 **emicarent:** as a lighthouse (the subjunctive expresses purpose).

It seems certain that Caligula claimed divinity. This was not as crazy as it might initially appear, since many provincials had worshipped Augustus and Tiberius as gods during their lifetimes, and Julius Caesar and Augustus were both officially deified after their deaths.

10 *He claimed divine honours, setting up statues of himself as a god, linking his palace to temples, instituting a cult of himself, and worse.*

22 General view of the Roman forum, looking over the Basilica Julia (dedicated in 46 BC) in the foreground on the right.

Admonitus et principum et regum se excessisse fastigium,
divinam maiestatem asserere sibi coepit. datoque negotio ut
simulacra numinum religione et arte praeclara apportarentur e
Graecia, quibus capite dempto suum imponeret, partem Palatii ad
forum usque promovit; atque, aede Castoris et Pollucis in 5
vestibulum transfigurata, consistens saepe inter fratres deos
adorandum se adeuntibus exhibebat. et quidam eum Iovem
consalutarunt. templum etiam numini suo proprium et sacerdotes et

excogitatissimas hostias instituit. in templo simulacrum stabat
aureum iconicum amiciebaturque cotidie veste quali ipse uteretur. 10
Magisteria sacerdotii ditissimus quisque licitatione maxima
comparabant. hostiae erant phoenicopteri, pavones, phasianae. et
noctibus plenam fulgentemque Lunam invitabat assidue in amplexus
atque concubitum. interdiu cum Capitolino Iove secreto fabulabatur,
modo insusurrans ac praebens invicem aurem, modo clarius nec 15
sine iurgiis. exoratus, ut referebat, et in contubernium invitatus,
ponte transmisso Palatium Capitoliumque coniunxit.

1 **admonitus:** probably he was reminded by his courtiers.

3 **praeclara:** could be nominative agreeing with *simulacra* (in which case *religione* and *arte* are causal ablatives) or ablative agreeing with *religione* and *arte* (which would then be ablatives of description). The reference is to the most revered and skilfully sculpted statues.

4 **quibus . . . imponeret:** a relative clause expressing purpose ('in order that, [their] heads having been removed, he might place his own [head] on them' = 'so that he could remove their heads and replace them with his own').

4–5 **ad forum usque** = *usque ad forum.*

5–6 Caligula extended his palace on the Palatine all the way down to the Temple of Castor and Pollux (twin sons of Jupiter who were minor gods especially associated with the protection of ships and sailors), which was on the south side of the forum Romanum and was transformed into a grand entrance hall for the emperor's palace.

7 **adorandum se . . . exhibebat:** i.e. he displayed himself for worship by visitors. *adeuntibus* (from *adeo*) is dative of agent with the gerundive *adorandum* (expressing obligation).

8 **consalutarunt** = *consalutaverunt.*

10 **veste . . . uteretur** = *tali veste quali ipse uteretur* (*uteretur* 'was using' = 'was wearing').

11 **magisteria sacerdotii:** i.e. positions as priest.

11 **ditissimus quisque:** 'each most rich person' = 'all the richest people' (hence the plural verb *comparabant* in 12). *ditissimus* is the superlative of *dives.*

13 **Lunam:** i.e. the moon regarded as a goddess.

14 **Capitolino:** Jupiter had a famous temple on the Capitoline Hill at Rome, not far from the Palatine Hill.

15 **praebens . . . aurem:** i.e. pressing his ear to the statue's mouth to hear its reply.

15 **modo clarius:** 'at another moment [speaking] more clearly/out loud'.

16 **contubernium** might mean simply the sharing of a home, but it would tie in more closely with the invitations to the Moon and be more outrageous and climactic if the word denoted concubinage (i.e. living together as lovers).

The plot to kill Caligula seems to have been motivated more by personal revenge than political principle.

23 Praetorian guardsmen on a relief of the second century AD. Soldiers like this carried out the assassination of Caligula and helped elevate both Claudius and Nero to the purple.

11 Caligula's excesses made many think of murdering him, and finally two tribunes of the praetorian guard (Cassius Chaerea and Sabinus) actually formed a plan to assassinate him. His death was foretold by various prodigies.

Ita bacchantem atque grassantem non defuit plerisque animus adoriri. duo consilium communicaverunt perfeceruntque (non sine conscientia potentissimorum libertorum praefectorumque praetori), quod suspectos se et invisos sentiebant. cum placuisset Palatinis ludis spectaculo egressum meridie adgredi, primas sibi partes 5 Cassius Chaerea (tribunus cohortis praetoriae) depoposcit, quem Gaius mollem et effeminatum denotare omni probro consuerat et agenti gratias osculandam manum offerre formatam commotamque in obscaenum modum.

Futurae caedis multa prodigia exstiterunt. Olympiae simulacrum 10 Iovis (quod transferri Romam placuerat) tantum cachinnum repente edidit ut machinis labefactis opifices diffugerint; supervenitque ilico quidam Cassius nomine, iussum se somnio affirmans immolare taurum Iovi. monuerunt et Fortunae Antiatinae ut a Cassio caveret; qua causa ille Cassium Longinum (Asiae tum proconsulem) 15 occidendum delegaverat, inmemor Chaeream Cassium nominari. pridie quam periret, somniavit consistere se in caelo iuxta solium Iovis impulsumque ab eo dextri pedis pollice et in terras praecipitatum. sacrificans respersus est phoenicopteri sanguine.

1–2 **ita . . . adoriri**: 'The intention to attack him [i.e. Caligula] . . . was not lacking to very many people'. The rhyme in *bacchantem* and *grassantem* stresses Caligula's excesses.

3 **libertorum . . . praetori**: the freedmen are Caligula's secretaries/advisers, and *praetori* is genitive singular of *praetorium*. This statement of support for the plot at the highest level is emphasized by alliteration, assonance and rhyme in 2–3.

4 **suspectos**: supply *esse*. They were suspected of complicity in an earlier plot against Caligula.

5 **spectaculo egressum**: 'having left the show'. The participle agrees with the understood *illum* which is the object of *adgredi*.

5 **primas . . . partes** = 'the leading part/role'.

6–7 **quem . . . consuerat**: 'whom Gaius was accustomed to disparage as . . .' *consuerat* = *consueverat*. Such syncopated forms will not be pointed out any more.

7–9 **et agenti . . . modum**: 'and to whom thanking him [Gaius was accustomed] to offer to be kissed his hand formed and moved in an obscene manner' (e.g. with the middle finger extended from the clenched hand like a penis, implying that Chaerea was a passive homosexual).

10 **Olympiae**: locative. The reference here is to one of the Greek statues that Caligula ordered brought to Rome so that his head could replace the god's.

11 **quod . . . placuerat**: 'which to be transferred to Rome had seemed good' = 'which Caligula had decided to have transferred to Rome'.

13 **iussum**: understand *esse* (in an accusative and infinitive construction after *affirmans*).

14 **Fortunae**: at Antium, there was a shrine of two sister goddesses of fortune, who warned Caligula to be on his guard against someone called Cassius.

15 **qua causa**: ablative of cause.

16 **occidendum delegaverat**: 'had ordered to be killed'.

16 **inmemor . . . nominari**: 'forgetting that Chaerea was named Cassius'.

17 **pridie quam periret**: 'on the day before he died'.

18–19 **impulsumque . . . praecipitatum**: supply *esse* each time (these are infinitives after *somniavit*).

12 The assassination took place as Caligula left the Palatine Games for lunch. His wife and daughter were also put to death.

VIIII Kal. Febr. cunctatus an ad prandium surgeret (marcente adhuc stomacho pridiani cibi onere), tandem suadentibus amicis egressus est. cum in crypta per quam transeundum erat pueri nobiles praepararentur, ut eos inspiceret hortareturque restitit. duplex dehinc fama est: alii tradunt adloquenti pueros a tergo 5 Chaeream cervicem gladio caesim graviter percussisse, dehinc Sabinum (alterum e coniuratis) ex adverso traiecisse pectus; alii Sabinum signum more militiae petisse et, Gaio 'Iovem' dante, Chaeream exclamasse 'Accipe ratum!' respicientique maxillam ictu discidisse. iacentem contractisque membris clamitantem se vivere 10 ceteri vulneribus triginta confecerunt. quidam etiam per obscaena ferrum adegerunt. lecticarii in auxilium accucurrerunt, mox Germani corporis custodes, ac nonnullos ex percussoribus, quosdam etiam senatores innoxios interemerunt.

Cadaver eius clam in hortos Lamianos asportatum et 15 tumultuario rogo semiambustum levi caespite obrutum est. satis constat hortorum custodes umbris inquietatos; in ea domo in qua occubuerit nullam noctem sine aliquo terrore transactam, donec ipsa domus incendio consumpta sit. perit una et uxor Caesonia gladio a centurione confossa et filia parieti inlisa. condicionem temporum 20 illorum per haec aestimare quivis possit: fuit suspicio ab ipso Gaio famam caedis simulatam et emissam ut hominum erga se mentes deprehenderet.

1 **VIIII Kal. Febr.**: 'on January 24th'.

1 **surgeret**: deliberative subjunctive in an indirect question.

2 **onere**: causal ablative (his stomach was upset because of the large amount of food he had consumed at dinner the day before).

3 **per . . . erat**: i.e. which he had to pass through.

3 **pueri**: i.e. boys who were to appear on the stage and were rehearsing.

5 **adloquenti**: possessive dative with *cervicem* (= 'the neck of him [Caligula] as he was talking to the boys').

7 **ex adverso**: 'from a point facing' = 'while facing Caligula'.

7 **alii**: understand *tradunt.*

8–9 Sabinus asked for the watchword according to military custom, and when Caligula gave him 'Jupiter' as the watchword, Chaerea shouted out, 'Accept it as fulfilled!' and split Caligula's jaw as he looked around (*respicienti* is possessive dative with *maxillam*). Jupiter was the god of the thunderbolt (i.e. sudden death), so Chaerea took Caligula's '*Iovem*' as an omen of Caligula's own death and promptly made the omen come true.

10 **contractisque membris**: i.e. curled up into a ball, in agony and/or self-defence.

13 **corporis custodes**: Caligula's German 'bodyguard'.

16 **levi caespite**: i.e. a light/thin covering of turf.

17–18 **inquietatos... transactam**: understand *esse* with both (these are infinitives after *satis constat*).

17 **domo**: i.e. the house in whose passageway he was murdered.

19 **una** is the adverb and means 'together' (with Caligula).

21 **possit**: potential subjunctive.

22 **simulatam et emissam**: supply *esse* (these are infinitives after *suspicio*). People suspected that Caligula made up and spread the report of his death to find out how men felt about him.

CALIGULA APPRECIATION

Passage 1 Suetonius Caligula *10–11.*

If just some of the stories about Tiberius' life on Capri are true, Caligula's experiences there (AD 31–7) could not have been good for the formation of his character. But Suetonius' view was that his nature was unchanging and evil from the start. So he talks twice of his inherent viciousness (in 6 and 9, with three strong adjectives to underline the point; compare *incredibili* in 3) and depicts here numerous failings in the young Caligula. Of these, *dissimulatio* receives stress, by means of two mentions, in 4 and 8 (this is not surprising in someone who to the biographer was wicked all along but managed to conceal his faults from many for a time). He also blackens Caligula firstly via close association with Tiberius, reminding us (at 9ff.) of how depraved and bizarre that emperor was (yet Caligula survived and in fact revelled in the murky waters of his court), and secondly via two memorable quotes (again the doublet for emphasis) – the *sententia nec servum... fuisse* in 5f. and the more full *exitio suo... educare* at 10ff. (which makes for an ominous close, as even Tiberius condemns Caligula). In the latter, the reference to Phaethon is still more suggestive than the metaphor of the snake. What are the correspondences between Caligula and Phaethon?

Passage 2 Suetonius Caligula *13–14.*

For Caligula's popularity at the start of his Principate, see Introduction section 7. Especially after Suetonius' remarks at 1.9ff. and his claim (just before this selection) that Caligula very probably murdered Tiberius, there is extensive irony here – in the universal support and joy (which also make Caligula's later conduct seem even worse), in people feeling sorry for Caligula's family being all but destroyed (soon they will be feeling sorry for themselves and wishing that it *had* been totally destroyed) and in people thanking the gods for Caligula (who will shortly amongst other things be posing as a god). The irony is underlined by pointers back to 1.11f. (at 1f., with the allusion to the Roman people and the whole world; at 7f., where the burning torches and *sidus* (which can also mean 'sun') recall Phaethon; and at 8, where *alumnum* calls to mind *educare* in 1.12). With hindsight, one can see other reverberations here as well: the stress on death seems apt for this murderous emperor; and in connection with the pet names in 8, stars (e.g. the dog-star) and other heavenly bodies designated by the word *sidus* were also believed to have a destructive and malefic influence; *pullum* and *pupum* highlight Caligula's (immature, irresponsible) youth, and instead of being a noun *pullum* could be an adjective, meaning 'dark, sombre'.

Passage 3 Suetonius Caligula *24–5.*

People often feel that knowledge of a person's sexual tastes provides a real insight into his or her character. Here (and later, in *Caligula* 36) Suetonius employs these anecdotes to portray Caligula as evil in private as well as public life, a monster who perverted natural affection and the natural role of a brother, husband, and father. For impact, he puts the more shocking crime of incest first and gives his treatment of that an arresting start via alliteration at 1f. and a series of sensational revelations at 1–7. Then he adds more and more counts against Caligula, which also involve other faults. Drusilla (named after Caligula's sister), a dreadful daughter of dreadful parents, attacking her playmates to her father's evident approval, provides a memorable climax. Caligula was fond of his sisters, especially Drusilla. When she died in AD 38, he was inconsolable and had her deified as Panthea (coin issues attest this deification). But do these actions prove incest? Or was he trying to proclaim a new family unity after Tiberius' divisive reign? Orators often made accusations of incest (e.g. Cicero *Pro Caelio* 32), so such charges against the hated emperor cannot be automatically accepted as true.

Passage 4 Suetonius Caligula *27–8.*

This time, we are shown Caligula the murderous tyrant with a sadistic sense of humour. As usual, Suetonius employs an apparently objective style of reporting (very little overt criticism of Caligula, no exclamations of sympathy for the victims etc.), so that he seems to be letting the facts speak for themselves. Of course, the 'facts' that he supplies are horrifying, and he also ensures that he gets his point across in more subtle ways. He introduces his anecdotes (grouped for cumulative impact) with a short, sharp sentence designed to get the attention and colour reactions from the start. He achieves stress by means of emphatic position, repetition (the mass murders at 1ff. and 15f.) and fulness of expression (in 15f. and 19). And there is a distinct climax at 16ff., of a personage as important as a senator. In each of these tales, the focus is on gruesomeness, and specific details such as names are few and flimsy. This typically vague list of victims must raise suspicions that we are dealing more with rumours than with established fact. We should certainly not conclude that Caligula was devoid of viciousness, but we must question whether he went about routinely executing 'a senator' or 'a knight' for no reason at all. For more lurid stories, see *Caligula* 27, 32, 38, 49, 55, and on the distortion and exaggeration in such tales, see Barrett 1989, xxff.

Passage 5 Suetonius Caligula *29–33.*

What people say reveals a lot about them, and the remarks here attributed to Caligula build up a picture of a bloodthirsty megalomaniac with a sick sense of humour and a penchant for brevity, bluntness, and a forceful and epigrammatic turn of phrase. Suetonius also puts across the idea that nobody was safe from Caligula's ferocity, which embraced even those closest to him. So a full four members of his family are mentioned at the start, and at the end there are the friend Apelles, the *uxor* and *amicula* at supremely tender moments and even his beloved Caesonia (the placement of these two groups is emphatic and ensures ring-structure). There is also a certain suspicious irony here, as several of these remarks appear to rebound on Caligula in Suetonius' version (in Passages 11 and 12) of his assassination: before his death, a statue of Jupiter laughed (at his presumption) and Caligula dreamed that Jupiter kicked him out of heaven; during the actual murder, he was wounded in the neck; swords were used on him, and he was finished off by means of many wounds (compare 5, 6f., 16f. and 19f.). But although some of Caligula's sayings here may have been embellished or made up, our only eyewitness account of Caligula's behaviour suggests that he really did have a nasty tongue: see Philo *Embassy To Gaius* 349ff.

Passage 6 Suetonius Caligula *37–8, 41–2.*

Suetonius here fills out his depiction of Caligula the monster with his extravagance, which involves more than simply spending large sums of money (e.g. there is much that is fantastic, abnormal, and unbalanced). Compare Passages 3–5 for the material's nature and presentation (which you can investigate on your own). Suspiciously, the Caligula of our sources has all the traits of the tyrant, a common type in Classical literature (see the *Philippics* of Demosthenes and Cicero, and Wardle 1994, 70ff.). The tyrant is extravagant with money and also has perverse and insatiable sexual appetites, is cruel in ingenious ways, makes savage statements, sometimes aspires to divinity and embarks on hare-brained schemes. But that these stories about Caligula are not wholesale fabrication was illustrated by the discovery in the 1920s of two pleasure barges, each over 200 ft long, at the bottom of Lake Nemi near Rome. They were dated to Caligula's reign by inscriptions, and showed evidence of marble panelling, mosaics, ivory inlay, piped water (the pipes were inscribed with Caligula's name), bronze fittings, gilded roof tiles and elaborate friezes. The barges were destroyed by fire in 1944, and all that remains of them are two beams, now in Rome's Vatican Museum.

Passage 7 Suetonius Caligula *50, 55.*

Suetonius' physical descriptions sharpen the picture and make the emperors come alive. At 1–7 (where Caligula's strange, repellent and extreme appearance complements his mental make-up), the biographer probably had in mind theories of physiognomy according to which the emperor's features would have indicated failings such as cowardice (paleness, thin neck and legs), promiscuity (thin legs, baldness, excessive body hair), and treachery (hollow eyes, hairy thighs). In connection with the mental abnormality (on which, see Introduction section 7), there is much absurdity (but always with a dark tinge) and a bleak irony (in this arch-criminal at 4f. designating the acts of others as crimes, and at 8f. in his beloved wife giving him a love potion, which causes madness instead of love). Here, as elsewhere, by not assigning motives, Suetonius intimates that Caligula was irrational (the ferocious expressions in 7 could have been due to Caligula feeling threatened, and the business with Incitatus could have been an elaborate joke). You may feel a bit sorry for Caligula over the love potion, the sleeplessness and the nightmares, but Suetonius expresses no sympathy at all; in view of his general depiction of Caligula, one infers instead satisfaction at a certain poetic justice in his promiscuity leading to the potion, and in this terrifying figure who tortured many being tortured and terrified himself.

Passage 8 Suetonius Caligula *43.*

We may be amused at this German campaign, but the Romans rated martial prowess highly (especially in their leaders), and so would have seen this as damning criticism of Caligula. He is presented as totally without military credentials and totally unsuited to command, having 'fought' only once, in an episode which is a blend of farce and lunacy, which is discreditable to himself and to Rome, and which is virtually an inversion of a military campaign (no objectives, enemy, fighting etc.). As there is no real logical link between supplementing Caligula's German bodyguard and a German expedition, the campaign would appear to have been conceived on a strange whim, while the emperor was sightseeing. The preparations at 4f. suggest something serious in the offing and great energy on the part of Caligula (who looks like a real general at this point), but the speed at 6 soon gives way to indolence, and the drama is deflated as Caligula behaves like no other Roman general (a point brought out also by the considered diction in 7: *segnis* can mean 'slothful', 'lacking energy' and 'slow', while *delicatus* can mean 'luxurious', 'self-indulgent', 'frivolous', 'fastidious', and 'foppish'). Elsewhere in Suetonius (*Galba* 6), this campaign is mentioned as a great military accomplishment. It is clear that once more the sources cannot be taken at face value and the hostile tradition about Caligula is exerting its influence on the depiction of events here (see further Woods 2000).

Passage 9 Suetonius Caligula *44–6.*

Of the four fraudulent victories here, the second and third are very similar, which makes them look particularly ludicrous and suggests that Caligula was short of ideas, while the most bizarre and crazy 'victory' is saved until last for a climax. At 1ff. there may well be an implicit contrast with Julius Caesar, who did actually invade Britain (in 55 and 54 BC) and had genuine military successes there. The behaviour at 14ff. recalls that of another megalomaniac and tyrant, the Persian King Xerxes, who invaded Greece in 480 BC, building two bridges of boats across the Hellespont (Caligula also built a boat-bridge, near Baiae) and reportedly claiming that he had enslaved the sea (throwing fetters into it, and lashing and branding it when it broke down his bridges). The reference to the lighthouse at Pharos in 17 links Caligula with its builder, King Ptolemy II (308–246 BC), a famous benefactor and cultural patron. But above all, one thinks of Caligula's father Germanicus. In fact, Suetonius begins his *Caligula* with six chapters on Germanicus, and so subsequently one cannot help contrasting the son with the father, especially here (because Suetonius had described Germanicus as possessing unequalled valour, often killing the enemy in hand-to-hand combat, winning a real victory in Germany and celebrating a triumph for it).

Passage 10 Suetonius Caligula *22.*

Again, Roman readers would have been appalled (not amused) at the impiety here (not to mention the concomitant faults). For similar sensational stories, see Cassius Dio 59.26–8 (deities were supposed to be immortal, so Dio remarks pointedly that Caligula discovered that he was not divine when he was assassinated). It seems clear that Caligula did demand to be worshipped as a god (see e.g. Philo *Embassy To Gaius* 349ff.). To make the demand was not in itself entirely crazed (though certainly megalomaniac). Humans who accomplished great deeds could be considered divine after their death. This happened with Alexander the Great, Romulus, Julius Caesar and Augustus. Indeed, in many parts of the empire, Augustus and Tiberius received worship while still alive, though not in Rome itself. This is the line Caligula crossed – by demanding to be worshipped as divine while alive, and by insisting this be done in Rome as well as elsewhere in the empire. So, once more, we encounter the familiar pattern – a basic claim (the demand for divinity) that appears factual but is then greatly embellished with 'crazy' details until it becomes almost a ludicrous pantomime. On Roman concepts of sanctity, piety, and the divine status of emperors, see Beard–North–Price 1998, I, 125ff., 140ff., 214ff.; II, 222ff., 253ff.

Passage 11 Suetonius Caligula *56–7.*

Caligula was the first Roman emperor to be assassinated openly. That he fell to his own praetorian guard suggests that his excessive and offensive behaviour finally became totally unacceptable. Suetonius imputes only personal motives to the assassins. Modern scholars wonder if political manipulators were behind the scenes, guiding events to their own benefit. However, we get little hint of this in surviving accounts, and all must remain speculation. Such, perhaps, is the very nature of conspiracies.

Suetonius' version has impact. For clarity, he provides context for the murder and in the course of passages 11 and 12 divides his narrative into separate sections on: the conspirators and their motivation; prodigies foreshadowing the death; the assassination itself, and the aftermath. Here, there is a build-up to the killing: the sense of inevitability in the first paragraph (*perfeceruntque* in 2, the highest support in 3, the determination of Chaerea at 5ff.) is reinforced in the second paragraph by the prodigies (which also hold back the action and make for an unsettling gloom). Suetonius also includes (in passages 11 and 12) details which are small and lively, striking and horrifying, and dramatic and sensational. Look for them.

Passage 12 Suetonius Caligula *58–60.*

The atmosphere overall is dispiriting. This is an appropriately ugly end to an ugly reign, and there is no quiet diminuendo close after Caligula's demise. Suetonius' account may seem objective, and he certainly does not condone openly the murder of the emperor of Rome, but there is a subtle colouring. Apart from the fact that there is no expression of sympathy for the victims or condemnation of the conspirators, he actually devotes more space to material which could be seen as justifying the assassination than he does to the deed itself. He does not gloss over the brutality of the murder, but one can infer easily enough that the death was not undeserved and that this was a case of brutality begetting brutality. In passage 11 at 4ff., we saw Caligula's own maltreatment of people rebounding on him, and at 10ff. there was allusion to his impiety and murderous streak (with Jupiter himself approving of his fall in the dream). That is followed here by reminders of his ludicrous German campaign (in 12) and various faults (at 2, 11, 12 and 21ff.). In 13f., his supporters are shown to be ferocious; at 17f., he is a terrifying monster even when dead (in death as in life); and his fatuous final words in 10 hardly show him in a good light either (to keep on shouting that you are still alive while surrounded by armed assassins is really asking for it).

CLAUDIUS

~

24 Coin depicting Claudius.

On Claudius, see section 8 of the Introduction.

1 *Suetonius presents a Claudius who was feeble-minded, despised by his family and (in Caligula's reign) the subject of various pranks.*

Per omne fere pueritiae atque adulescentiae tempus variis et tenacibus morbis conflictatus est adeo ut, animo simul et corpore hebetato, ne progressa quidem aetate ulli publico privatoque muneri habilis existimaretur.

Mater Antonia portentum eum hominis dictitabat, nec absolutum a natura, sed tantum incohatum; ac si quem socordiae argueret, stultiorem aiebat filio suo Claudio. avia Livia pro despectissimo semper habuit, non affari nisi rarissime, non monere nisi acerbo et brevi scripto aut per internuntios solita. soror Livilla cum audisset quandoque imperaturum, tam iniquam et tam indignam sortem populo Romano palam et clare detestata est.

Quotiens post cibum addormisceret (quod ei fere accidebat), olearum aut palmularum ossibus incessebatur, interdum ferula flagrove velut per ludum excitabatur a copreis. solebant et manibus stertentis socci induci, ut repente expergefactus faciem sibimet confricaret. 15

3 **ne progressa quidem aetate:** *progressa* is ablative, agreeing with *aetate*, and *ne . . . quidem* means 'not even'. Even when he had reached the proper age to begin a public career, Claudius was thought to be unfit for such a thing and even for performing a minor private role.

5 **portentum eum hominis dictitabat:** understand *esse*; *portentum . . . hominis* means 'a monster of a man'.

6 **tantum** is the adverb.

6 **argueret:** the subjunctive is here employed in a generalizing condition containing the idea of repetition (similar to the frequentative subjunctive with *quotiens* in 12). The genitive *socordiae* denotes what she was accusing the person of each time.

7 **stultiorem aiebat:** understand *eum esse.*

7–8 *pro* with *habeo* means to treat somebody as being something.

8 **non affari nisi rarissime:** this infinitive (like *monere*) depends on *solita* (from *soleo*) in 9. *non nisi* ('not except') = 'only'.

10 with *imperaturum* ('be emperor') understand *eum esse.*

12 **quod** = *id quod* ('something which').

14 **velut per ludum:** 'as though in jest'.

14–15 **solebant . . . induci:** literally, 'slippers were accustomed to be put on the hands of him snoring'.

15–16 **faciem sibimet confricaret:** *sibimet* = *sibi* ('he might rub his face [with them]').

2 *According to Suetonius, Claudius had great physical defects, which were matched by other flaws, such as immoderate appetites and stupidity (he was tricked by one party in a lawsuit into removing the man's opponent, and he actually had in mind a very strange decree).*

Auctoritas dignitasque formae non defuit illi, verum stanti vel sedenti ac praecipue quiescenti; ceterum ingredientem destituebant poplites minus firmi, et remisse quid vel serio agentem multa dehonestabant – risus indecens, ira turpior (spumante rictu, umentibus naribus), linguae titubantia caputque maxime tremulum. 5

Cibi vinique quocumque et tempore et loco appetentissimus. nec temere umquam triclinio abscessit nisi distentus ac madens et ut statim supino ac per somnum hianti pinna in os inderetur ad exonerandum stomachum. somni brevissimi erat (nam ante mediam noctem plerumque vigilabat), ut tamen interdiu nonnumquam in 10 iure dicendo obdormisceret vixque ab advocatis de industria vocem augentibus excitaretur. libidinis in feminas profusissimae, marum omnino expers. aleam studiosissime lusit, de cuius arte librum

quoque emisit, solitus etiam in gestatione ludere, essedo alveoque
adaptatis ne lusus confunderetur. 15

Unus ex litigatoribus seducto in salutatione affirmavit vidisse se
per quietem occidi eum a quodam. dein paulo post, quasi
percussorem agnosceret, libellum tradentem adversarium suum
demonstravit; confestimque is ad poenam raptus est. Claudius dicitur
etiam meditatus edictum quo veniam daret flatum crepitumque 20
ventris in convivio emittendi, cum periclitatum quendam prae
pudore ex continentia repperisset.

1–2 **verum stanti . . . quiescenti**: 'but [to him] standing . . . lying down' = 'but only when he was standing . . . lying down'.

3 **minus firmi**: Claudius stumbled and limped.

4 **ira**: nominative, another one of the many (*multa*) disagreeable traits of Claudius listed here.

6 **et . . . et**: 'both . . . and'.

7 **temere**: 'readily', 'willingly'.

7–9 **ut . . . stomachum**: i.e. with the intention of being made to vomit during his sleep (*supino* and *hianti* are dative, agreeing with an *illi* to be supplied) to relieve his stomach of its burden.

9 **somni brevissimi**: genitive of quality/description, denoting what Claudius required.

10 **ut tamen**: 'with the result, however, that'.

10–11 **in iure dicendo**: i.e. while presiding in court.

12 **libidinis . . . profusissimae**: understand *erat*. This is a genitive of quality/description denoting a characteristic of Claudius, and *in* means 'towards'.

12 **marum**: from *mas* (Claudius was not a homosexual).

14 **solitus**: from *soleo*.

16 **seducto** is dative (i.e. to Claudius having been taken aside) and goes with *affirmavit*.

17 **per quietem**: i.e. in a dream.

17 **paulo post**: 'a little later'. *post* is the adverb.

17–18 **quasi percussorem agnosceret**: the man (exploiting Claudius' suspicious and gullible nature) claims that his opponent was the one he saw in his dream murdering the emperor.

20 **meditatus** (understand *esse*) goes with *dicitur*.

20 **quo veniam daret**: a relative clause expressing purpose.

20–1 **flatum . . . emittendi**: the gerund depends on *veniam* ('leave to emit'). With *flatum crepitumque* it appears that Claudius intended to give people leave to fart silently or loudly.

21 with *periclitatum* supply *esse*. *quendam* is from *quidam*.

25 Statue of Valeria Messalina holding her son Britannicus (born AD 41).

Claudius' third wife was Valeria Messalina, a girl in her mid-to-late teens when she married the already middle-aged Claudius in AD *38 or 39, as he was approaching fifty. Her status at court was greatly enhanced by the birth of Claudius' son and prospective heir, Britannicus, in* AD *41. Our sources portray her as a pouting, amoral nymphomaniac, easily able to bamboozle her gullible husband.*

3 *Tacitus begins his account of the downfall of Messalina by explaining how she was distracted from attacking a rival by her wild passion for the handsome Silius.*

Novo et furori proximo amore distinebatur. nam in C. Silium, iuventutis Romanae pulcherrimum, ita exarserat ut Iuniam Silanam, nobilem feminam, matrimonio eius exturbaret vacuoque adultero poteretur. neque Silius flagitii aut periculi nescius erat. sed certo, si abnueret, exitio, et nonnulla fallendi spe, simul magnis praemiis, 5
operire futura et praesentibus frui pro solacio habebat. illa non furtim sed multo comitatu ventitare domum, egressibus adhaerescere, largiri opes, honores. postremo, velut translata iam fortuna, servi liberti paratus principis apud adulterum visebantur.

1 *proximus* + dative = nearest to (i.e. bordering on).

1 **C.** = *Gaium.*

3 **matrimonio eius**: 'from [her] marriage to him'.

3–4 **vacuoque adultero poteretur**: 'seized [for herself] an adulterer [now] without a wife'.

4–5 there are three ablative absolutes here, with the imaginary present participle of *sum* to be understood each time: 'with death [being] certain, if . . . , and with [there being] . . .'

6 **operire futura . . . pro solacio habebat**: 'he regarded it as a solace to conceal [from thought] future events' = 'he took comfort in banishing thoughts of the future'.

7 **domum**: i.e. to the house of Silius.

7–8 **egressibus adhaerescere**: i.e. kept close to him when he went out.

9 **fortuna** denotes the rank of emperor.

4 *The process whereby Claudius finally discovers his wife's adultery now begins, as Silius proposes to her that they seize power and promises to marry her, and she accepts the offer of marriage to him.*

Flagitia uxoris noscere ac punire adactus est, ut deinde ardesceret in nuptias incestas. iam Messalina, facilitate adulteriorum in fastidium versa, ad incognitas libidines profluebat, cum abrumpi dissimulationem Silius urgebat: quippe non eo ventum ut senectam principis opperirentur; flagitiis manifestis subsidium ab audacia petendum; adesse conscios paria metuentes; se caelibem, orbum, nuptiis et adoptando Britannico paratum; mansuram eandem Messalinae potentiam, addita securitate, si praevenirent Claudium, ut insidiis incautum, ita irae properum. 5

Segniter eae voces acceptae, non amore in maritum, sed ne Silius summa adeptus sperneret adulteram. nomen tamen matrimonii concupivit ob magnitudinem infamiae (cuius apud prodigos novissima voluptas est). nec ultra exspectato quam dum sacrificii gratia Claudius Ostiam proficisceretur, cuncta nuptiarum sollemnia celebrat. 10 15

1–2 the *ut* introduces a result clause = 'only to become eager subsequently for an incestuous marriage' (to his niece Agrippina, his fourth wife).

3 **versa**: nominative.

4–9 **quippe** etc.: the arguments used by Silius here appear as reported statement, with *esse* to be supplied with *ventum* (4), *petendum* (6), *paratum* and *mansuram* (7).

4–5 **non eo . . . opperirentur**: 'it had not been come to the point that they were awaiting the outcome of the emperor's old age' (i.e. they were not reduced to waiting for Claudius to die). *ventum (esse)* is impersonal, and *eo* is the adverb.

5–6 **flagitiis . . . petendum**: i.e. their affair was exposed and they needed to take bold steps to save themselves. *flagitiis manifestis* is dative with *subsidium* ('help for . . .'), and *petendum* is a gerundive expressing obligation.

7 **nuptiis . . . paratum** = ready to marry her and adopt Britannicus (her son by Claudius).

8–9 **ut . . . properum**: 'although not on his guard against treachery, yet quick to grasp hold of anger' (i.e. quick to anger). The adverbs *ut* and *ita* often head contrasting clauses like this. *irae* is genitive of reference.

10 **amore**: ablative of cause.

10 **ne**: 'for fear that'.

11 **summa** (neuter accusative plural) denotes supreme power.

11 **nomen . . . matrimonii**: i.e. being called Silius' wife.

12–13 **cuius . . . est**: 'of which the pleasure is most extreme among the unrestrained' = 'the voluptuary's ultimate pleasure'.

13 **nec . . . dum**: ablative absolute (*exspectato* is impersonal): 'with it not having been waited longer than until' = 'waiting only until'.

14 **Ostiam**: this was Rome's port nearby.

5 It may seem incredible that Silius and Messalina went through all the formalities of a marriage ceremony in a gossipy place like Rome, but it is true.

Haud sum ignarus fabulosum visum iri tantum ullis mortalium securitatis fuisse in civitate omnium gnara et nihil reticente; nedum consulem designatum cum uxore principis, praedicta die, adhibitis

qui obsignarent, convenisse; atque illam audisse auspicum verba,
subisse flammeum, sacrificasse apud deos; discubitum inter 5
convivas, oscula complexus, noctem denique actam licentia coniugali.
sed nihil compositum miraculi causa, verum audita scriptaque
senioribus tradam.

1 **haud . . . visum iri:** 'I am not unaware that it will seem incredible that . . .' *visum iri* is the future passive infinitive of *video* (*videor* = 'seem'). The reported statement extends down to line 6.

1–2 *mortalium* (partitive genitive) goes with *ullis* (dative), *securitatis* (partitive genitive) goes with *tantum* (= 'so much complacent negligence') and *omnium* goes with *gnara* (ablative).

2 **nedum** = 'and still more incredible that . . .'

3 **consulem designatum** refers to Silius.

3–4 **adhibitis qui obsignarent:** 'with people having been brought in to sign [the wedding contract as witnesses]'. There is an ablative absolute and a relative clause expressing purpose here.

5 **subisse:** (from *subeo*) 'went under' = 'put on'.

5 **discubitum:** supply *esse ab illis* with this impersonal expression.

6 with *oscula [et] complexus* supply *fuisse*, and with *actam* understand *esse*.

7 *causa* is ablative and governs *miraculi*, while *verum* means 'but'.

8 **senioribus:** dative of agent.

6 *The freedmen (ex-slaves) who are chief secretaries in the emperor's household now see Silius as a threat to their power.*

Igitur domus principis inhorruerat, maximeque quos penes
potentia et, si res verterentur, formido fremere iuvenem nobilem
dignitate formae, vi mentis ac propinquo consulatu maiorem ad spem
adcingi; nec enim occultum quid post tale matrimonium superesset.
subibat sine dubio metus reputantes hebetem Claudium et uxori 5
devinctum multasque mortes iussu Messalinae patratas. rursus ipsa
facilitas imperatoris fiduciam dabat si atrocitate criminis
praevaluissent, posse opprimi damnatam ante quam ream.

1–2 **quos penes . . . formido:** '[those] amongst whom there was power and reason for alarm if the state were subverted' (i.e. the freedmen, who had much to fear if Silius took over as emperor). The *illi* which is to be supplied as the antecedent of *quos* is the subject of the historic infinitive *fremere*.

3 **dignitate . . . vi . . . propinquo consulatu:** ablatives of description, attaching to *iuvenem nobilem* (i.e. the consul designate Silius).

4 **adcingi** has a reflexive force ('was readying himself').

4 **occultum:** understand *esse*.

5 **reputantes** = *illos reputantes* (the freedmen when they bore in mind . . .).

7–8 **fiduciam** is followed by indirect statement: 'confidence that if . . . , she could be condemned [and] destroyed before a defendant [= before being put on trial]'. The pluperfect subjunctive represents a future perfect indicative in the original direct statement.

7 The freedmen wonder if instead of openly accusing Messalina they could get her to end the affair by threatening her with exposure. Two of them withdraw in fear of her. The remaining plotter (Narcissus) drops the idea of threats and moves directly to accusation of her.

Ac primo Callistus, iam mihi circa necem Gai narratus, et
Appianae caedis molitor Narcissus flagrantissimaque eo in tempore
gratia Pallas agitavere num Messalinam secretis minis depellerent
amore Silii, cuncta alia dissimulantes. dein metu ne ad perniciem
traherentur desistunt Pallas per ignaviam, Callistus prioris quoque 5
regiae peritus et potentiam cautis quam acribus consiliis tutius
haberi. perstitit Narcissus, solum id immutans ne quo sermone
praesciam criminis et accusatoris faceret. ipse ad occasiones intentus,
longa apud Ostiam Claudi mora, duas paelices, quarum is corpori
maxime insueverat, largitione ac promissis et uxore deiecta plus 10
potentiae ostentando perpulit delationem subire.

1 **Callistus:** this freedman had held a powerful position under Caligula (Gaius) and was involved in his assassination.

1 **mihi:** dative of agent.

2 **Appianae caedis:** Appius Junius Silanus had become Messalina's stepfather and had refused to yield to her sexual advances, so Narcissus and Messalina claimed that they had both dreamed of Appius attacking Claudius, and the gullible emperor ordered his execution.

2–3 **flagrantissima . . . gratia:** ablative of description.

3 **secretis** = made to her in private.

4 **amore:** the ablative = 'from'.

4 **cuncta alia:** i.e. the plot by Messalina to depose Claudius.

4 **metu ne:** metu is a causal ablative, and *ne* introduces a (positive) fear clause.

5–7 *peritus* ('having knowledge') here takes two constructions: firstly, a genitive (having knowledge of Caligula's court); secondly, an accusative and infinitive (having knowledge that when it comes to retaining power, cautious measures are better than vigorous ones).

7–8 **solum . . . faceret:** 'changing only this' [= making just this modification] – that he would not make [her] aware in advance of the charge and of [her] accuser by means of any (*quo*) conversation [with her]'. He decided not to threaten her in private in case that gave the game away.

9 **longa . . . mora:** ablative absolute.

9–10 **quarum is corpori maxime insueverat:** 'to whose bodies [*corpori* is singular for plural] he [Claudius] had become most accustomed', i.e. his two favourite mistresses.

10–11 **uxore . . . ostentando:** 'by showing more of power, with the wife having been deposed' = 'by holding out the prospect of more power [for them] when his wife was deposed'.

8 One of Claudius' mistresses informs him of Messalina's marriage to Silius. This is corroborated by another mistress, and Narcissus tells him that this means that unless Claudius acts quickly, Silius is the new ruler of Rome.

Exim Calpurnia (id enim paelici nomen), ubi datum secretum, genibus Claudi provoluta, nupsisse Messalinam Silio exclamat; simul Cleopatram (quae id opperiens adstabat) an comperisset interrogat; atque, illa adnuente, cieri Narcissum postulat. is veniam in praeteritum petens quod Vettios, Plautios dissimulavisset, nec nunc adulteria obiecturum ait, nedum domum, servitia et ceteros paratus fortunae reposceret. frueretur immo his, set redderet uxorem rumperetque tabulas nuptiales. 'An discidium,' inquit, 'tuum nosti? nam matrimonium Silii vidit populus et senatus et miles; ac ni propere agis, tenet urbem maritus.'

26 General view of the Roman forum.

2 **genibus**: 'at the knees' (knees were clasped in supplication).

3 **an comperisset**: 'whether she had discovered [that this was true]'.

4–5 **in praeteritum**: 'for the past' (i.e. for his former concealment of Messalina's adultery).

5 **Vettios, Plautios**: 'men like Vettius [and] Plautius' (men with whom Messalina had committed adultery).

5–6 nec nunc . . . ait: 'said that not even now would he [Narcissus] throw in her face her adulterous affairs' (he would not reproach Messalina with such things, because there was something more serious to be attended to – her marriage to Silius, which threatened Claudius' position as emperor). With *obiecturum* understand *esse se*.

6–7 nedum . . . reposceret: 'still less should he [Claudius] demand back . . .' The subjunctive here (like the others in 7) represents a command in the original direct speech.

7 fortunae: the rank of emperor.

7 frueretur . . . uxorem: Silius is the subject of the verbs, while *uxorem* denotes the wife of Claudius and of Silius.

8 an . . . nosti: Narcissus is claiming that Messalina has divorced Claudius. *nosti* is the second person singular of *novi*.

9 miles: singular for plural, referring to the troops in Rome (the praetorian guard).

10 maritus: Messalina's new husband.

9 *While the terrified emperor is urged to secure the support of the praetorian guard, Messalina and Silius are enjoying themselves with friends at a wild Bacchanalian revel.*

Tum potissimum quemque amicorum vocat, primumque rei
frumentariae praefectum Turranium, post Lusium Getam
praetorianis impositum percontatur. quis fatentibus, certatim ceteri
circumstrepunt: iret in castra, firmaret praetorias cohortes, securitati
ante quam vindictae consuleret. satis constat eo pavore offusum 5
Claudium ut identidem interrogaret an ipse imperii potens, an Silius
privatus esset.

At Messalina, non alias solutior luxu, adulto autumno simulacrum
vindemiae per domum celebrabat. urgeri prela, fluere lacus; et
feminae pellibus accinctae adsultabant ut sacrificantes vel 10
insanientes Bacchae; ipsa crine fluxo thyrsum quatiens, iuxtaque
Silius, hedera vinctus, gerere cothurnos, iacere caput, strepente
circum procaci choro. ferunt Vettium Valentem, lascivia in praealtam
arborem conisum, interrogantibus quid aspiceret respondisse
tempestatem ab Ostia atrocem. 15

1 potissimum quemque amicorum: i.e. all of Claudius' closest friends.

1 vocat: the subject of this verb (and of *percontatur* in 3) is Narcissus (he was the subject of *inquit* at the end of the last passage, and he is still controlling events here).

1–2 primumque . . . post: these are adverbs.

3 quis fatentibus: *quis* = *quibus* in this ablative absolute = 'when they admitted [that the story was true]'. Note how the danger is stressed at 3–5 by the alliteration and the brisk brevity and asyndeton.

3 certatim: i.e. trying to outshout each other.

4–5 iret . . . consuleret: the subjunctives represent commands in the original direct speech.

5 satis constat: 'it is well enough known that . . .'

5 eo is the adverb.

7 **privatus** is the noun (i.e. not emperor).

8 **non alias solutior luxu:** 'not at another time more unrestrained in extravagance' (= 'at her most extravagant and uninhibited').

8–9 **simulacrum vindemiae:** i.e. a mimic celebration of the vintage (grape-harvest).

9 **per domum:** i.e. in the grounds of Silius' house.

9 **lacus** refers to the vats of new wine.

10 **ut:** 'like'.

11 with *ipsa* (i.e. Messalina) understand *aderat* ('was present') or *adsultabat.*

12 the ivy garland and high boots were worn by the god of wine, Bacchus, who also tossed his head in ecstasy (*iacere* is from *iacio*).

13 **ferunt** introduces indirect speech.

13 **lascivia:** ablative of manner.

14 **interrogantibus:** 'to those asking' (indirect object of *respondisse*).

10 *The party suddenly breaks up as troops arrive and arrest people. Messalina decides to soften up Claudius by meeting him in person, sending their two children to him and getting the senior priestess of Rome to appeal to him to be merciful to her.*

Non rumor interea sed undique nuntii incedunt, qui gnara Claudio cuncta et venire promptum ultioni adferrent. igitur Messalina Lucullianos in hortos, Silius dissimulando metu ad munia fori digrediuntur. ceteris passim dilabentibus, adfuere centuriones, inditaque sunt vincla, ut quis reperiebatur in publico aut per (5) latebras.

Messalina tamen, quamquam res adversae consilium eximerent, ire obviam et aspici a marito (quod saepe subsidium habuerat) haud segniter intendit, misitque ut Britannicus et Octavia in complexum patris pergerent. et Vibidiam, virginum Vestalium vetustissimam, (10) oravit pontificis maximi auris adire, clementiam expetere. atque interim, tribus omnino comitantibus, spatium urbis pedibus emensa, vehiculo quo purgamenta hortorum excipiuntur Ostiensem viam intrat, nulla cuiusquam misericordia, quia flagitiorum deformitas praevalebat. (15)

1 **non . . . sed** = 'not only . . . but also'.

1–2 with *gnara* understand *esse*, and with *venire* understand *Claudium.*

2 **adferrent:** the subjunctive expresses purpose.

3 **dissimulando metu:** dative of purpose.

5 **inditaque:** from *indo.*

5–6 **ut . . . latebras:** i.e. as (wherever) individuals were found, in the open or in hiding.

7 **quamquam . . . eximerent** = the sudden catastrophe meant that she did not have time to and/or was too shaken to come up with a fully thought out plan.

8 quod...habuerat: 'something [a course of action] which she had often employed as a help [found helpful]'.

9 misitque ut: 'and she sent orders that...'

10 Vibidia was the chief Vestal Virgin (these were priestesses who watched over the sacred fire in the temple of the goddess Vesta and who could intervene on behalf of people accused of a crime).

11 pontificis...adire: *auris* is not genitive. The emperor was *pontifex maximus* (head of the priests called *pontifices*, and also the one who appointed and disciplined the Vestal Virgins).

12 spatium urbis = 'the [whole] breadth of the city' (from the Lucullan Gardens to the road to Ostia). The Gardens were on the Pincian Hill, while the Ostian Gate was on the far side of Rome beyond the Aventine Hill (about two miles away as the crow flies).

14 nulla cuiusquam misericordia: ablative absolute (i.e. with nobody pitying her). *cuiusquam* is genitive of *quisquam*.

15 praevalebat: i.e. had more weight in people's minds.

11 *Narcissus offers to take over command of the praetorian guard for the day as the only way of saving the emperor, and secures himself a place in Claudius' carriage with his travelling companions.*

Trepidabatur nihilo minus a Claudio: quippe Getae praetorii
praefecto haud satis fidebant. ergo Narcissus, adsumptis quibus idem
metus, non aliam spem incolumitatis Claudi adfirmat quam si ius
militum uno illo die in aliquem libertorum transferret, seque offert
susceptūrum. ac ne, dum in urbem revehitur, ad paenitentiam a L. 5
Vitellio et Largo Caecina mutaretur, in eodem gestamine sedem
poscit adsumiturque.

1 trepidabatur...Claudio: 'it was feared by no amount less on the side of Claudius', i.e. just as much apprehension was felt by Claudius and his advisers (the Latin identifies the manipulated emperor with his advisers).

2–3 adsumptis...metus = *illis, quibus idem metus erat, adsumptis.*

3 non aliam...quam si: '[that there would be] no other hope of... than if' = 'that the only hope of... was for him to'. Supply *futuram* esse with *spem.*

4 transferret: the imperfect subjunctive represents a future indicative in the original direct statement.

5 suscepturum = *suscepturum esse.*

5 L. is an abbreviation for the Roman name Lucius.

12 *Claudius' companions offer only non-committal responses to his contradictory remarks about Messalina, and Narcissus manages to head off Messalina and her children and the Vestal Virgin Vibidia.*

Crebra post haec fama fuit inter diversas principis voces, cum
modo incusaret flagitia uxoris, aliquando ad memoriam coniugii et
infantiam liberorum revolveretur, non aliud prolocutum Vitellium

quam 'o facinus! o scelus!' instabat quidem Narcissus aperire ambages, sed non pervicit quin suspensa responderet exemploque eius Largus Caecina uteretur. 5

Et iam erat in aspectu Messalina clamitabatque audiret Octaviae et Britannici matrem, cum obstrepere accusator, Silium et nuptias referens; simul codicillos libidinum indices tradidit, quis visus Claudi averteret. nec multo post urbem ingredienti offerebantur 10 communes liberi, nisi Narcissus amoveri eos iussisset. Vibidiam depellere nequivit quin multa cum invidia flagitaret ne indefensa coniunx exitio daretur. igitur auditurum principem et fore diluendi criminis facultatem respondit; iret interim virgo et sacra capesseret.

2 **modo . . . aliquando**: 'at one moment . . . at another moment'.

3 **prolocutum** = *prolocutum* esse in an accusative and infinitive construction after *fama*.

5 **non pervicit quin . . .**: 'he did not prevail so that he didn't . . .' = 'he did not persuade him [Vitellius] not to . . . and Largus Caecina not to . . .' The conjunction *quin* introduces a clause with a negative force after a main clause that is negative (or virtually negative).

7 **clamitabatque audiret**: 'and kept on shouting out that he [Claudius] should listen to . . .' In indirect commands with *clamito* we find the subjunctive on its own (as here) and *ut* plus the subjunctive.

8 **obstrepere accusator**: *obstrepere* is historic infinitive, and the *accusator* is Narcissus.

9 **quis visus**: *quis* = *quibus*, and *visus* (the noun) is plural for singular.

10 **averteret**: the subjunctive expresses purpose.

10 **post**: is the adverb.

10 *ingredienti* refers to Claudius.

10 **offerebantur**: the imperfect tense denotes an action begun but not completed = 'the children began to be brought forward (and would have actually been brought forward), if Narcissus had not . . .'

12 **depellere . . . quin**: 'stop . . . from'.

13 **exitio daretur**: i.e. be executed.

13 **fore** = *futuram esse* ('there would be').

14 **iret . . . capesseret**: the subjunctives represent third person commands in indirect speech.

13 *Now back in Rome, Narcissus shows Claudius Silius' house with the emperor's possessions in it and gets Claudius to address the praetorian guard, and then the executions of the conspirators begin,*

Mirum inter haec silentium Claudi, Vitellius ignaro propior: omnia liberto oboediebant. patefieri domum adulteri atque illuc deduci imperatorem iubet. ac demonstrat quidquid avitum in pretium probri cessisse. incensumque et ad minas erumpentem castris infert, parata contione militum. apud quos, praemonente Narcisso, pauca 5 verba fecit: nam, etsi iustum, dolorem pudor impediebat. continuus dehinc cohortium clamor, nomina reorum et poenas flagitantium; admotusque Silius tribunali non defensionem, non moras temptavit,

27 Interior of the Senate House (Curia Julia) in the Roman forum, Rome. Although built and dedicated by Julius Caesar in 46 BC, the current structure dates from the reign of Diocletian (AD 284–305).

precatus ut mors accelераretur. eadem constantia et inlustres equites Romani. et Titium Proculum (custodem a Silio Messalinae datum et indicium offerentem), Vettium Valentem confessum, et Pompeium Urbicum ac Saufeium Trogum ex consciis tradi ad supplicium iubet. Decrius quoque Calpurnianus vigilum praefectus, Sulpicius Rufus ludi procurator, Iuncus Vergilianus senator eadem poena adfecti. 10

1 **Vitellius ignaro propior:** 'Vitellius [was] closer to an ignorant person', i.e. Vitellius seemed not to know what was going on.

3 **quidquid avitum:** i.e. all of Claudius' ancestral possessions.

3–4 **in pretium probri cessisse:** 'had gone [there] with a view to payment/reward for [his] offence', i.e. had been sent there by Messalina to pay/reward Silius for his adulterous affair with her.

6 **dolorem pudor impediebat:** i.e. he was so ashamed that he could hardly express his indignation.

7 **flagitantium:** agrees with *cohortium.*

9 **eadem constantia:** understand *fuerunt* with this ablative of description.

10 **custodem:** a guardian appointed to ensure the fidelity of a wife (this was a common enough practice in Rome).

12 **iubet:** the subject is Claudius.

13 **vigilum praefectus:** a man of equestrian rank was in charge of the *vigiles* (a combined fire brigade and police force).

13–14 **ludi procurator:** men of equestrian rank superintended the training of gladiators who fought at games put on by the emperor.

14 *Two more executions are ordered (one after some hesitation), and finally two men are pardoned.*

Solus Mnester cunctationem attulit, dilaniata veste clamitans
aspiceret verberum notas, reminisceretur vocis qua se obnoxium
iussis Messalinae dedisset: aliis largitione aut spei magnitudine, sibi
ex necessitate culpam; nec cuiquam ante pereundum fuisse, si Silius
rerum poteretur. commotum his et pronum ad misericordiam 5
Claudium perpulere liberti ne, tot inlustribus viris interfectis,
histrioni consuleretur. ne Trauli quidem Montani (equitis Romani)
defensio recepta est. is (modesta iuventa, sed corpore insigni) accitus
ultro noctemque intra unam a Messalina proturbatus erat. Suillio
Caesonino et Plautio Laterano mors remittitur, huic ob patrui 10
egregium meritum; Caesoninus vitiis protectus est, tamquam in illo
foedissimo coetu passus muliebria.

1 Mnester was a pantomime actor with whom Messalina became infatuated. When he resisted her advances, she got Claudius to order Mnester to obey her every command, pretending that she wanted his help for some other purpose. So Mnester slept with her when she told him to, thinking that Claudius wanted this.

1–2 **clamitans . . . notas:** 'shouting repeatedly that he [Claudius] should look at the marks of the whips/floggings' (he had been flogged for resisting Messalina).

2–3 **se . . . dedisset:** *se* refers to Mnester, and Claudius is the subject of the verb.

3–4 **aliis . . . culpam:** supply *fuisse*, i.e. he said that others had done wrong because of . . . but he had done wrong out of necessity. The two ablatives in 3 are causal. The antithesis is pointed.

4 **nec cuiquam . . . fuisse:** i.e. he said that he would have been the first who had to die. The impersonal gerundive *pereundum* expresses the idea of future necessity (and *cuiquam* is dative of agent with it), while *poteretur* in 5 represents a future indicative in the original direct speech.

6–7 **ne . . . histrioni consuleretur:** i.e. that an actor should not be spared. *consuleretur* (the verb takes the dative) is an impersonal expression.

8 modesta...insigni: ablatives of description.

9 *ultro* means that the invitation was unsought.

10 **huic** refers to Plautius Lateranus, whose uncle had successfully invaded Britain for Claudius.

12 **passus muliebria**: 'he submitted to the female role' (i.e. he was the passive partner in homosexual intercourse). *passus* is from *patior.*

15 *While Messalina writes a letter pleading for her life, Claudius dines and begins to soften towards her, so Narcissus sends some soldiers to kill her, pretending that this is on Claudius' orders.*

Interim Messalina Lucullianis in hortis prolatare vitam, componere preces, nonnulla spe et aliquando ira (tantum inter extrema superbiae gerebat). ac ni caedem eius Narcissus properavisset, verterat pernicies in accusatorem. nam Claudius domum regressus et tempestivis epulis delenitus, ubi vino (5) incaluit, iri iubet nuntiarique miserae dicendam ad causam postero die adesset. quod ubi auditum et languescere ira, redire amor, prorumpit Narcissus denuntiatque centurionibus et tribuno, qui aderat, exsequi caedem: ita imperatorem iubere.

Custos et exactor e libertis Euodus datur. Isque raptim in hortos (10) praegressus repperit fusam humi, adsidente matre Lepida, quae florenti filiae haud concors supremis eius necessitatibus ad miserationem evicta erat suadebatque ne percussorem opperiretur: transisse vitam neque aliud quam morti decus quaerendum. sed animo per libidines corrupto nihil honestum inerat. lacrimaeque et (15) questus inriti ducebantur, cum impetu venientium pulsae fores adstititque tribunus per silentium, at libertus increpans multis et servilibus probris.

2 **spe...ira**: ablatives of manner (= 'with').

2 **tantum**: goes with the partitive genitive *superbiae* in 3.

4 **verterat**: 'would have rebounded' (the pluperfect indicative instead of subjunctive vividly represents what would have happened as actually having happened, to stress how close the occurrence was).

6–7 **iri...nuntiarique**: impersonal expression (i.e. he ordered someone to go and instruct the poor woman to appear...).

7 **languescere...redire**: the *ubi* clause has first a perfect indicative and now historic infinitives.

9 **ita imperatorem iubere**: reported statement (of what Narcissus said to the soldiers).

10 **custos et exactor**: the freedman was to prevent Messalina's escape and make sure that Narcissus' order was carried out.

12 **florenti filiae haud concors**: 'not in agreement with her flourishing daughter' = 'although she had been estranged from her daughter when she was at the height of her power'.

14 **neque aliud . . . quaerendum:** i.e. she said that all she [Messalina] should look for was a dignified death.

17 **per silentium:** 'with silence' = 'in silence'.

16 Messalina is executed. When Claudius is told of her death, he carries on with his dinner, and he does not even show any reaction on subsequent days either.

Tum primum fortunam suam introspexit ferrumque accepit, quod
frustra iugulo aut pectori per trepidationem admovens ictu tribuni
transigitur. corpus matri concessum. nuntiatumque Claudio epulanti
perisse Messalinam, non distincto sua an aliena manu. nec ille
quaesivit, poposcitque poculum et solita convivio celebravit. ne 5
secutis quidem diebus odii gaudii, irae tristitiae, ullius denique
humani adfectus signa dedit, non cum laetantis accusatores aspiceret,
non cum filios maerentis. iuvitque oblivionem eius senatus censendo
nomen et effigies privatis ac publicis locis demovendas. decreta
Narcisso quaestoria insignia. 10

1 **quod:** from *qui.*

2 **iugulo aut pectori** = 'now to her throat and now to her breast'.

2–3 note the curt brevity and harsh alliteration in *ictu tribuni transigitur* and *corpus matri concessum.*

3 **nuntiatumque:** impersonal expression.

4 **non distincto . . . manu:** ablative absolute plus indirect double question ('with it not having been specified whether [she died] by her own hand or another's').

5 **solita convivio celebravit:** i.e. he did what one normally does at a banquet (*solita* is neuter accusative plural and means 'things customary').

8 **filios:** 'his children' (his son and daughter).

9 **nomen et effigies . . . demovendas:** Messalina's name was to be deleted from inscriptions; statues of her were to be removed etc.

10 **quaestoria insignia:** although only a freedman, Narcissus was rewarded with an honorary quaestorship (= the status of an administrative official and member of the senate).

Despite his mother's death, Britannicus stood next in line. But his position was undermined and eventually overturned by Claudius' formidable fourth wife, his niece Agrippina the Younger (she was the sister of Caligula, against whom she had conspired in AD *39). Following her marriage to Claudius in* AD *49, she worked tirelessly to have her adolescent son Nero advanced over Britannicus and adopted by Claudius, as he was in* AD *50. By the time Nero had reached his sixteenth year, he and (more so) his mother were already in control. Claudius, if anything, was a hindrance to their further plans.*

17 When Claudius remarks that he is fated first to endure his wives' outrages and then to punish them, Agrippina becomes frightened and decides to act quickly – to kill him and replace him with her son Nero. But first she disposes of Lepida (mother of Messalina and aunt of Nero, and a rival for control of him).

Agere et celerare statuit, perdita prius Lepida, quia Lepida parem
sibi claritudinem credebat. nec forma, aetas, opes multum distabant;
et utraque impudica, infamis, violenta. enimvero certamen
acerrimum, amita potius an mater apud Neronem praevaleret: nam
Lepida blandimentis ac largitionibus iuvenilem animum 5
devinciebat, truci contra ac minaci Agrippina, quae filio dare
imperium, tolerare imperitantem nequibat. ceterum obiecta sunt
quod coniugem principis devotionibus petivisset quodque parum
coercitis per Calabriam servorum agminibus pacem Italiae turbaret.
ob haec mors indicta, multum adversante Narcisso, qui (Agrippinam 10
magis magisque suspectans) prompsisse ferebatur certam sibi
perniciem, seu Britannicus rerum seu Nero poteretur; Britannico
successore nullum principi metum, at novercae insidiis domum
omnem convelli; ne impudicitiam quidem abesse, Pallante adultero,
ne quis ambigat decus, pudorem, corpus regno viliora habere. 15

1–2 **quia... credebat**: supply *esse* (Lepida thought that her family connections made her as distinguished as Agrippina).

3–4 **certamen acerrimum**: ('the fiercest/most serious point of contention [was]') introduces an indirect double question.

6 **truci... Agrippina**: ablative absolute.

6 **dare**: understand *quibat* ('was able') from *nequibat* in 7.

7–9 the actual charges against Lepida were that she had tried to kill Agrippina by magic and was disturbing the peace by not controlling the large gangs of armed herdsmen on her estates in south Italy. The two *quod* clauses are the subjects of *obiecta sunt.*

11 **prompsisse ferebatur**: 'was said to have...' Narcissus had engineered the death of Britannicus' mother (Messalina) and was an opponent of Nero's mother, so things looked bad for him whoever succeeded.

12–13 **Britannico successore**: ablative absolute (like *Pallante adultero* in 14).

13 **nullum principi metum**: i.e the emperor had nothing to fear. Supply *esse* in the indirect statement here (which continues in the following lines).

13 **novercae**: i.e. Agrippina (stepmother of Britannicus).

13 **domum**: i.e. the imperial household.

15 **ne quis... habere**: 'so that nobody could doubt that she regarded her... as of less importance than political control'.

18 When Narcissus leaves Rome for health reasons, Agrippina acts: a poisoned mushroom is served up to Claudius by his food-taster.

Tum Agrippina, sceleris olim certa et oblatae occasionis propera nec ministrorum egens, de genere veneni consultavit, ne repentino et praecipiti facinus proderetur. exquisitum aliquid placebat, quod turbaret mentem et mortem differret. deligitur artifex talium Locusta. eius mulieris ingenio paratum virus, cuius minister e spadonibus fuit Halotus, inferre epulas et explorare gustu solitus. 5

Adeoque cuncta mox pernotuere ut temporum illorum scriptores prodiderint infusum delectabili boleto venenum, nec vim medicaminis statim intellectam, socordiane an vinolentia; simul soluta alvus subvenisse videbatur. igitur exterrita Agrippina 10 provisam iam sibi Xenophontis medici conscientiam adhibet. ille, tamquam nisus evomentis adiuvaret, pinnam rapido veneno inlitam faucibus eius demisisse creditur.

1 **sceleris**: i.e. the crime of killing Claudius.

2 **ne**: fear is implied in *consultavit.*

2–3 **repentino et praecipiti**: supply *veneno.*

4 **turbaret mentem**: so that Claudius would not realize that he was being poisoned. Why subjunctive?

5 **cuius minister**: i.e. the person who administered the poison.

8–9 **infusum . . . intellectam**: supply *esse* with both. With the second infinitive understand *a consciis* ('by the accomplices').

9 **socordiane an vinolentia**: 'whether because of dullness or drunkenness' (i.e. either because of his normal cretinous torpor or because he was befuddled with drink, the conspirators could not see any ill effects on Claudius' faculties, which the poison was supposed to upset at once). *socordia* could refer to dullness on the part of the accomplices, but that is less pointed.

10 **soluta alvus**: i.e. a bowel movement (which could get rid of the poisoned mushroom).

11 **provisam . . . adhibet**: Agrippina had already secured Claudius' doctor as an accomplice, and now she got him to help.

12 **nisus evomentis**: i.e. Claudius' struggles to vomit (presumably, as in passage 2, he is vomiting to relieve his stomach of all the food and drink he has imbibed). *evomentis* is genitive singular.

19 Claudius' children are detained, and Claudius is reported as being ill but improving until Nero emerges from the palace to be hailed as the new emperor by the praetorian guard.

Agrippina, velut dolore victa et solacia conquirens, tenere amplexu Britannicum, veram paterni oris effigiem appellare ac variis artibus demorari, ne cubiculo egrederetur. Antoniam quoque et Octaviam (sorores eius) attinuit, et cunctos aditus custodiis clauserat,

crebroque vulgabat ire in melius valetudinem principis. tunc medio 5
diei tertium ante Idus Octobris, foribus palatii repente diductis,
comitante Burro Nero egreditur ad cohortem quae excubiis adest. ibi,
monente praefecto, faustis vocibus exceptus inditur lecticae.
inlatusque castris Nero, promisso donativo ad exemplum paternae
largitionis, imperator consalutatur. sententiam militum secuta 10
patrum consulta, nec dubitatum est apud provincias. caelestesque
honores Claudio decernuntur.

2 **veram paterni oris effigiem**: i.e. (Agrippina called him) the very image of his father.

3 **Antoniam**: Britannicus and Octavia were Claudius' children by Messalina, whereas Antonia was his daughter by an earlier marriage.

4 **aditus** refers to approaches to the palace.

6 **tertium . . . Octobris**: 'on the thirteenth of October'.

7 **Burro**: commander of the praetorian guard (and an accomplice in the plot).

7 **excubiis**: dative of purpose.

8 **faustis vocibus exceptus**: i.e. Nero was cheered by the soldiers.

9 **castris**: the camp of the praetorian guard.

9–10 **promisso . . . largitionis**: i.e. Nero promised to match Claudius' generous gift to the troops of 15,000 sesterces each on his accession. *ad* means 'in accordance with'.

10 **largitionis, imperator**: the juxtaposition is pointed.

11 **patrum consulta** = 'senatorial decrees'.

12 **nec dubitatum est** means that there was no hesitation in accepting Nero as emperor.

11–12 **caelestesque honores**: Claudius was declared to have become a god on his death, and a temple to him was begun in Rome.

20 *Seneca describes to his Roman readers how Claudius recently died and turned up in heaven (as a new god) but was so inarticulate and deformed that nobody could work out who or what he was.*

Ultima vox eius haec inter homines audita est, cum maiorem
sonitum emisisset illa parte qua facilius loquebatur: 'vae me, puto,
concacavi me.' quod an fecerit, nescio; omnia certe concacavit.

Quae in terris postea sint acta, supervacuum est referre. scitis
enim optime: nemo felicitatis suae obliviscitur. in caelo quae acta 5
sint, audite. nuntiatur Iovi venisse quendam bonae staturae, bene
canum; nescioquid illum minari (assidue enim caput movere), pedem
dextrum trahere; quaesisse se cuius nationis esset; respondisse
nescioquid perturbato sono et voce confusa; non intellegere se
linguam eius: nec Graecum esse nec Romanum nec ullius gentis 10
notae. tum Iuppiter Herculem (qui totum orbem terrarum
pererraverat et nosse videbatur omnes nationes) iubet ire et

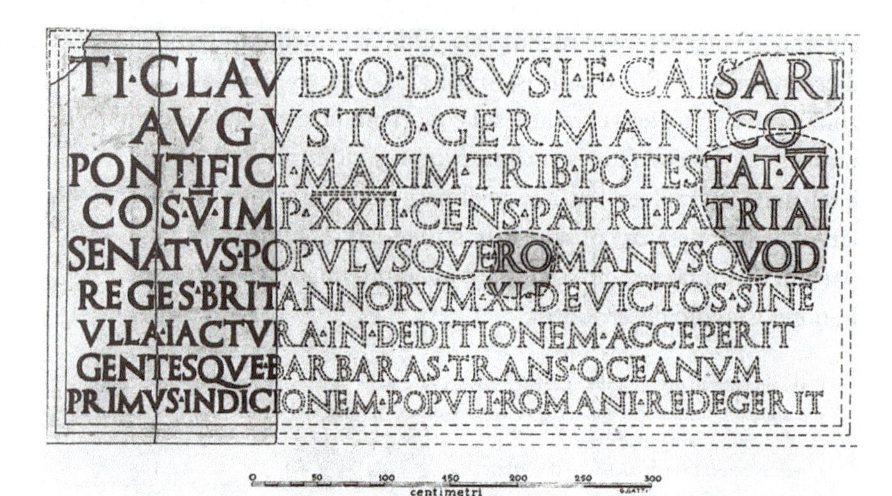

28 Reconstruction of the inscription from Arch of Claudius at Rome commemorating his conquest of Britain. Translated, it reads as follows: 'The Senate and People of Rome [dedicate this monument] to Tiberius Claudius, son of Drusus, Caesar Augustus Germanicus, *pontifex maximus*, holding the power of a tribune for the eleventh time, consul for the fifth time, *imperator* for the twenty-second time, censor, father of his country, because he conquered without any loss of life and accepted the surrender of eleven kings of the Britons and because he was the first to bring the barbarian races across the Ocean under the sway of the Roman People.'

explorare quorum hominum esset. tum Hercules primo aspectu sane perturbatus est, ut qui non omnia monstra timuerit. ut vidit novi generis faciem, insolitum incessum, vocem nullius terrestris (15) animalis, putavit sibi tertium decimum laborem venisse. diligentius intuenti visus est quasi homo.

1 **maiorem:** 'rather loud' or 'louder' [than his words].

2 **illa parte:** i.e. his anus.

3 *quod* ('which thing' = 'that') is the object of *fecerit* inside an indirect question. The verb on which the indirect question depends (*nescio*) comes after it, as is also the case in lines 4 and 5–6.

3 **omnia certe concacavit:** 'he certainly made a mess of all things' = 'it is certain that he always did make a mess of things'.

6 **nuntiatur:** impersonal expression, introducing indirect statement that extends down to 11. The person (the *se* of 8 and 9) making the report to Jupiter will be some sort of doorkeeper at the entrance to heaven.

6 **quendam bonae staturae:** genitive of quality/description. Claudius was fairly tall.

7 **assidue . . . movere:** Claudius' involuntary twitch is taken as a threatening movement of the head.

10 **Graecum** does not qualify (feminine) *linguam.*

11 **Herculem:** the great hero who travelled throughout the world, especially while performing the twelve arduous tasks laid on him known as the Labours.

12 **nosse videbatur:** 'was deemed to know'. *nosse* is the infinitive of *novi.*

13 **quorum hominum esset** = 'to what race of humans he belonged'.

14 **ut qui... timuerit**: 'even though he had not been afraid of...' (he had encountered every monster in the world and had not been frightened by any of them).

14 **ut**: 'when'.

16 **tertium decimum**: 'thirteenth'.

16–17 **diligentius... homo**: i.e. when Hercules looked more closely at him, Claudius seemed to be something similar to a human being.

CLAUDIUS APPRECIATION

Passage 1 Suetonius Claudius *2, 3, 8.*

This passage and the next give a typical ancient picture of Claudius. According to the Classical sources he was a malformed cretin, completely under the control of his wives and freedmen advisors, and a greedy drunkard, addicted to gambling and directly or indirectly responsible for countless executions during his Principate – in short, a ludicrous disaster of an emperor. The modern popular image of Claudius has been deeply coloured by Robert Graves' novels *I, Claudius* and *Claudius the God*. There, the emperor is portrayed as physically handicapped but intellectually sound, a basically decent human being who negotiates the troubled waters of imperial politics with skill but is forced by circumstances into some horrible acts, such as the execution of his beloved but devious wife Messalina. The BBC serialization of the novels (called *I, Claudius*) is available on video, and the episodes entitled *Fool's Luck* and *A God in Colchester* provide an interesting contrast with Tacitus' version of Messalina's downfall (excerpted in passages 3–16 below).

Passage 2 Suetonius Claudius *30, 32–3, 37.*

A third view of Claudius sees him as not the moron here depicted but (instead of Graves' sympathetic figure) an astute and calculating politician. Levick 1990 argues that Claudius was frustrated in early life when relatives excluded him from politics because of his embarrassing physical handicaps, became a manipulative usurper grasping for power (possibly involved in the death of Caligula), and as emperor was concerned about the wellbeing of Rome and also his own survival. In passages 3–16 (on the downfall of Messalina), it is clear that the portrayal of Claudius is coloured to make him fit the stereotypical picture of a passive, contemptible idiot. What evidence can you find in those passages that might suggest a more active and decisive role in events for Claudius?

Passage 3 Tacitus Annals *11.12.*

On the fall of Messalina, see Introduction section 8. In the very first line, *furori* sets the keynote (there is an insanity to the whole affair with Silius as Tacitus presents it), and at 6ff. that is quickly reinforced by Messalina's unbalanced conduct. There is also an abnormal inversion of roles: in ancient love affairs, the male was the one who burned with passion, pursued the beautiful beloved, dealt with rivals, possessed the object of his desires and bestowed gifts, but here (reflecting her personality and position) Messalina does all that. So too, she is the one acting (subject of the verbs) at the start; several strong words are applied to her there, and *poteretur* in 4 blends various pointed senses ('seize', 'win sexually', 'obtain control over', and 'exercise control over'). If Messalina is motivated by frenzied lust, there is no real love on the part of Silius either, who seems calculating. *adulter* (in 3 and 9, repeated for stress) and *flagitii* (4) bring out that this is a sordid liaison (no dashing romance).

Passage 4 Tacitus Annals *11.25–6.*

There is irony at 1f., with Claudius himself burning (*ardesceret*) like Messalina (*exarserat* in 3.2), and the punisher of an illicit marriage moving on to an illicit marriage himself. At 2ff., there is a dramatic progression, from an adulterous affair to thoughts of a coup, as Silius starts to assert himself. His arguments at 4ff. are not too specific (presumably he doesn't quite trust Messalina), but they are emphatic (the brevity, the alliteration in 9) and calculating (he tries to scare her into agreement by alluding to danger in 5, 6 and 9, and at the same time he reassures her). With a blackly comic touch, this carefully thought out speech merely arouses suspicion and Messalina seizes on the part about marriage, and does so not out of love (and love had not figured in his arguments earlier) but out of decadent perversity. She is still firmly in control (subject of the main verbs at 12ff.), as the passage ends with the lunacy of a formal wedding (and the quick progression to that implies a reckless impulsiveness).

Passage 5 Tacitus Annals *11.27.*

The fact that Tacitus takes a whole chapter to assure us that Messalina and Silius did actually wed intimates how bizarre and deranged an act that was, and this notion is reinforced by structure and expression. There is ring composition, with the incredible nature of events brought out at the start and end for stress. The chapter is made up of just two sentences. The first has cumulative impact, as startling point after point is added, taking us all the way through the marriage process down to the wedding night. This long sentence listing all the unbelievable details is followed by a short one crisply confirming them (and the contrast in length heightens its impact).

Passage 6 Tacitus Annals *11.28.*

The focus suddenly shifts to rather sinister unnamed forces, and palace intrigue begins. What was (we were told in Passage 4) largely a whimsical bid for notoriety by Messalina now develops into something very serious (literally, a life-and-death struggle), as the freedmen put two and two together. There is a grim humour in Messalina crazily failing to consider the natural inferences likely to be drawn by the courtiers. Also grim, but not so humorous for Roman readers (among whom class and ethnic prejudice was common), is this picture of the freedmen concerned to protect Claudius' position, not due to any love for their emperor or Rome but purely through self-interest, and of a head of the Roman empire who is stupid, completely unaware of what is going on around him and manipulated by non-Roman ex-slaves and his unbalanced whore of a wife.

Passage 7 Tacitus Annals *11.29.*

Events progress here, as one main opponent emerges from the freedmen, decides on and initiates his plan. It is a crafty plan too: by not threatening Messalina and by using others as informers, Narcissus conceals his own role in case of adverse reaction by Claudius or retaliation by his wife, and he employs not just one but two accusers (for reinforcement), selecting women likely to have inspired some affection and trust. The stress on the corrupt nature of the freedmen amounts to harsh criticism of Claudius (for surrounding himself with such criminals and letting them dominate him) and represents the struggle against Messalina not as good versus evil but as cunning evil against reckless evil. Ironically, Claudius is himself an adulterer and will learn of his wife's adultery from his own partners in adultery.

Passage 8 Tacitus Annals *11.30.*

In line with the assessment at 6.5ff. of Claudius as able to be swayed by a really serious charge, Narcissus undermines Messalina's position and gets the gravity of the situation across by means of a flurry of rapidly successive blows. First, Calpurnia intimately touches Claudius' knees, and goes on to make not the expected entreaty but a brief, bald and loud announcement of the wedding. That claim is corroborated at once by the other mistress, and then by Narcissus. He begins with a disarming appeal for forgiveness, then reveals that there have been other lovers (naming some), and that Silius has actually been given various imperial possessions. Intriguingly, he condones that, since there is something even worse – Claudius has been divorced and virtually deposed! In 8ff. there is a vivid quote of his conclusion, aimed at alarming and enraging Claudius (how?).

Passage 9 Tacitus Annals *11.31.*

At 1ff., for further reinforcement, Narcissus summons men who would be credible (and who had much to lose if Claudius was deposed), and they stress the danger even more strongly, leaving Claudius panicked and befuddled (i.e. malleable). In 8, with an abrupt change of scene and mood, we are taken from seriousness and efficiency to frivolity and play-acting, from the scheming Narcissus and the terrified Claudius to the relaxed and unsuspecting Messalina enjoying herself with the fatuous Silius. There is dark humour in this rather eccentric and very unsuitable revelling. There is also much that is apt – the bizarre nature of the proceedings, Messalina acting like a raving Bacchante, and Silius posing as Bacchus (which suggests his ambition, shows him simply playing at being powerful and ominously represents the kind of *hybris* (insolence towards the gods) which was supposed to attract severe punishment). Also ominous is the terrible storm at the close (Claudius and Narcissus are at Ostia).

Passage 10 Tacitus Annals *11.32.*

The storm soon breaks, with another effective switch (back to grim efficiency, scheming and terror). At 1ff. Narcissus is a sinister force in the background, moving swiftly and possessing excellent intelligence. At 7ff., his adversary also acts quickly, coming up with three different ways for her to manipulate Claudius herself, on a personal and an official level. She is determined and desperate enough to travel on foot and on a refuse-cart to get to Claudius before he is totally hardened against her and access to him is denied. Her means of transport is grotesque but wryly appropriate (she is rubbish from the Lucullan Gardens). In case we pity her (a very different figure now from the reveller of Passage 9), 14 reminds us of her crimes.

Passage 11 Tacitus Annals *11.33.*

Outrageously, a Greek ex-slave takes on the command of the praetorian guard and *demands* a seat in Claudius' carriage. Ironically, Claudius (who still hardly figures in the narrative) is superseded by one person to prevent him being superseded by another. The focus now shifts back to Narcissus, who is shrewdly attentive to the all-important troops and the unstable emperor's state of mind, and who (despite 9.1ff.) trusts nobody. So too *trepidabatur* (1) and *metus* (3) are reminders that this is a very dangerous game. There is drama in that, and in the way in which the two protagonists (each with three companions on a conveyance) are now converging with diametrically opposed purposes (while

Messalina's present inferiority to Narcissus is reflected in her mode of transport and anonymous associates).

Passage 12 Tacitus Annals *11.34.*

1ff. present the emperor as a maundering fool (again) and two free-born, high-ranking administrators in his court as evasive and inert (especially in contrast to the ex-slave). With sardonic neatness, the deliberately vague '*o facinus! o scelus!*' in fact sums up acutely the whole proceedings and the part played in them by everybody – by Messalina, Narcissus, Claudius and Vitellius. At 7ff., when the protagonists meet, Narcissus easily wins the encounter, blocking Messalina's personal appeal aurally and visually (her use of the two children is countered by the twofold *Silium et nuptias*, while the documentary evidence of her immorality is to distract and alienate). Next, the brevity at 11f. underlines the ease with which Claudius' own children are kept from him. Vibidia (whose forceful demand represents the judgement of religion and morality) causes more of a problem, but she too is disposed of, with a lie (13f.), and also with insolence (*virgo* and *sacra capesseret* imply that she knows nothing about marriage and adultery, and should mind her own business).

Passage 13 Tacitus Annals *11.35.*

There is a smooth progression to the executions: first, Claudius is taken to the scene of the crime and shown his possessions there (*quidquid avitum* is exaggerated; *pretium probri* is inflammatory); then, duly incensed, he is moved on to the camp for a stage-managed meeting; finally, amid troops baying for punishment, the malefactors are produced (the chief culprit first). Silius, who recently played god, is reduced to praying and is seen to be all too mortal. But he does show dignity and bravery (unlike others, such as Claudius and later Messalina). The killing of Silius and the distinguished Romans at 9ff. (apparently without the formal trial before the Senate that might have been expected) is engineered by a freedman out to protect his own skin. As name after name rings out, extensive corruption in the upper echelons of Roman society is intimated, and so is extensive dissatisfaction with Claudius as emperor. Amid the grim roll-call in 10, there is more lunacy, in Silius imagining that anyone could ensure Messalina's fidelity (in her bigamous marriage to him).

Passage 14 Tacitus Annals *11.36.*

Here, there are still more executions, and one is led to question further the justice of these proceedings. Mnester (who conjures up, aptly, Claudius' absurd gullibility) makes a strong case, which does actually sway Claudius, until he is taken in hand by the freedmen again – and their grounds for condemnation are illogical and involve laughable snobbery on the part of ex-slaves. Next, although adultery with the empress counted as treason, it seems rather hard to lump in the presumed lover Montanus with those who are being presented as having plotted a coup, especially in view of 9. Finally, two of the accused are let off, but the mercy is soured (how exactly?). As it is presented here, the punishment seems almost as bad as the crime.

Passage 15 Tacitus Annals *11.37.*

At last we are taken back to Messalina (having been left to wonder about her for quite a while), and after the previous flurry of executions, this death scene is prolonged (why?). Once more, Tacitus cuts with effective contrasts – firstly to the gardens of Lucullus (where Messalina grimly tries to save her life and feels anger), then to the palace (where Claudius enjoys a sumptuous banquet, and his anger is abating, and where two powerful freedmen plot Messalina's death), and finally back to the gardens (where two powerless women contemplate Messalina's death, one urging it; one putting it off). The passage has a cliff-hanging end, with the sinister silent tribune and the intimidating freedman in a dominant position. Insanity and grotesquerie are evident again: Messalina in this situation is actually angry, and Claudius is even on the point of letting her off (comically, Narcissus' hard work is nearly wasted because the moronic emperor becomes drunk), and Narcissus in preserving Claudius' position totally usurps that position himself. Tacitus also tries to arouse mixed feelings with his presentation of the death of Messalina. It is a far from noble end, but there is some pathos. In this connection, analyse the ways in which we are we prejudiced against Messalina in this passage, and the impact of Lepida at 11ff. and the freedman at 17f.

Passage 16 Tacitus Annals *11.38.*

This is a dispiriting close to the whole sorry episode. Nobody comes out of it well. Messalina, decadent to the end, is put to death ingloriously. There is a callousness to the suddenness of that and the curtness with which her corpse is passed on to her mother. While she is being murdered, the emperor is obliviously banqueting. When Narcissus unscrupulously fudges the news of her death, Claudius does not react in a normal way, not even when he sobers up and sees his children mourning (a particularly repugnant touch). He comes across as a befuddled and brutish half-wit, unfeeling and interested only in food and drink. Finally, the spineless Senate condones the murder, and the despicable Narcissus is actually rewarded.

Passage 17 Tacitus Annals *12.64–5.*

On Claudius' marriage to Agrippina and his death, see the Introduction section 8. Tacitus depicts the freedmen as getting rid of one bad wife, only to replace her with an even worse wife, one who is more calculating and focused, and who actually succeeds in deposing Claudius. Tacitus' vivid sketch of Agrippina employs direct characterization in 2, 3 and 6 and indirect characterization elsewhere (her actions show her to be vigorous, ruthless, proud etc.). Although he sees her as also motivated by self-preservation and jealousy of Lepida, he foregrounds her lust for power (through her son), to satisfy which she sleeps with an ex-slave (to ensure his support) and kills. Here, as the first step in the coup, she carefully secures her own base by removing her rival for control over the future emperor swiftly and shamelessly (Lepida is accused of attempted murder and disturbing the peace while Agrippina is in the process of bringing about the death of Claudius and (13f.) convulsing his household).

Passage 18 Tacitus Annals *12.66–7.*

Phase two of the plot is the assassination. Here, Agrippina's character is developed further and she becomes a really memorable and formidable figure. She chooses her agents well (experts and people in the right positions), craftily exploits Claudius' greed in administering the poison via the mushroom, and when that seems not to work acts promptly and decisively under stress, falling back on another accomplice prudently suborned in advance. There is cruel humour – Claudius being poisoned by his food-taster; the emperor being so moronic/drunk that no derangement of his wits by the poison can be perceived; all Agrippina's meticulous planning apparently upset by a bowel movement; the bizarre methods of execution (a mushroom and a feather!). There is also revulsion, in the grotesque and undignified exit so apt for Tacitus' Claudius – excreting and retching, insensible and manipulated to the end.

Passage 19 Tacitus Annals *68–9.*

Phase three is the succession of Nero, which is smoothly orchestrated. First, inside the palace Agrippina neutralizes Claudius' children (and their supporters), playing her part with panache and quite possibly with malicious wit (to call Britannicus the image of his father is a back-handed compliment and may well hint at him being similarly ignorant, controlled, and doomed). Then, outside the palace her well-chosen accomplice Burrus handles the vital praetorians, initially securing the support of the cohort on guard and then letting Nero bribe the rest. Faced with that, the Senate and the provinces follow suit, and as a final outrage Claudius (the crapping, puking fool) is declared a god.

Agrippina's role here recalls that of Tacitus, Livia at the death of Augustus (and in Tacitus Livia too later found her son hard to handle). There are also echoes of the accession of Claudius (he too was hailed by troops at the palace, put in a litter and taken to the camp of the praetorians, where he was acclaimed emperor and gave them a large gift of money), which suggest that the new ruler may be rather like the incompetent clown who preceded him.

Passage 20 Seneca Apocolocyntosis *4–5.*

On the genre and the work, see Introduction section 12. The Romans despised weakness. This attitude lies behind the gladiatorial games and permeates Roman society. Dwarves are common in Roman art as comic elements, and in the arena dwarves, blind people and cripples were sometimes forced to fight each other, as a droll variant on the standard bouts. The 'physically challenged' (like Claudius) were to the Romans objects of contempt. Particularly cruel are Claudius' last words here. The deaths of (especially celebrated) people were often described in literature of the first century AD (see e.g. the ends of the emperors in these selections, and the grim final hours of Vitellius in Tac. *Hist.* 3.84f., and compare also Pliny *Letters* 5.5.3, 8.12.4). And there was an ancient tradition of ascribing famous last words to notable figures. Alexander the Great, when asked to whom his empire should be bequeathed, said, 'To the strongest' and then died. Julius Caesar is reported to have said, 'You too, my child?' as he was stabbed by Brutus (not the Shakespearean, 'Et tu, Brute?'). The emperor Vespasian's remark prior to his death and deification was: 'Oh dear, I think I'm turning into a god.' Claudius' final utterance may reflect the contemplated edict to allow farting at table and also the bowel movement that frustrated the first attempt to poison him.

NERO

~

29 Coin depicting Nero.

On Nero, see section 9 of the Introduction.

His first five years in power (called the quinquennium*) were surprisingly good, while his mother and chief advisors (Seneca and Burrus) kept a rein on his impulses. After the removal of these restraints, however, Nero's reign descended into chaotic farce.*

1 *In Suetonius' account, Nero begins his reign as emperor (in* AD *54) with some acts to show his goodness and win him popularity.*

Orsus a pietatis ostentatione, Claudium apparatissimo funere elatum laudavit et consecravit. atque ut certiorem adhuc indolem ostenderet, ex Augusti praescripto imperaturum se professus, neque liberalitatis neque clementiae exhibendae ullam occasionem omisit. graviora vectigalia aut abolevit aut minuit. spectaculorum plurima et varia genera edidit, commisitque etiam camelorum quadrigas; notissimus eques Romanus elephanto supersidens per catadromum decurrit; sparsa et populo missilia omnium rerum per omnes dies –

milia avium cuiusque generis, vestis, aurum, argentum, gemmae,
margaritae, tabulae pictae, mancipia, iumenta atque etiam 10
mansuetae ferae, novissime naves, insulae, agri.

1 **orsus a** = 'beginning with'.

1 **pietatis:** *pietas* denotes dutiful respect towards family, friends, gods etc. (here towards Nero's adoptive father, Claudius).

2 **elatum:** from *effero.*

2 **laudavit** refers to a funeral speech praising Claudius.

6 **commisitque . . . quadrigas:** i.e. he put on races between chariots drawn by four camels.

8 **missilia omnium rerum** are tokens entitling people to all kinds of things (listed at 9–11). At the games, emperors often threw such tokens (balls etc. inscribed with the names of prizes) to the crowd, who scrambled for them.

8 **per omnes dies:** i.e. every day of the games put on by Nero.

10 **tabulae pictae:** i.e. paintings.

11 11 **insulae** does not mean 'islands' here.

2 *Soon (in AD 55), Agrippina quarrels with Nero and begins to speak of Claudius' son Britannicus as the one who should have succeeded him as emperor. Tacitus describes how Nero promptly has Britannicus murdered.*

30 Coin depicting Agrippina Minor.

Quia nullum crimen neque iubere caedem fratris palam audebat,
occulta molitur pararique venenum iubet, ministro praetoriae
cohortis tribuno, cuius cura attinebatur damnata veneficii Locusta.
primum venenum ab ipsis educatoribus accepit, tramisitque exsoluta
alvo parum validum. sed Nero lenti sceleris impatiens minitari 5
tribuno, iubere supplicium veneficae. promittentibus dein
praecipitem necem, cubiculum Neronis iuxta decoquitur virus
rapidum.

Mos habebatur principum liberos vesci in aspectu propinquorum propria et parciore mensa. illic epulante Britannico, quia cibos potusque eius delectus ex ministris gustu explorabat, ne utriusque morte proderetur scelus, talis dolus repertus est. innoxia adhuc et praecalida et libata gustu potio traditur Britannico; dein, postquam fervore aspernabatur, frigida in aqua adfunditur venenum, quod ita cunctos eius artus pervasit ut vox pariter et spiritus raperentur. trepidatur a circumsedentibus, diffugiunt imprudentes. at quibus altior intellectus resistunt defixi et Neronem intuentes. ille, reclinis et nescio similis, solitum ita ait per comitialem morbum, quo prima ab infantia adflictaretur Britannicus, et redituros paulatim visus sensusque. at Agrippinae pavor, quamvis vultu premeretur, emicuit: quippe sibi supremum auxilium ereptum et parricidii exemplum intellegebat. Octavia quoque (quamvis rudibus annis) dolorem, caritatem, omnis adfectus abscondere didicerat. ita post breve silentium repetita convivii laetitia.

Nox eadem necem Britannici et rogum coniunxit, proviso ante funebri paratu, qui modicus fuit. in Campo tamen Martis sepultus est, adeo turbidis imbribus ut vulgus iram deum portendi crediderit adversus facinus. tradunt plerique eorum temporum scriptores crebris ante exitium diebus illusum isse pueritiae Britannici Neronem, ut iam non praematura neque saeva mors videri queat, quamvis (ne tempore quidem ad complexum sororum dato) ante oculos inimici properata sit in illum supremum Claudiorum sanguinem, stupro prius quam veneno pollutum.

1 **quia nullum crimen**: understand *erat* (Nero had no grounds for charging, and executing, his stepbrother Britannicus).

2–3 **ministro . . . tribuno**: ablative absolute.

3 **cuius cura attinebatur**: 'by whose supervision was detained' = 'who was in charge of the detained prisoner . . .'

4 Britannicus is the subject of the verbs.

5 *parum* ('not') *validum* refers to the *venenum.*

6 **promittentibus**: understand *tribuno et venefica.*

7 **cubiculum Neronis iuxta**: *iuxta* is the preposition and governs *cubiculum.*

9 **mos . . . vesci**: 'The custom was observed that the emperors' children ate . . .' = 'It was an established custom for the emperors' children to eat . . .'

11 **delectus ex ministris**: one of Britannicus' servants chosen to taste his food and drink and so detect any poison in it.

11 **utriusque**: i.e. of both Britannicus and the taster.

14 **fervore**: ablative of cause.

16–17 quibus altior intellectus = *ei quibus altior intellectus erat* (i.e. those who, unlike the *imprudentes*, realized what was going on).

18 nescio is an adjective here (in the dative).

18 solitum ita ait: supply *esse* (= 'said that it was normal so', i.e. said that this kind of thing was normal for Britannicus).

21–2 quippe... intellegebat: understand *esse* with *ereptum* (Britannicus had been her final support) and with *parricidii exemplum* (= 'there was [now] a precedent for matricide', i.e. because Nero had just murdered one close relative he could easily go on to murder another – his mother).

22 Octavia... annis: Octavia was Britannicus' young sister. With *rudibus annis* (ablative of description) supply *esset.*

23 didicerat is from *disco.*

25 nox... coniunxit: i.e. Britannicus was killed and cremated on the same night.

26 Britannicus' ashes were placed in the Mausoleum of Augustus (which was located in the area of Rome called the Campus Martius, or Field of Mars).

27 adeo turbidis imbribus: ablative of attendant circumstances (= 'to the accompaniment of').

27 deum = *deorum.*

29–30 illusum... Neronem: 'that Nero went to use for sexual pleasure the boyhood of Britannicus [= the boy Britannicus]', i.e. Nero went to the thirteen-year-old Britannicus and forced himself on him. *isse* is from *eo*, and *illusum* is the supine in -um expressing purpose.

30 ut introduces a consecutive (result) clause.

30–3 even though, as his enemy Nero watched, death was hurriedly inflicted on Britannicus (who had been raped before he was poisoned), death could appear as a kindness to Britannicus (the last in the line of the Claudii family) which came none too soon. In 31 *tempore... dato* is an ablative absolute, and in 32 the subject of *properata sit* is *mors.* Note the forceful alliteration in 32–3.

3 *The young Nero also wandered Rome of a night, disguised as a slave and with a gang, robbing tradesmen and beating up people.*

Nero itinera urbis et lupanaria et deverticula veste servili in
dissimulationem sui compositus pererrabat, comitantibus qui
raperent venditioni exposita et obviis vulnera inferrent. deinde ubi
Neronem esse qui grassaretur pernotuit, augebanturque iniuriae
adversus viros feminasque insignis, et quidam sub nomine Neronis 5
inulti propriis cum globis eadem exercebant, in modum captivitatis
nox agebatur. Iuliusque Montanus senatorii ordinis, congressus forte
per tenebras cum principe, quia vi attemptantem acriter reppulerat,
deinde adgnitum oraverat, quasi exprobrasset, mori adactus est. Nero
tamen metuentior in posterum milites sibi et plerosque gladiatores 10
circumdedit, qui rixarum initia modica sinerent; si a laesis validius
ageretur, arma inferebant.

1–2 in... compositus: 'modified in order to cause concealment of himself' = 'disguised to conceal his identity'.

2–3 comitantibus qui... inferrent: supply *viris* with *comitantibus* in an ablative absolute construction. The subjunctives in the relative clause express purpose.

5 sub nomine Neronis: i.e. calling themselves Nero.

6 in modum captivitatis: i.e. just as in a captured city (nights in Rome were violent and dangerous, filled with looting and assaults).

7–9 The senator Julius Montanus was violently attacked by Nero in the dark and fought him off, then recognized him and begged his pardon; this was taken as a reproach (presumably acknowledging Nero as the assailant was taken to imply criticism of him for the attack), and so Montanus was forced to commit suicide. In 8 *attemptantem* and in 9 *adgnitum* agree with an understood *illum* and refer to Nero.

11 qui . . . sinerent: the subjunctive expresses purpose (they were not to intervene when brawls began with a moderate amount of violence).

11–12 si . . . ageretur: 'if it was ever acted/ proceeded' (if the injured parties ever fought back too vigorously, there was armed intervention by the soldiers and gladiators). The subjunctive is used in a generalizing condition containing an idea of repetition.

4 *Nero subsequently progressed to the murder of his own mother, and Tacitus describes here how that all began with the evil influence on him of the beautiful and bad Poppaea Sabina.*

Insignis impudicitia magnorum rei publicae malorum initium
fecit. erat in civitate Sabina Poppaea. huic mulieri cuncta alia fuere
praeter honestum animum. quippe mater eius, aetatis suae feminas
pulchritudine supergressa, gloriam pariter et formam dederat; opes
claritudini generis sufficiebant. sermo comis nec absurdum 5
ingenium; modestiam praeferre et lascivia uti; rarus in publicum
egressus, idque velata parte oris, ne satiaret aspectum, vel quia sic
decebat. famae numquam pepercit; neque adfectui suo aut alieno
obnoxia, unde utilitas ostenderetur, illuc libidinem transferebat.
igitur agentem eam in matrimonio equitis Romani, ex quo filium 10
genuerat, Otho pellexit iuventa ac luxu et quia flagrantissimus in
amicitia Neronis habebatur. nec mora quin adulterio matrimonium
iungeretur.

1 impudicitia: 'case/instance of immorality'.

2–9 In the character sketch here there is much to take the attention – the blunt *huic . . . animum* (2–3), generally brisk expression, extensive balance (doublets, and parallel arrangement of words), chiasmus (of nouns and adjectives) in *sermo . . . ingenium* at 5–6, and pointed antithesis in 6.

4 With *dederat* understand *ei*; *opes* refers to the wealth of Poppaea Sabina.

6 praeferre . . . uti: historic infinitives.

7 idque . . . oris: supply *fecit* (i.e. when she did appear in public, it was with part of her face veiled).

7 ne satiaret aspectum: i.e. so that men would be intrigued and want to see more of her face.

8 famae . . . pepercit: i.e. she never cared about making herself more notorious. *pepercit* is from *parco*.

8–9 neque . . . obnoxia: she had no feelings for others and did not care about their feelings for her (*suo* = 'in herself' and *alieno* = 'in anyone else'). *obnoxia* means 'vulnerable' (to).

9 unde . . . transferebat: i.e. she moved from man to man, having affairs with those who would be useful to her (*illuc . . . unde* = 'to the man by whom . . .'; such adverbs are often used as shorthand for prepositional phrases).

10 agentem . . . matrimonio: 'living in marriage to . . .' = 'while married to . . .'

11–12 flagrantissimus . . . habebatur: i.e. he was regarded as being the most popular of Nero's friends.

12–13 nec mora . . . iungeretur: they had an adulterous affair and then quickly got married to each other ('And [there was] no delay so as to prevent . . .'). Here, as often, *quin* introduces a clause with negative force after a negative main clause devoting the absence of delay. *adulterio* is dative.

5 *Nero becomes interested in Poppaea when Otho praises her. Soon, she is admitted to the emperor's presence and seduces him.*

Otho, sive amore incautus, laudare formam elegantiamque uxoris
apud principem, sive ut accenderet ac, si eadem femina potirentur, id
quoque vinculum potentiam ei adiceret. saepe auditus est
(consurgens e convivio Neronis) se ire ad illam, sibi concessam
dictitans nobilitatem, pulchritudinem, vota omnium. his atque 5
talibus inritamentis non longa cunctatio interponitur. sed, accepto
aditu, Poppaea primum per blandimenta et artes valescere, imparem
cupidini se et forma Neronis captam simulans, mox, acri iam principis
amore, ad superbiam vertens, si ultra unam alteramque noctem
attineretur, nuptam se esse dictitans nec posse matrimonium 10
amittere, devinctam Othoni per genus vitae quod nemo adaequaret;
illum animo et cultu magnificum; at Neronem, paelice ancilla
devinctum, nihil e contubernio servili nisi abiectum et sordidum
traxisse. deicitur familiaritate sueta, post congressu et comitatu Otho,
et ad postremum, ne in urbe aemulatus ageret, provinciae 15
Lusitaniae praeficitur.

1 amore: ablative of cause.

2–3 sive . . . adiceret: i.e. or (as an alternative to *sive amore incautus*) with the deliberate intention of making Nero fall in love with her and so that the additional bond of them sharing the same woman would increase Otho's power.

5 vota omnium = 'what all men desire' (like *nobilitatem* and *pulchritudinem* this refers to Poppaea).

5–6 his . . . inritamentis: ablative of cause.

7–8 imparem cupidini: i.e. too weak to resist her desire [for Nero].

8–9 acri . . . amore: ablative absolute.

9 ultra . . . noctem: i.e. for more than a second night.

12–14 illum . . . traxisse: all these words are also part of the indirect speech after *dictitans.* Understand *esse* with *illum.*

12 paelice ancilla: Nero was at this time married to Octavia (sister of Britannicus) but was having an affair with an ex-slave called Acte (here and in 13 contemptuously referred to as still a slave by Poppaea).

13 nihil . . . nisi: i.e. only.

13 **abiectum et sordidum:** the neuters are used as nouns here (= 'what was sordid and degrading').

14 *post* is the adverb. All the nouns in this line refer to Otho's relations with Nero and are ablatives (= 'from') going with *deicitur.*

15 **aemulatus ageret:** i.e. be a rival.

6 In AD 59, Nero decides to go ahead with the murder of his mother because of the taunts of Poppaea, who believes that she will not manage to get Nero to divorce his wife Octavia and marry her in the face of Agrippina's opposition.

Diu meditatum scelus non ultra Nero distulit, flagrantior in dies
amore Poppaeae. quae (sibi matrimonium et discidium Octaviae
incolumi Agrippina haud sperans) crebris criminationibus, aliquando
per facetias incusare principem et pupillum vocare qui, iussis alienis
obnoxius, non modo imperii sed libertatis etiam indigeret. cur enim 5
differri nuptias suas? formam scilicet displicere et triumphalis avos.
an fecunditatem et verum animum? si nurum Agrippina non nisi
filio infestam ferre posset, redderetur ipsa Othonis coniugio. ituram
quoquo terrarum, ubi audiret potius contumelias imperatoris quam
viseret, periculis eius inmixta. haec atque talia lacrimis et arte 10
adulterae penetrantia nemo prohibebat, cupientibus cunctis infringi
potentiam matris, et credente nullo usque ad caedem eius duratura
filii odia.

1 **meditatum:** although *meditor* is a deponent, the perfect participle (as often with deponents) has a passive sense here.

1 **distulit** is from *differo.*

1 **in dies:** 'day by day'.

2 **sibi . . . Octaviae:** the two opponents are at the far ends of this chiasmus and are separated by marriage and divorce.

3 **incolumi Agrippina:** ablative absolute.

4 **incusare . . . vocare:** this chiasmus brings together the alliterating *principem* and *pupillum* to sharpen the barb.

4 **alienis** refers to Agrippina.

5 **non modo . . . indigeret:** i.e. not only was he not in charge of the empire but also he did not have personal liberty.

5–10 **cur . . . inmixta:** this is all indirect speech, representing what Poppaea said to Nero.

6 **differri:** infinitive because this is a rhetorical question (not really expecting an answer) = 'why was her wedding [to Nero] being . . . ?'

6 **scilicet:** shows that Poppaea is being ironical here.

7 **an . . . animum:** supply *displicere* ('Or did her . . . displease [him]?'). Poppaea had a son, whereas Octavia had not given birth.

7 **non nisi** : 'only'.

8 **filio:** is dative and goes with *infestam.*

8 **redderetur ipsa:** 'let her [i.e. Poppaea] be restored to . . .'

8–9 **ituram quoquo terrarum:** with *ituram* understand *se esse*; *terrarum* is a partitive genitive ('she would go anywhere of [= on] earth'). The allusion is to distant Lusitania, where her husband Otho had been sent, or anywhere else that he might be sent by Nero.

9–10 **audiret . . . viseret:** potential subjunctives (elsewhere she would only hear about insults to the emperor rather than actually witness them in person at Rome).

10 **eius** refers to Nero.

11 **penetrantia:** understand *animum Neronis* as the object of this verb.

12–13 **usque . . . odia:** i.e. that Nero's hatred of Agrippina would make him go so far as to kill her.

7 Tacitus relates the story that Agrippina tried to keep power by committing incest with Nero but was foiled by one of Nero's chief ministers (Seneca).

Tradit Cluvius ardore retinendae Agrippinam potentiae eo usque
provectam ut medio diei, cum Nero per vinum et epulas incalesceret,
offerret se saepius temulento comptam et incesto paratam; iamque
lasciva oscula et praenuntias flagitii blanditias adnotantibus
proximis, Senecam contra muliebres inlecebras subsidium a femina 5
petivisse, immissamque Acten libertam, quae deferret pervulgatum
esse incestum, gloriante matre, nec toleraturos milites profani
principis imperium. Fabius Rusticus non Agrippinae sed Neroni
cupitum id memorat eiusdemque libertae astu disiectum. sed quae
Cluvius eadem ceteri quoque auctores prodidere, et fama huc 10
inclinat, seu concepit animo tantum immanitatis Agrippina, seu
credibilior novae libidinis meditatio in ea visa est quae exercita est
ad omne flagitium patrui nuptiis.

1 **Cluvius** was a politician and historian who acted as a herald for Nero.

1 **ardore retinendae . . . potentiae:** the order is suggestive (*Agrippina* is completely enveloped by these words).

1–2 **eo usque provectam ut:** i.e. was driven so far as to . . . (*eo* is the adverb). With *provectam* understand *esse*. The indirect statement continues at 3–8.

3 **offerret se saepius temulento:** *temulento* agrees with *Neroni* (to be understood, the indirect object), and *saepius* = 'rather often'.

5 **proximis:** used as a noun here (= 'their closest companions') in an ablative absolute construction.

6 **Acten:** she was Nero's mistress. Seneca is presumably using her because he does not want Agrippina's influence over Nero to undermine his own position.

6 **quae deferret:** the subjunctive expresses purpose, and the verb introduces indirect statement.

7 **milites:** Nero needed the troops' support if he was to keep his position as emperor.

8 **Fabius Rusticus** was a historian and had Seneca as his patron.

8–9 **non . . . id:** *id* refers to the incestuous relationship, and *Agrippinae* and *Neroni* are datives of agent. Understand *esse* with *cupitum* (and with *disiectum* later in 9).

9–10 quae Cluvius: supply *prodidit.*

11–13 seu . . . nuptiis: i.e. whether Agrippina actually did form such a monstrous plan or it seemed quite credible that a woman as depraved as her might have formed such a plan.

11 immanitatis: partitive genitive, with *tantum.*

8 Nero now avoids his mother, and as he ponders the best way to kill her without being found out, Anicetus suggests a collapsible boat which would simulate an accident at sea.

Igitur Nero vitare secretos eius congressus, abscedentem in hortos
aut in agrum laudare, quod otium capesseret. postremo, ubicumque
haberetur, praegravem ratus, interficere constituit, hactenus
consultans – veneno an ferro vel alia via. placuitque primo venenum.
sed inter epulas principis si daretur, referri ad casum non poterat, 5
tali iam Britannici exitio; et ministros temptare arduum videbatur
mulieris usu scelerum adversus insidias intentae; atque ipsa
praesumendo remedia munierat corpus. ferrum et caedes quonam
modo occultaretur, nemo reperiebat; et ne quis illi tanto facinori
delectus iussa sperneret metuebant. 10

Obtulit ingenium Anicetus libertus, classi apud Misenum
praefectus et pueritiae Neronis educator ac mutuis odiis Agrippinae
invisus. navem posse componi docet cuius pars ipso in mari per
artem soluta effunderet ignaram: nihil tam capax fortuitorum quam
mare; et si naufragio intercepta sit, quem adeo iniquum ut sceleri 15
adsignet quod venti et fluctus deliquerint? additurum principem
defunctae templum et aras et cetera ostentandae pietati.

1–2 in hortos aut in agrum: i.e. to her gardens in Rome, or to an estate of hers in the country.

2–3 ubicumque haberetur: 'wherever she was kept'.

3 ratus: from *reor.*

3–4 hactenus consultans . . . via: i.e. Nero discussed only the method of killing her (not the question of whether she should be killed at all).

6 tali iam Britannici exitio: ablative absolute, with a causal force (i.e. because Britannicus had already been killed by poison).

6 ministros temptare: i.e. to suborn Agrippina's own servants to poison her in her home.

7 usu scelerum: ablative of cause (her experience of crime had put Agrippina on her guard against such plots).

8 munierat corpus: i.e. she had strengthened her resistance to poison.

8 ferrum et caedes (= 'death by the sword') belongs inside the indirect question (*quonam modo occultaretur*), in which *occultaretur* is deliberative or potential subjunctive.

9 ne introduces a fear clause.

11 obtulit ingenium: the verb is *offero,* and the noun means 'a clever scheme'.

12 **Agrippinae:** is dative and goes with *invisus* in 13.

13–14 **cuius ... ignaram:** i.e. part of the ship would be designed to collapse while the ship was actually out at sea, to catch Agrippina unawares (*ignaram*) and to send her overboard (*effunderet*, which is potential subjunctive).

14–17 **nihil ... pietati:** this is all indirect speech, representing what Anicetus went on to say. With *nihil* understand *esse.*

15–16 **quem ... deliquerint:** i.e. who would be so unfair/prejudiced as to believe that an offence committed by winds and waves was a crime by a human? The accusative and infinitive (*quem adeo iniquum* [*futurum esse*]) is used because the question is rhetorical (not really expecting an answer). *quod = id quod.*

17 **defunctae** (referring to the dead Agrippina) is dative and goes with *additurum* (whose subject is Nero).

17 **ostentandae pietati:** dative of purpose.

9 Nero lures Agrippina to the seaside resort of Baiae, escorts her to her nearby villa (called Bauli) and invites her to dinner back in Baiae, providing the collapsible boat as transport. When she comes by litter instead (because warned of a plot), he allays her suspicions at dinner and sends her back to Bauli in the collapsible ship (which has meanwhile been brought round to Baiae for her to use).

Placuit sollertia, tempore etiam iuta, quando Quinquatruum festos
dies apud Baias frequentabat. illuc matrem elicit, ferendas
parentium iracundias et placandum animum dictitans, quo rumorem
reconciliationis efficeret acciperetque Agrippina facili feminarum
credulitate ad gaudia. venientem dehinc obvius in litora excepit 5
manu et complexu, ducitque Baulos. stabat inter alias navis ornatior,
tamquam id quoque honori matris daretur. ac tum invitata ad epulas
erat, ut occultando facinori nox adhiberetur. satis constitit exstitisse
proditorem et Agrippinam, auditis insidiis, an crederet ambiguam,
gestamine sellae Baias pervectam. ibi blandimentum sublevavit 10
metum: comiter excepta superque ipsum collocata. modo familiaritate
iuvenili Nero et rursus adductus, quasi seria consociaret, tracto in
longum convictu, prosequitur abeuntem, artius oculis et pectori
haerens, sive explendae simulationi, seu periturae matris supremus
aspectus quamvis ferum animum retinebat. 15

1 **sollertia** alludes to Anicetus' clever plan.

1 **iuta:** perfect participle passive of *iuvo.*

2–3 Understand *esse* with *ferendas* and *placandum. animum* refers to the bad temper of parents.

3 **quo:** introduces a purpose clause.

4–5 **facili ... gaudia:** 'with the ready credulity of women in response to joy [= good news]'. The ablative is one of manner.

6 manu: i.e. with outstretched hands.

6 Baulos: 'to Bauli'.

6 inter alias: supply *naves.*

8 occultando facinori: dative of purpose.

9 crederet is deliberative subjunctive ('she should believe [him]') in an indirect question after *ambiguam.*

10 gestamine sellae: *sellae* is genitive of definition ('consisting of').

10 Baias pervectam: understand *esse.*

11 superque ipsum collocata: i.e. at dinner, Agrippina was given the place of honour 'above' Nero (i.e. to the left of him). Normally, three couches holding three guests each were placed around a table (one on the left, one on the right, and one at the bottom of the table), but the Latin here suggests that Nero and Agrippina occupied the bottom couch on their own, and she reclined on his left.

11–13 *modo familiaritate iuvenili* and *rursus adductus* belong with *tracto in longum convictu* (Nero long protracted the banquet, being boyishly intimate at some points (*modo*) and at other points (*rursus*) being serious). Instead of the ablative absolute, *traxit in longum convictum et* would have been a more normal expression.

13–14 artius . . . haerens: 'hanging on her gaze and clinging to her breast rather closely' (or 'more closely' than usual).

14–15 sive . . . aspectus: 'either to put the final touch to his play-acting [dative of purpose], or else the last sight . . .'

15 quamvis ferum animum: 'his [i.e. Nero's] heart, brutal though it was'. *quamvis* does not always take a subjunctive; it often modifies adjectives like this.

10 *When Agrippina sails off, the roof of the boat collapses on top of her, but the sides of the couch on which she and a friend are reclining take the weight and she is only injured. The ship is then capsized, but she swims off silently and gets back safe to her villa.*

Noctem sideribus inlustrem et placido mari quietam, quasi
convincendum ad scelus, di praebuere. nec multum erat progressa
navis, duobus e numero familiarium Agrippinam comitantibus (ex
quis Crepereius Gallus haud procul gubernaculis adstabat, Acerronia
super pedes cubitantis reclinis paenitentiam filii et reciperatam 5
matris gratiam per gaudium memorabat), cum, dato signo, ruere
tectum multo plumbo grave. pressusque Creperieus et statim
exanimatus est. Agrippina et Acerronia eminentibus lecti parietibus
protectae sunt. nec dissolutio navigii sequebatur, turbatis omnibus et
quod plerique ignari etiam conscios impediebant. visum dehinc 10
remigibus unum in latus inclinare atque ita navem submergere. sed
neque ipsis promptus consensus, et alii contra nitentes dedere
facultatem lenioris in mare iactus. verum Acerronia, imprudentia
dum se Agrippinam esse utque subveniretur matri principis clamitat,
contis et remis et, quae fors obtulerat, navalibus telis conficitur. 15
Agrippina silens eoque minus adgnita (unum tamen vulnus umero

excepit) nando, deinde occursu lenunculorum Lucrinum in lacum vecta villae suae infertur.

2 **convincendum ad scelus** = *ad scelus convincendum* (expressing purpose).

2–7 **nec ... grave:** this is a long and complex sentence, in which Tacitus is essentially saying that the ship had not gone far when the roof collapsed. After the main verb *erat progressa* in 2, he adds an ablative absolute (*duobus ... comitantibus*) and then a long parenthesis in brackets (explaining the positions and actions of Agrippina's two companions) before coming to the *cum* (meaning 'when') in 6, which is followed by an ablative absolute (*signo dato*) and a historic infinitive (*ruere*).

4 **quis** = *quibus*.

5 **super pedes *cubitantis* reclinis:** with *cubitantis* understand *Agrippinae*; *reclinis* is nominative (Acerronia was on or beside Agrippina's couch, and was leaning over Agrippina's feet).

8 **eminentibus:** the sides of the couch jutted up above the level of the two women's heads.

9 **dissolutio navigii:** it seems that the falling weight (perhaps also meant to crush Agrippina to death) was supposed to knock a hole in the bottom of the boat and so break it up and sink it, with help from those on board who were in on the plot.

9 **turbatis omnibus:** this ablative absolute has a causal force.

10–11 **visum ... remigibus:** 'it seemed good to the rowers' = 'the rowers decided'.

12 **contra ... dedere:** i.e. the others ran to the opposite side of the ship and brought their weight to bear there, so that Agrippina and Acerronia were thrown overboard less violently. *dedere* is from *do*.

13 **imprudentia:** causal ablative, belonging inside the *dum* clause. It is positioned in front of the clause for emphasis.

14 **dum ... clamitat:** *clamitat* governs firstly an indirect statement and then an indirect command (in which *subveniretur* is an impersonal expression). Acerronia did not realize that there was a plot to kill Agrippina, and thought that she would get help by pretending to be the emperor's mother.

15 **quae ... telis:** i.e. whatever ship's gear came to hand was used as weapons on her. *obtulerat* is from *offero*.

16 **eoque minus adgnita:** 'and because of that not generally recognized'.

17 **nando:** gerund of *no*.

17–18 Apparently, Agrippina was taken by boat to the Lucrine Lake (to the north of Baiae) and then was carried in a litter overland from there to her villa Bauli.

11 *Agrippina realizes that Nero has tried to kill her, but decides that the safest course of action is to feign ignorance of the plot.*

Illic reputans ideo se fallacibus litteris accitam et honore
praecipuo habitam, quodque litus iuxta, non ventis acta, non saxis
impulsa, navis summa sui parte velut terrestre machinamentum
concidisset, observans etiam Acerroniae necem, simul suum vulnus
aspiciens, solum insidiarum remedium esse sensit si non 5
intellegerentur. misitque libertum Agerinum, qui nuntiaret filio
benignitate deum et fortuna eius evasisse gravem casum; orare ut,
quamvis periculo matris exterritus, visendi curam differret; sibi ad

praesens quiete opus. atque interim, securitate simulata,
medicamina vulneri et fomenta corpori adhibet. testamentum 10
Acerroniae requiri bonaque obsignari iubet – id tantum non per
simulationem.

1 **reputans** ('reflecting') is followed by indirect statement, expressed firstly by accusatives and infinitives (supply *esse* with *accitam* and *habitam*) and then by a *quod* clause (= 'on the fact that').

1 **ideo:** i.e. to bring about her death.

2 **iuxta** is the preposition and governs *litus.*

3 **summa sui parte:** 'in the upper part of itself' = 'from the top' (*summa* ... *parte* is ablative of respect).

3 **velut terrestre machinamentum:** i.e. not like a ship at sea. The reference may be to stage machinery and/or mechanisms in private houses which suddenly parted ceilings and showered guests with flowers or presents.

5–6 **solum ... intellegerentur:** *remedium* is defined by the *si* clause ('she felt that the only remedy for the plot was if it was not recognized [by her] as existing').

6 **nuntiaret:** why subjunctive?

7 **benignitate ... eius:** *deum* = *deorum*, and *Fortuna* (causal ablative) refers to Nero's lucky star.

7 **evasisse ... orare:** understand *se* (referring to Agrippina) with both these infinitives (in indirect speech after *nuntiaret*).

8 **visendi curam:** 'the attentiveness of visiting [her]' = 'an attentive visit'.

9 **opus:** understand *esse.*

11 **bonaque obsignari:** Acerronia's effects are to be sealed up because Agrippina expects that she has been left something in the will and wants to make sure that she gets all of her legacy.

11 **id tantum:** supply *fecit. tantum* is the adverb.

12 *When Nero hears that Agrippina is only wounded, he panics and turns to his chief ministers for help. They can only suggest that Anicetus (who proposed the trick boat) should keep his promise to dispose of her. He is sent off to murder her, while Nero tries to make her messenger look like an assassin sent by her to kill him.*

At Neroni nuntios patrati facinoris opperienti adfertur evasisse
ictu levi sauciam. tum pavore exanimis et iam iamque adfore
obtestans vindictae properam, sive servitia armaret vel militem
accenderet, sive ad senatum et populum pervaderet, naufragium et
vulnus et interfectos amicos obiciendo; quod contra subsidium sibi? 5
nisi quid Burrus et Seneca. quos statim acciverat. longum utriusque
silentium. post Seneca hactenus promptius ut respiceret Burrum ac
sciscitaretur an militi imperanda caedes esset. ille praetorianos toti
Caesarum domui obstrictos memoresque Germanici nihil adversus
progeniem eius atrox ausuros respondit; perpetraret Anicetus 10
promissa. qui, nihil cunctatus, poscit summam sceleris. Nero illo sibi

die dari imperium auctoremque tanti muneris libertum profitetur;
iret propere duceretque promptissimos ad iussa. ipse, audito venisse
nuntium Agerinum, scaenam criminis parat, gladiumque (dum
mandata perfert) abicit inter pedes eius. tum quasi deprehenso 15
vincla inici iubet, ut exitium principis molitam matrem et pudore
deprehensi sceleris sponte mortem sumpsisse confingeret.

1 **adfertur** = 'news is brought that'.

2 **tum pavore exanimis**: supply *ille erat.*

2 **adfore** = *adfuturam esse.*

3 **vindictae**: genitive of reference, going with *properam.*

3 **armaret**: Agrippina is the subject of this and the following verbs.

3 **militem**: singular for plural, referring to the praetorian guard.

5 **obiciendo**: this is the instrumental ablative of the gerund, equivalent to the present participle *obiciens* (= 'charging him with . . . ').

5–6 **quod . . . Seneca**: the indirect statement continues. *contra* is the adverb. Understand *esse* in the (rhetorical) question and a verb of saying after *nisi* ('unless Burrus and Seneca [suggested] anything').

7 **hactenus promptius ut**: supply *egit* ('acted'), i.e. so far took the lead as to look round at . . .

8 **militi . . . esset**: i.e. whether they should order the praetorian guard to kill Agrippina.

9 **Germanici**: the soldiers were loyal to Agrippina because of their love for her father, the great general Germanicus.

10 **ausuros** = *ausuros esse.*

10 **perpetraret**: the subjunctive represents in indirect speech an original command (like *iret* and *duceretque* in 13).

12 **auctoremque**: understand *esse.*

13 **audito**: impersonal ablative absolute ('it having been heard that . . . ').

15 **mandata**: i.e. the message Agerinus was told to deliver by Agrippina.

15 In *perfert* and *eius* and *deprehenso* (dative with *inici*) the reference is to Agerinus.

16 **molitam** = *molitam esse.* The subject of this infinitive and of *sumpsisse* is *matrem.*

13 *People gather to congratulate Agrippina on her escape but are scattered by Anicetus and his men, who enter her villa and kill her.*

Interim vulgato Agrippinae periculo, ut quisque acceperat,
decurrere ad litus. hi molium obiectus, hi proximas scaphas scandere;
alii, quantum corpus sinebat, vadere in mare; quidam manus
protendere; questibus, votis, clamore diversa rogitantium aut incerta
respondentium omnis ora compleri; adfluere ingens multitudo cum 5
luminibus, atque ubi incolumem esse pernotuit, ad gratandum sese
expedire, donec aspectu armati et minitantis agminis disiecti sunt.

Anicetus villam statione circumdat, refractaque ianua obvios
servorum abripit, donec ad fores cubiculi veniret; cui pauci
adstabant, ceteris exterritis. cubiculo modicum lumen inerat et 10

ancillarum una, magis ac magis anxia Agrippina quod nemo a filio ac
ne Agerinus quidem: aliam fore laetae rei faciem; nunc solitudinem
ac repentinos strepitus et extremi mali indicia. abeunte dehinc
ancilla, 'tu quoque me deseris' prolocuta respicit Anicetum, trierarcho
et centurione classiario comitatum. circumsistunt lectum 15
percussores, et prior trierarchus fusti caput eius adflixit. iam
centurioni ferrum destringenti protendens uterum, 'ventrem feri'
exclamavit multisque vulneribus confecta est.

1 **ut quisque acceperat**: 'as each person had heard [the news]'. *quisque* is also the subject of the historic infinitive *decurrere.*

2 **hi . . . hi** denote different groups of people.

2 **molium obiectus**: the embankments that formed a barrier against the sea (reclaiming land for building etc.).

3 **quantum corpus sinebat**: 'as far as their bodies allowed' (i.e. as far as they could before the water became too deep for them). *quantum* (= *tantum quantum*) is accusative of extent.

4–5 **questibus . . . respondentium**: the two participles depend on the three ablative nouns, and *rogitantium* (= 'those frequently asking') has *diversa* as its object, while *respondentium* (= 'those saying in reply') has as its object *incerta.*

6 **incolumem esse**: understand *eam.*

9 **servorum**: partitive genitive ('those of the slaves in his way').

9 **cui**: (dative with *adstabant*) refers to *cubiculi.*

11 **anxia Agrippina**: ablative absolute.

11–12 **quod . . . quidem**: supply *venisset* with both nominatives.

12–13 **aliam . . . indicia**: this is indirect statement, representing Agrippina's thoughts. *laetae rei* denotes a successful state of affairs (i.e. if all had gone well, things would look different), and after *nunc* (= 'as it was') *esse* is to be understood.

14–15 **trierarcho . . . classiario**: these are ablatives of accompaniment (= 'by'). Anicetus uses sailors because he cannot rely on the praetorian guard to kill Agrippina.

17 **centurioni . . . uterum**: *centurioni* is indirect object and *uterum* is direct object of *protendens.* Agrippina wants her womb struck (*feri*, from *ferio*) because it gave birth to the son who ordered her murder.

14 *Agrippina is hastily cremated and Nero, finally realizing the full horror of his crime, spends the night in terror. But the next day officers of the praetorian guard congratulate him on his escape from his mother's attempt on his life, and then his friends, nearby towns and the leading men at Rome thank the gods for his deliverance.*

Aspexeritne matrem exanimem Nero et formam corporis eius
laudaverit, sunt qui tradiderint, sunt qui abnuant. cremata est nocte
eadem exsequiis vilibus; neque, dum Nero rerum potiebatur,
congesta aut clausa humus. mox domesticorum cura levem tumulum

accepit. hunc sui finem multos ante annos crediderat Agrippina 5
contempseratque. nam consulenti super Nerone responderunt
Chaldaei fore ut imperaret matremque occideret; atque illa 'occidat'
inquit 'dum imperet'.

Sed a Nerone perfecto demum scelere magnitudo eius intellecta
est. reliquo noctis, modo per silentium defixus, saepius pavore 10
exsurgens et mentis inops, lucem opperiebatur tamquam exitium
adlaturam. atque eum, auctore Burro, prima centurionum
tribunorumque adulatio ad spem firmavit, prensantium manum
gratantiumque quod discrimen improvisum et matris facinus
evasisset. amici dehinc adire templa, et proxima municipia victimis 15
et legationibus laetitiam testari. ipse diversa simulatione maestus et
morti parentis inlacrimans. quia tamen non, ut hominum vultus, ita
locorum facies mutantur, obversabaturque maris illius et litorum
gravis aspectus (et erant qui crederent sonitum tubae collibus circum
planctusque tumulo matris audiri), Neapolim concessit. miro 20
certamine procerum decernuntur supplicationes apud omnia
pulvinaria.

1–2 As *sunt qui tradiderint, sunt qui abnuant* is virtually equivalent to *incertum est* ('it is uncertain'), Tacitus has an indirect question (*aspexeritne* ...) instead of reported statement. Translate: 'As to the question whether ..., some have related that he did, some deny it'. *tradiderint* and *abnuant* are subjunctives in generic relative clauses, like *crederent* in 19.

4 **congesta aut clausa** refers to the heaping up of earth in a burial mound and the enclosure of it in a stone tomb (i.e. Agrippina's ashes were buried in the ground but not given a proper grave).

4 **mox domesticorum cura**: *mox* here means 'later on', the *domestici* are members of Agrippina's household, and *cura* is ablative.

5 **hunc sui finem**: understand *futurum esse* ('that this would be her end').

5 **multos ante annos**: 'many years earlier'.

7 **fore ut ... occideret**: *fore ut* + subjunctive was a way of expressing a future infinitive in indirect statement.

7–8 **occidat ... dum imperet**: *occidat* is jussive subjunctive, and *dum* means 'provided that'.

8 **a Nerone**: goes with *intellecta est.*

10 **reliquo noctis**: Tacitus was fond of the ablative (instead of the accusative) to express duration of time.

10 **per silentium**: 'in silence'.

12 **adlaturam**: (from *affero*) has *exitium* as its object.

12 **prima**: adverbial ('first of all').

16 **diversa simulatione maestus**: supply *erat.* The ablative is one of manner (i.e. Nero was pretending to be sad, while the others were pretending to be happy).

17–18 **non ... mutantur**: i.e. the features of a landscape do not change as obligingly as the expressions of men do.

19–20 **collibus ... tumulo**: these are local ablatives (= *e collibus* and *e tumulo*).

21 **certamine procerum**: i.e. competition/rivalry among the leading citizens at Rome.

15 No longer restrained by his mother, Nero at last indulges his deplorable ambition to race in a chariot and play the lyre on stage.

Vetus illi cupido erat curriculo quadrigarum insistere, nec minus foedum studium cithara ludicrum in modum canere. concertare equis regium et antiquis ducibus factitatum memorabat, idque vatum laudibus celebre; enimvero cantus Apollini sacros. nec iam sisti poterat cum Senecae et Burro visum, ne utraque pervinceret, alterum concedere. clausumque valle Vaticana spatium in quo equos regeret, haud promisco spectaculo. mox vocari populus Romanus laudibusque extollere. ne tamen adhuc publico theatro dehonestaretur, instituit ludos Iuvenalium vocabulo; feminae inlustres deformia meditari; exstructaque conventicula et cauponae, et posita veno inritamenta luxui. inde gliscere flagitia et infamia, nec ulla moribus olim corruptis plus libidinum circumdedit quam illa conluvies. postremum ipse scaenam incedit, multa cura temptans citharam. accesserat cohors militum, centuriones tribunique et maerens Burrus ac laudans. tuncque primum conscripti sunt equites Romani cognomento Augustianorum. ii dies ac noctes plausibus personare, formam principis vocemque deum vocabulis appellantes.

2 **cithara ... canere**: 'to sing to [his own accompaniment on] the lyre in a theatrical manner' (i.e. on a public stage as a professional).

2–3 **concertare ... memorabat**: i.e. he used to say that to race with horses was a pursuit of kings and heroes. *antiquis ducibus* is dative of agent. Mythological heroes were depicted as competing in chariot-races at funeral games, and in historical times kings and princes entered chariots in the various Greek games (Olympian etc.).

3 **vatum**: poets such as Pindar and Bacchylides wrote odes celebrating victories in the Greek games.

5 **visum**: supply *est* (= 'it seemed good') in this inverted *cum* clause (in such clauses A is happening when B happens).

5–6 **utraque ... alterum**: both words refer to Nero's wishes.

6 **valle Vaticana**: in Rome (St Peter's now stands where Nero raced).

7 **regeret**: why subjunctive?

7 **haud promisco spectaculo**: ablative absolute.

8 **extollere**: understand *Neronem* as the object.

9 **Iuvenalium vocabulo** = 'called the Juvenalia' (*Iuvenalium* is genitive of definition). Nero could perform before an audience at these games without appearing before the general public in a theatre.

10 **deformia**: i.e. indecent parts on the stage.

11 **posita veno**: 'were set out for sale' (*veno* is a predicative dative).

11–12 **nec ulla**: supply *conluvies* (*illa conluvies* refers to all the disreputable people present at Nero's games).

12 **moribus olim corruptis** refers to Roman morals, which had long been corrupt. *Moribus* (dative) is indirect object of *circumdedit* ('contributed'), while *plus libidinum* is the direct object.

15 maerens Burrus ac laudans: Burrus is secretly unhappy at the sight of the emperor on stage but has to praise his performance.

16 ii: masculine nominative plural of *is*.

17–18 deum vocabulis appellantes: i.e. they used the names and/or epithets of gods in describing Nero's handsomeness and voice (likening him to Apollo and Hercules).

16 Nero kept up these interests and several years later (in AD 66), because the Greeks who held musical contests craftily gave prizes to him despite his absence and flattered his singing, he sets off on a tour of Greece. After being awarded victory after victory in the games there, he returns to Rome amid extravagant celebrations in imitation of the solemn and revered military triumph.

Instituerant civitates, apud quas musici agones edi solent, omnes citharoedorum coronas ad ipsum mittere. eas adeo grate recipiebat ut legatos, qui pertulissent, non modo primos admitteret sed etiam familiaribus epulis interponeret. a quibusdam ex his rogatus ut cantaret super cenam, exceptusque effusius, solos scire audire 5 Graecos solosque se et studiis suis dignos ait. nec profectione dilata, certamina obiit omnia (nam quae diversissimorum temporum sunt cogi in unum annum iussit).

Cantante eo, ne necessaria quidem causa excedere theatro licitum est. itaque et enixae quaedam in spectaculis dicuntur et multi 10 taedio audiendi laudandique (clausis portis) aut furtim desiluisse de muro aut, morte simulata, funere elati. quam autem trepide anxieque certaverit, quanta adversariorum aemulatione, quo metu iudicum, vix credi potest. adversarios, quasi plane condicionis eiusdem, observare, captare, infamare secreto, nonnumquam maledictis 15 incessere ac, si arte praecellerent, corrumpere etiam solebat. in certando ita legi oboediebat ut, numquam exscreare ausus, sudorem frontis bracchio detergeret; atque in tragico quodam actu, cum elapsum baculum cito resumpsisset, pavidus et metuens ne ob delictum certamine summoveretur, non aliter confirmatus est quam 20 adiurante hypocrita non animadversum id inter exsultationes succlamationesque populi. ac ne cuius alterius hieronicarum memoria aut vestigium exstaret usquam, subverti et unco trahi abicique in latrinas omnium statuas et imagines imperavit. aurigavit

quoque plurifariam, sed Olympiis excussus curru ac rursus 25
repositus, cum perdurare non posset, destitit ante decursum; neque
eo setius coronatus est. decedens deinde provinciam universam
libertate donavit simulque iudices civitate Romana et pecunia grandi.

Reversus e Graecia, introiit Romam eo curru quo Augustus olim
triumphaverat, et in veste purpurea distinctaque stellis aureis 30
chlamyde, coronamque capite gerens Olympiacam, praeeunte pompa
ceterarum cum titulis, sequentibus currum plausoribus, Augustianos
militesque se triumphi eius clamitantibus. incedenti passim victimae
caesae, sparso per vias identidem croco, ingestaeque aves ac lemnisci
et bellaria. sacras coronas in cubiculis circum lectos posuit, item 35
statuas suas citharoedico habitu.

3 **pertulissent:** from *perfero* (so *dilata* in 6 is from *differo*). Why is it subjunctive?

3 **admitteret:** i.e. admitted to an audience with him.

5 **scire audire** = 'knew how to listen properly'.

6 **se...suis:** both words refer to Nero. Supply *esse* here.

7–8 So that he could compete at all the contests during his year-long tour of Greece, Nero had them all put on in that year (even those that were not due to be held until a year or two later). *quae* = *ea [certamina] quae.*

9 **necessaria...causa:** ablative of cause (like *taedio* in 11).

10 **enixae** = *enixae esse.*

12 **funere elati:** supply *esse.* The reference is to people being carried out for burial.

12–14 There are three indirect questions here. Understand *certaverit* in the second and third ones (*quanta*...and *quo*...). *aemulatio* + genitive = 'rivalry towards...'.

18 **bracchio detergeret:** the use of a handkerchief was not permitted.

20–1 **non aliter...hypocrita:** i.e. he was only reassured by an actor who swore that Nero's slip had not been noticed.

22 **cuius alterius:** 'of anyone else' (from *quis* and *alter*).

24 **omnium** = of all other victors in the games.

26–7 **neque eo setius:** 'but none the less for that' = 'but all the same'.

28 **iudices:** also object of *donavit,* this denotes the judges at the games where Nero had competed.

32 **ceterarum cum titulis:** i.e. the other wreaths which Nero had won, together with inscriptions on placards explaining where he had won them, what songs he had performed etc.

32–3 **Augustianos...eius:** understand *esse* in this indirect statement (after *clamitantibus*).

35 **cubiculis** denotes Nero's sleeping-quarters.

36 **citharoedico habitu:** ablative of description.

A few years earlier, in AD *62, Burrus had died and Seneca had withdrawn from public life. Nero was then free of all restraining influences and proceeded to divorce Octavia and marry Poppaea.*

17 Poppaea gets one of Octavia's servants to accuse his mistress of adultery with a slave. Tigellinus (one of the new commanders of the praetorian guard) conducts the examination of Octavia's maids, but most of them maintain her innocence. Nero then divorces her.

Exturbat Octaviam, sterilem dictitans; exim Poppaeae coniungitur. ea (diu paelex, et adulteri Neronis, mox mariti potens) quendam ex ministris Octaviae impulit servilem ei amorem obicere. actae ob id de ancillis quaestiones et, vi tormentorum victis quibusdam ut falsa adnuerent, plures perstitere sanctitatem dominae tueri. ex quibus 5
una instanti Tigellino castiora esse muliebria Octaviae respondit quam os eius. amovetur tamen civilis discidii specie; mox in Campaniam pulsa est, addita militari custodia.

1 With *sterilem* supply *eam esse.*

2 **mariti**: understand *Neronis* (= 'Nero as her husband', as *adulteri Neronis* = 'Nero as her lover'). The genitives go with *potens.*

4 **vi tormentorum**: slaves were examined under torture for evidence in connection with their owners.

4 **falsa** denotes false confessions.

7 **civilis discidii specie**: 'under the pretence of a legal divorce' (the charge of adultery, which for the emperor's wife was tantamount to a charge of treason, could not be substantiated, so Nero just divorced Octavia, on the grounds of infertility).

31 General view of the Roman forum toward the Palatine Hill beyond. The structures in the foreground are of medieval date.

18 The Roman people disapprove of this. When a rumour spreads that Nero has taken Octavia back, they are delighted and surge on to the Palatine Hill (where Nero's residence was) until soldiers disperse them. Poppaea, afraid that Nero may abandon her, claims that they are in danger from Octavia and her supporters, and that he must kill her.

Inde crebri questus per vulgum; . . . tamquam Nero paenitentia flagitii coniugem revocarit Octaviam. exim laeti Capitolium scandunt deosque tandem venerantur. effigies Poppaeae proruunt, Octaviae imagines gestant umeris, spargunt floribus, foroque ac templis statuunt. itur etiam in principis laudes. iamque et Palatium 5
multitudine complebant, cum emissi militum globi verberibus et intento ferro turbatos disiecere, et Poppaeae honos repositus est. quae, metu atrox ne Nero inclinatione populi mutaretur, provoluta genibus eius ait sibi vitam in extremum adductam a clientelis et servitiis Octaviae, quae plebis sibi nomen indiderint, ea in pace ausi 10
quae vix bello evenirent; arma illa adversus principem sumpta; ducem tantum defuisse; qui facile reperiretur, modo in urbem ipsa pergeret, ad cuius nutum tumultus cierentur; ille consuleret securitati iusta ultione.

1 **. . . tamquam:** some words have been lost from the text here. Tacitus will have said something like: 'a false rumour spread to the effect that (*tamquam*) Nero had recalled Octavia as his wife . . . '

1 **paenitentia:** ablative of cause ('out of regret for his . . .').

2 **scandunt:** various members of the Roman people form the subject of this and the following plural verbs.

3 **deosque tandem venerantur:** i.e. after all the wrongs of Nero's reign, at last they had reason to believe in divine justice and to thank the gods.

5 **itur . . . laudes:** i.e. they even resorted to praising Nero. *itur* (impersonal) is from *eo.*

7 **intento:** from *intendo.*

8 **ne:** introduces a fear clause after *metu* (which is ablative of cause).

9 **genibus:** 'at his knees' (clasped in supplication).

9–11 **sibi . . . sumpta:** Poppaea is claiming that the crowd that had just flocked to the Palatine Hill in spontaneous support of Octavia really consisted of Octavia's slaves and clients (people who attached themselves to a more powerful figure for protection and support), masquerading as the people of Rome, trying to rise against the emperor and threatening the lives of Nero and Poppaea.

9 **extremum** denotes the verge of destruction.

10 **quae** refers to *clientelis* and (neuter plural) *servitiis.*

10 **ea** is neuter accusative plural (object of *ausi*) and is picked up by *quae* in 11.

10 **ausi:** masculine because *clientelis* and *servitiis* really = (masculine) *clientes* and *servi.*

11 **bello evenirent:** *bello* is ablative of time, and *evenirent* is potential or generic subjunctive.

11 **sumpta:** supply *esse* (the indirect statement continues here and in the rest of this sentence).

12–13 Poppaea is claiming that the recent 'uprising' had come to nothing because a leader alone was missing (*defuisse*, from *desum*) in Rome, but a leader would easily be found if Octavia (who was behind the unrest) came to Rome in person from Campania.

12–13 qui ... pergeret: '[she said that] who [= a leader] would easily be found – only let her come [i.e. if only she came] to Rome'.

13–14 ille ... ultione: i.e. Nero should ensure his own safety by executing Octavia in revenge, as she deserved.

19 Duly persuaded by Poppaea's words, Nero decides that an actual confession is needed, and gets Anicetus to pretend that he committed adultery with Octavia. Anicetus is then banished to Sardinia, where he lives in comfortable exile until his death (from natural causes).

Sermo ad metum atque iram accommodatus terruit simul
audientem et accendit. sed parum valebat suspicio in servo et
quaestionibus ancillarum elusa erat. ergo confessionem alicuius
quaeri placet. et visus idoneus maternae necis patrator Anicetus
(classi praefectus). igitur accitum eum Nero operae prioris admonet: 5
solum incolumitati principis adversus insidiantem matrem
subvenisse; locum haud minoris gratiae instare, si coniugem
infensam depelleret; nec manu aut telo opus: fateretur Octaviae
adulterium. magna ei praemia et secessus amoenos promittit; vel, si
negavisset, necem intentat. ille plura etiam quam iussum erat fingit 10
fateturque apud amicos quos velut consilio adhibuerat princeps. tum
in Sardiniam pellitur, ubi non inops exilium toleravit et fato obiit.

1 ad ... accommodatus: i.e. playing on.

2 suspicio in servo: i.e. suspicion in the case of the slave with whom Octavia was accused of committing adultery.

4 placet: 'it was pleasing for a ...' = 'he decided to have a ...'

6–9 solum ... adulterium: indirect statement after *admonet. solum* refers to Anicetus.

7 locum + genitive: i.e. 'an opportunity for'.

8 nec ... opus: i.e. there was no need for Anicetus to resort to violence or bloodshed.

8 fateretur represents a command in the original direct speech.

9–10 si ... intentat: i.e. Nero threatened that he would kill Anicetus if he refused to help.

11 velut consilio: 'as if for [= as] a council of state'. Since the time of Augustus, the emperor used selected friends as an advisory or judicial council, but *velut* here implies that this was a sham council.

12 fato: 'through [the ordinary course of] fate', i.e. he died a natural death.

20 Nero announces in an edict that Octavia seduced Anicetus in an attempt to seize power, and exiles her to the island of Pandateria, where she is put to death shortly afterwards.

At Nero praefectum in spem sociandae classis corruptum et
(incusatae paulo ante sterilitatis oblitus) abactos partus conscientia

libidinum edicto memorat, insulaque Pandateria Octaviam claudit.
non alia exul visentium oculos maiore misericordia adfecit. huic
nuptiarum dies loco funeris fuit, deductae in domum in qua nihil 5
nisi luctuosum haberet, erepto per venenum patre et statim fratre;
tum Poppaea nupta; postremo crimen omni exitio gravius. ac puella
vicesimo aetatis anno, inter centuriones et milites, praesagio
malorum iam vitae exempta, nondum tamen morte adquiescebat.
paucis dehinc interiectis diebus mori iubetur, cum iam viduam se et 10
tantum sororem testaretur. restringitur vinclis venaeque eius per
omnis artus exsolvuntur; et quia pressus pavore sanguis tardius
labebatur, praefervidi balnei vapore enecatur. additurque atrocior
saevitia: caput amputatum latumque in urbem Poppaea vidit.

1 **in spem sociandae classis**: 'with a view to [= in order to realize] the hope of winning over the fleet' (i.e. Nero maintained that the commander Anicetus had been seduced by Octavia as a way of gaining the support of his fleet in her attempt to seize power).

2 **incusatae . . . sterilitatis** denotes Nero's recent charge that Octavia was infertile.

2–3 **conscientia** + genitive = guilty conscience over something. This is an ablative of cause.

5 **loco** + genitive = 'tantamount to'.

5–6 **deductae . . . haberet**: i.e. since she was married into the kind of house (that of Nero and Agrippina) in which she had only grief.

6 **patre . . . statim fratre**: Claudius and Britannicus (who was poisoned soon after Claudius).

7 **nupta** is from *nubo* and refers to marriage to Nero.

7 **crimen**: i.e. the accusation of 1–2.

8 **vicesimo aetatis anno**: actually she was at least twenty-two, so there is probably something wrong with the text here.

8–9 **praesagio . . . adquiescebat**: because she could tell in advance that she would be executed, she was no longer among the living, but she still did not enjoy the peace of death (she was as good as dead, but was left in fear and suspense for several days before she was actually put to death). *exempta* is from *eximo*.

10–11 **cum . . . testaretur**: *cum* means 'although' here. Because of the divorce she was not Nero's wife any more, only (*tantum*) his sister (Nero had been adopted by her father Claudius), and so represented no threat to his relationship with Poppaea.

12–13 **pressus . . . labebatur**: i.e. her terror arrested the movement of her blood and made it flow too slowly.

13 **praefervidi . . . enecatur**: i.e. heat was used to speed the flow of blood, so that she could bleed to death.

Poppaea bore Nero one child (which died after four months), then in AD *65, pregnant again, she died herself, reportedly when kicked by Nero in a fit of temper.*

21 *Shortly before the great fire of Rome* (AD *64), Tigellinus puts on an outdoor orgy and Nero gets married to a man.*

In stagno Agrippae fabricatus est ratem, cui superpositum convivium navium aliarum tractu moveretur. naves auro et ebore distinctae; remigesque exoleti per aetates et scientiam libidinum componebantur. volucris et feras diversis e terris et animalia maris Oceano abusque petiverat. crepidinibus stagni lupanaria adstabant 5
inlustribus feminis completa, et contra scorta visebantur nudis corporibus. iam gestus motusque obsceni; et postquam tenebrae incedebant, circumiecta tecta consonare cantu et luminibus clarescere. ipse per licita et inlicita foedatus nihil flagitii reliquerat, quo corruptior ageret, nisi paucos post dies uni ex illo 10
contaminatorum grege denupsisset. inditum imperatori flammeum; dos et genialis torus et faces nuptiales; cuncta denique spectata quae etiam in femina nox operit.

1–2 **cui . . . moveretur**: the subjunctive expresses purpose ('so that the guests put aboard it could be moved around . . .').

3 **remigesque**: 'and as rowers'.

3 **per**: 'according to'.

5 **Oceano abusque petiverat** = *abusque Oceano petiverat* (the subject is Tigellinus).

9 **ipse**: i.e. Nero.

9–10 **nihil . . . ageret**: 'had left untried no sexual abomination by means of which he might live more depraved' = 'had tried every sexual abomination to heighten the depravity of his existence'. *Flagitii* is partitive genitive, and *quo* introduces a purpose clause.

10–11 **nisi . . . denupsisset** = 'except for marriage to . . .' *paucos post dies* = *post paucos dies.*

13 **etiam in femina**: i.e. even in the case of a female bride, even at a normal wedding (the reference in *cuncta* and the relative clause is to sex on the wedding night).

22 *Next comes the worst fire ever in Rome, causing great terror, confusion, and loss of life – and possibly started on Nero's orders.*

Sequitur clades (forte an dolo principis incertum) omnibus quae huic urbi per violentiam ignium acciderunt gravior atque atrocior. initium in ea parte Circi quae Palatino Caelioque montibus contigua est. impetu pervagatum incendium plana primum, deinde in edita

adsurgens, et rursus inferiora populando, anteiit remedia velocitate 5
et obnoxia urbe artis itineribus hucque et illuc flexis. ad hoc lamenta
paventium feminarum; fessa senum aut rudis pueritiae aetas; quique
sibi quique aliis consulebant, dum trahunt invalidos aut opperiuntur,
cuncta impediebant. et saepe, dum in tergum respectant, lateribus
aut fronte circumveniebantur; vel, si in proxima evaserant, illis 10
quoque igni correptis, etiam quae longinqua crediderant in eodem
casu reperiebant. postremo quid vitarent, quid peterent ambigui,
complere vias, sterni per agros. quidam amissis omnibus fortunis, alii
caritate suorum (quos eripere nequiverant), quamvis patente effugio,
interiere. nec quisquam defendere audebat, crebris multorum minis 15
restinguere prohibentium, et quia alii palam faces iaciebant atque
esse sibi auctorem vociferabantur, sive ut raptus licentius exercerent
seu iussu.

1 **forte ... incertum** = *incertun est utrum* ('whether') *forte an dolo principis illa clades evenerit* ('happened')

1 **omnibus** = *omnibus cladibus* (ablative of comparison).

2 the gravity of the disaster is brought out by fullness of expression, alliteration, assonance, and emphatic placement.

4 **impetu**: ablative of manner.

4–5 **plana ... edita ... inferiora**: these refer to various areas of the city.

5 **populando**: equivalent to the present participle in the nominative.

6 **obnoxia ... flexis**: ablative absolute with causal force followed by ablatives of cause (= 'due to the fact that the city was vulnerable because of its ...').

6 **ad**: could mean 'in addition to' or 'in response to'.

7 **fessa ... aetas**: there were weary old men or inexperienced boys (both feeble and helpless groups).

10 **proxima** denotes 'neighbouring districts' (also referred to by *illis*), which they imagined were far away from the fire and so remote from danger.

11 **igni**: ablative of instrument.

12 **vitarent ... peterent**: deliberative subjunctives in indirect questions.

14 **caritate**: causal ablative.

15 **defendere**: understand *ignem* as the object.

15 **crebris ... minis**: ablative absolute with a causal force.

17 **esse sibi auctorem**: i.e. that they were acting under authority.

23 *Nero takes various relief measures, but wins no gratitude for them because of a rumour that on his private stage he had sung of the destruction of Troy as Rome was destroyed around him.*

Eo in tempore Nero Antii agens non ante in urbem regressus est
quam domui eius ignis propinquaret. sed populo exturbato ac
profugo Campum Martis ac hortos suos patefecit et subitaria aedificia

exstruxit, quae multitudinem inopem acciperent; subvectaque
utensilia ab Ostia, pretiumque frumenti minutum. quae (quamquam 5
popularia) in inritum cadebant, quia pervaserat rumor ipso tempore
flagrantis urbis inisse eum domesticam scaenam et cecinisse
Troianum excidium, praesentia mala vetustis cladibus adsimulantem.

1 **Antii:** locative. Antium was a town not far from Rome.

1–2 **ante . . . quam** = *antequam* ('before').

3 **Campum Martis:** the Campus Martius was a large open space in Rome on the banks of the Tiber.

4 **acciperent:** why subjunctive?

8 Troy (in modern Turkey) was the city of King Priam, and it was captured and burnt down by the Greeks at the end of the legendary Trojan War.

24 *The conflagration is ended by means of a fire-break, but then starts up again. The devastation is widespread and serious.*

Sexto demum die finis incendio factus, prorutis per immensum
aedificiis, ut continuae violentiae campus occurreret. necdum positus
metus aut redierat plebi spes; rursum grassatus ignis, patulis magis
urbis locis, eoque strages hominum minor; delubra deum et porticus
latius procidere. plusque infamiae id incendium habuit, quia 5
praediis Tigellini proruperat, videbaturque Nero condendae urbis
novae et cognomento suo appellandae gloriam quaerere.

In regiones quattuordecim Roma dividitur, quarum quattuor
integrae manebant, tres solo tenus deiectae; septem reliquis pauca
tectorum vestigia supererant, lacera et semusta. Domuum et 10
insularum et templorum quae amissa sunt numerum inire haud
promptum fuerit. sed aedesque Statoris Iovis Numaeque regia
exusta, iam opes tot victoriis quaesitae et Graecarum artium decora,
exim monumenta ingeniorum antiqua. quamvis in tanta resurgentis
urbis pulchritudine, multa seniores meminerant quae reparari 15
nequibant.

1 **immensum:** denotes a vast area.

2 **necdum . . . positus:** understand *erat. necdum* = 'But not yet', and *pono* here means 'lay aside'.

3–4 **patulis . . . locis:** local ablative.

4 **eoque** = *et eo* (adverb).

6–7 **videbaturque Nero . . . quaerere:** because Tigellinus was one of Nero's supporters, people thought that the fire started up again on Nero's orders, so that he could found a new city on the site of Rome and name it after himself.

9 **solo tenus deiectae:** i.e. were levelled to the ground.

12 **fuerit:** potential subjunctive. The perfect tense has the same force as the present tense ('it would be').

12 **aedesque . . . regia:** the temple of Jupiter Stator was vowed by Romulus, and Numa was the second King of Rome, so these were very ancient and venerable buildings.

13 **iam opes . . . decora:** *iam* ('further/besides') introduces some more items in the list of things destroyed by the fire. *opes* denotes precious objects of all kinds taken as spoils of war, while *decora* (from *decus*) denotes artistic masterpieces in particular.

14 **monumenta ingeniorum antiqua:** 'ancient records/documents of genius/men of genius' (i.e. works of great authors).

14–15 **quamvis . . . pulchritudine:** i.e. although the city when rebuilt was very beautiful. *in* = 'amidst'.

32 Coin of Gordian III (AD 238–44) depicting the Colossus of Nero, which stood at the entrance to his Golden House complex and later gave its name to the adjacent amphitheatre, the Colosseum.

25 *Nero profits from the devastation by building himself a palace on a large tract cleared by the fire, but he also rebuilds the rest of Rome on safer principles.*

Ceterum Nero usus est patriae ruinis exstruxitque domum, in qua
haud perinde gemmae et aurum miraculo essent quam arva et stagna
et hinc silvae, inde aperta spatia et prospectus. urbis quae domui
supererant non passim erecta sed latis viarum spatiis cohibitaque
aedificiorum altitudine ac patefactis areis additisque porticibus, 5
quae frontem insularum protegerent. porticus Nero sua pecunia
exstructurum pollicitus est. ea decorem quoque novae urbi attulere.
erant tamen qui crederent veterem illam formam salubritati magis
conduxisse, quoniam angustiae itinerum et altitudo tectorum non
perinde solis vapore perrumperentur. 10

1 **domum:** this is the famous *domus aurea* ('Golden House'), a lavish palace with extensive grounds (of the type normally found in country estates) in the very centre of Rome.

2 **haud perinde . . . quam:** 'not as much . . . as'.

2 **miraculo essent:** the subjunctive expresses (Nero's) purpose, and the dative is predicative ('would be for a marvel' = 'would cause amazement').

3 **hinc . . . inde** refer to different areas of the grounds.

3–4 **urbis . . . supererant:** the parts of Rome that were not taken over for the Golden House. *quae = illa quae.*

4 **latis viarum spatiis:** i.e. with broad streets.

5 **areis:** i.e. courtyards inside the apartment blocks or spaces around/in front of them (to hinder the spread of fire).

6 **protegerent** alludes to protection from the weather and traffic passing by.

7 **exstructurum:** supply *se* and *esse.*

7 **ea:** refers to all the features of the rebuilding just mentioned, which were not just utilitarian.

26 *Despite Nero's generosity and offerings to appease the gods (as if they had caused the fire) people still believe that he had ordered it, so he makes the Christians scapegoats and executes many of them.*

Mox petita dis piacula. sed non largitionibus principis aut deum
placamentis decedebat infamia quin iussum incendium crederetur.
ergo abolendo rumori Nero subdidit reos et quaesitissimis poenis
adfecit quos (per flagitia invisos) vulgus Christianos appellabat.
multitudo ingens haud perinde in crimine incendii quam odio 5
humani generis convicti sunt. et pereuntibus addita ludibria, ut
ferarum tergis contecti laniatu canum interirent, aut crucibus adfixi
aut flammati, atque ubi defecisset dies in usum nocturni luminis
uterentur. hortos suos ei spectaculo Nero obtulerat et circense

33 Octagonal hall (*triclinium?*) of Nero's Domus Aurea, Rome. A curious labyrinth of 142 rooms and corridors, the Golden House was a massive experiment in concrete-centered design principles, conducted by architects Severus and Celer.

ludicrum edebat, habitu aurigae permixtus plebi vel curriculo insistens. unde miseratio oriebatur, tamquam non utilitate publica sed in saevitiam unius absumerentur. 10

1 **dis . . . deum**: dative plural and genitive plural of *deus*.

2 **quin . . . crederetur**: 'so as to prevent the fire from being believed to have been ordered'. Here, as often, *quin* introduces a clause with a negative force after a negative main clause denoting the ineffectiveness of counter-measures.

3 **abolendo rumori**: dative of purpose.

4 **quos** = *illos quos*.

4 **flagitia**: the Christians were believed to be guilty of infanticide, cannibalism and incest amongst other things.

5 **haud perinde . . . quam**: 'not so much . . . as'.

5 **incendii** = 'arson'.

5–6 **odio humani generis**: causal ablative. The Christians were supposed to hate mankind because they had different moral standards, kept away from social gatherings, would not sacrifice to gods other than their own, and so on.

6 **convicti sunt**: the subject is *multitudo ingens*, which denotes plurality (= *plurimi*) – hence the plural verb here.

6 **ut** introduces a consecutive (result) clause.

7–8 **aut . . . flammati**: supply *interirent*. People were set on fire by being dressed in the *tunica molesta*, a tunic covered with pitch.

8–9 in usum . . . uterentur: i.e. they were employed to serve as torches at night.

9 obtulerat: from *offero*.

9 circense: Nero had his own circus (a place for holding games such as chariot-racing) in his gardens.

11 unde: i.e. as a result of Nero's cruelty.

11 tamquam: 'on the grounds that'.

11 utilitate publica: causal ablative.

12 in: 'with a view to' (i.e. so as to gratify).

34 Frescoed corridors in Nero's Domus Aurea, Rome. The walls and vaults of the Golden House were once fantastically decorated with frescoes and moulded stucco (plaster). Today, they are badly faded.

27 Believing the assurances (based solely on a dream) of a lunatic from Carthage that he has found a cave filled with gold, Nero becomes more extravagant than ever and squanders his resources.

Inlusit Neroni fortuna per vanitatem ipsius et promissa Bassi, qui (origine Poenus, mente turbida) nocturnae quietis imaginem ad spem haud dubiae rei traxit, vectusque Romam, principis aditum emercatus, expromit repertum in agro suo specum altitudine immensa, quo magna vis auri contineretur; Dido, condita 5 Carthagine, illas opes abdidisse, ne novus populus nimia pecunia lasciviret aut reges Numidarum cupidine auri ad bellum accenderentur. igitur Nero, non auctoris, non ipsius negotii fide satis spectata, auget rumorem mittitque qui praedam adveherent. ab oratoribusque materia in laudem principis adsumpta est: non enim 10 solitas tantum fruges gigni, sed nova ubertate provenire terram et obvias opes deferre deos. gliscebat interim luxuria spe inani, consumebanturque veteres opes. Bassus, effosso agro suo latisque circum arvis (dum hunc vel illum locum promissi specus adseverat), tandem posita vaecordia, non falsa antea somnia sua seque tunc 15 primum elusum admirans, pudorem et metum morte voluntaria effugit.

2 **origine**: ablative of respect.

2 **mente turbida**: ablative of description (like *altitudine immensa* in 4–5).

2–3 **ad spem . . . traxit**: i.e. took as a promise of something certain.

4 **repertum**: supply *esse.*

5 **Dido**: accusative, in a continuation of the indirect statement. Dido was the legendary queen who founded the city of Carthage in Numidia (in north Africa) and who committed suicide after being left by her lover Aeneas (a Trojan survivor of the fall of Troy and the famous ancestor of the Roman race). The story was told in Virgil's epic poem called the *Aeneid.*

9 **spectata**: from *specto* ('examine').

9 **qui praedam adveherent**: understand *Romam* here; the subjunctive expresses purpose ('men to . . .').

10 **materia**: supply *haec* ('this topic was employed for . . .').

10 **enim**: introduces the praise of Nero by the orators (at the Neronian Games) in indirect statement.

11 **tantum**: goes with *non* ('not only . . .').

12 **obvias**: 'in our way' = 'without being searched for'.

13 **effosso**: agrees with *agro* (the nearest noun) but also applies to *arvis.*

14 **hunc vel illum locum**: understand *esse* ('that this [place] or that was the location of . . .').

16 **posita vaecordia**: i.e. Bassus finally recovered from his delusion (but he was still amazed that for the first time a dream of his had proved to be false and he had been fooled by it).

By such antics, Nero, though popular with the masses, alienated the upper classes and the army. In AD 65, a large conspiracy was unearthed that comprised senators, knights and praetorians. The plot was ruthlessly suppressed and any suspected of involvement were executed, exiled, or forced to commit suicide. Seneca was one of those who ended his own life like this. Another conspiracy followed in AD 66 and was also suppressed. But Nero's position now hung by a thread. Grumblings in the army caused an open revolt in Gaul in the spring of AD 68, which was put down by the legions in Germany. But, spurred by the Gallic uprising, the army in Spain declared against Nero, and the German legions soon followed. The praetorian guard and the Senate then deserted Nero, and he was declared a public enemy (hostis).

28 As his death approaches, Nero is terrified by bad dreams and omens. On the day of his death, he finds himself isolated, flees to a freedman's villa and finally commits suicide.

Terrebatur evidentibus portentis somniorum et ominum. vidit
per quietem navem sibi regenti extortum gubernaculum trahique se
ab Octavia uxore in artissimas tenebras et pinnatarum formicarum
multitudine oppleri; asturconem (quo maxime laetabatur) posteriore
corporis parte in simiae speciem transfiguratum ac tantum capite 5
integro hinnitus edere canoros. de Mausoleo, sponte foribus
patefactis, exaudita vox est nomine eum cientis.

Ad mediam fere noctem excitatus, ut comperit stationem militum
recessisse, prosiluit e lecto misitque circum amicos; et quia nihil a
quoquam renuntiabatur, ipse cum paucis hospitia singulorum adiit. 10
verum clausis omnium foribus, respondente nullo, in cubiculum
rediit, unde iam et custodes diffugerant, direptis etiam stragulis. ac
statim Spiculum murmillonem vel quemlibet alium percussorem,
cuius manu periret, requisiit, et nemine reperto, 'Ergo ego,' inquit,
'nec amicum habeo nec inimicum?' procurritque, quasi 15
praecipitaturus se in Tiberim.

Sed revocato rursus impetu, aliquid secretioris latebrae ad
colligendum animum desideravit, et (offerente Phaonte liberto
suburbanum suum) nudo pede et tunicatus, paenulam obsoleti coloris
superinduit; adopertoque capite et ante faciem optento sudario 20
equum inscendit, quattuor solis comitantibus, inter quos Sporus erat.
statimque tremore terrae et fulgure adverso pavefactus audiit e

proximis castris clamorem militum et sibi adversa et Galbae prospera
ominantium. equo autem ex odore abiecti in via cadaveris
consternato, detecta facie agnitus est a quodam missicio praetoriano 25
et salutatus. dimissis equis, inter fruticeta ac vepres aegre ad
aversum villae parietem evasit. aquam ex lacuna poturus manu
hausit et 'Haec est,' inquit, 'Neronis decocta.' dein divolsa sentibus
paenula quadripes per angustias effossae cavernae receptus in
proximam cellam decubuit super lectum modica culcita instructum. 30

Tunc uno quoque instante ut quam primum se impendentibus
contumeliis eriperet, scrobem coram fieri imperavit, flens atque
identidem dictitans 'Qualis artifex pereo!' inter moras perlatos a
cursore Phaonti codicillos praeripuit, legitque se hostem a senatu
iudicatum et quaeri ut puniatur more maiorum, interrogavitque 35
quale id genus esset poenae. et cum comperisset nudi hominis
cervicem inseri furcae, corpus virgis ad necem caedi, conterritus duos
pugiones (quos secum extulerat) arripuit, temptataque utriusque acie
rursus condidit, causatus nondum adesse fatalem horam. ac modo
Sporum hortabatur ut lamentari ac plangere inciperet, modo orabat 40
ut se aliquis ad mortem capessendam exemplo iuvaret, interdum
segnitiem suam his verbis increpabat: 'Vivo deformiter, turpiter.'

Iamque equites appropinquabant, quibus praeceptum erat ut
vivum eum adtraherent. quod ut sensit, ferrum iugulo adegit,
iuvante Epaphrodito. semianimisque adhuc irrumpenti centurioni 45
et (paenula ad vulnus adposita) in auxilium se venisse simulanti non
aliud respondit quam 'Sero!' et 'Haec est fides!' atque in ea voce
defecit, exstantibus rigentibusque oculis usque ad horrorem
formidinemque visentium.

1–2 **vidit per quietem**: i.e. he dreamed that.

2 **navem**: object of *regenti*. According to the ship of state metaphor, someone running a country was said to be in charge of the helm of government (there may also be allusion here to the attempt to kill Agrippina by means of the collapsible boat).

2 **sibi . . . extortum**: *sibi* is dative of disadvantage with *extortum* (*esse*).

4–5 **posteriore . . . parte**: ablative of respect.

5 **tantum** is the adverb.

6 **hinnitus . . . canoros**: i.e. the horse's head was whinnying a tune.

6 **Mausoleo**: the Mausoleum of Augustus, a large and ornate tomb in which many of the imperial family were laid to rest.

7 **vox . . . cientis**: 'the voice of someone summoning'.

8 **ut**: 'when'.

8 **stationem militum** denotes the cohort of the praetorian guard on duty at the palace.

9 **misitque circum amicos:** 'and he sent [men] around his friends' (to summon them to him).

10 **hospitia:** probably refers to rooms in the palace used as accommodation for his friends (as this paragraph seems centred on the palace) but could denote houses in Rome where his friends were.

12 **custodes:** may refer to sentries inside the palace, or servants acting as caretakers.

14 **cuius manu periret:** the subjunctive expresses purpose.

15 **amicum ... inimicum:** i.e. a friend prepared to put him out of his misery, or an enemy who would be glad to kill him.

17 **aliquid secretioris latebrae ad:** 'something of a [= some sort of] more secluded hiding-place for the purpose of ...'

21 **Sporus:** this was a boy whom Nero had reportedly castrated and married.

23 **proximis castris:** the camp of the praetorian guard, who are probably acclaiming the rebel Galba as the new emperor.

23 **sibi:** refers to Nero.

28 **decocta:** an invention of Nero in more luxurious times, this was a pure and refreshing drink made by boiling water and then chilling it by plunging it into snow.

29 **quadripes ... cavernae:** i.e. crawling on all fours through a narrow tunnel which had been dug into the villa.

31 **uno quoque:** 'each one' (of his companions). *quoque* is from *quisque.*

33 **qualis artifex pereo:** i.e. what a great artist the world is losing in me.

34 **hostem:** a public enemy (who could be lawfully put to death by any citizen).

35 **quaeri ... maiorum:** 'that it was being aimed that he would be punished according to the custom of their ancestors' = 'that the aim was for him to be punished ...'

36–7 **nudi ... caedi:** the criminal was stripped, had his neck inserted into a forked framework (and his arms fastened to the projecting ends) and was flogged to death.

41 **se ... iuvaret:** i.e. help Nero to take his own life by setting him the example of committing suicide.

42 **vivo deformiter, turpiter:** i.e. how ugly and vulgar my life has become.

43 **quibus:** dative, with the impersonal *praeceptum erat* (which is followed by an indirect command).

44 **quod ut sensit:** *quod* is the relative and *ut* means 'when'.

45 **Epaphrodito:** Nero's private secretary.

45 **centurioni:** indirect object with *non aliud respondit quam* ('replied nothing other than' = 'replied only ...').

48–9 **usque ad ... visentium:** 'up to the point of horror and dread of those looking' = 'to the absolute horror of the onlookers'.

NERO APPRECIATION

Passage 1 Suetonius Nero *9–11.*

During the *quinquennium*, Augustan standards of government were proclaimed; the Senate's role was revitalized; the influence of the hated imperial freedmen was curtailed; clemency characterized the emperor's actions, and on the frontiers there were military successes. The main reason adduced by Tacitus (*Ann.* 13.2–4) is the influence of the praetorian prefect Burrus and the emperor's tutor Seneca, who diverted Nero's nastier impulses down the paths of least offensiveness, while also opposing Agrippina's domineering incursions (on which, see Introduction section 9). For instance, Burrus dissuaded a drunken

Nero from a decision to kill his mother, and Seneca composed Nero's inaugural speech with its high principles of government. Remarkably, these principles were implemented, and Nero, at least on official occasions, behaved decently and seemed a good emperor. But there were also worrying signs right from the start (compare passages 2–6 below, and see further *Ann.* 13.3–25).

Passage 2 Tacitus Annals *13.15–17.*

Despite some scholarly doubts (see Barrett 1996 170–2), it is most likely that Britannicus was murdered. His sudden and timely end, amid a mop-up of former sources of influence at court (such as Pallas), makes foul play a very strong likelihood, and Britannicus, as the natural son of the previous emperor, was a threat to Nero's position. Other inconvenient siblings in Roman history suffered similar fates. This murder foreshadows the killings of Agrippina and Octavia, but it is particularly illuminating to compare and contrast it with the assassination of Britannicus' father Claudius by Agrippina (in *Claudius* passage 18). Numerous points of similarity (can you see them?) make for bleak and eerie echoes, suggest that Nero is a true son of his mother, and bring out the irony of him taking against the very one who made him emperor and using her own methods in a way contrary to her interests. There are also important differences: e.g. the villain here is even more horrifying – a murderer just seventeen years old who sodomizes his victim first, and who (unlike the fearful Agrippina in *Claudius* 18) is brazen, unafraid, and actually terrifies others. And Tacitus builds up sympathy for Britannicus (how exactly?), rather than the revulsion he aroused for Claudius. The grim (but not certain) detail of the rape is held back until line 29 for added shock and forms part of the final sentence's powerful climax, with cumulative impact in the piling up of outrage after outrage.

Passage 3 Tacitus Annals *13.25.*

Suetonius, in his *Nero* 26, has similar stories (with the added details of pilfered goods being put on sale in the palace and people as they returned from dinner being stabbed and thrown into sewers), and he says that such conduct was not just youthful horseplay but indicative of the true (deeply flawed) character of Nero. Tacitus (who describes these actions as *foeda lascivia* 'disgraceful excesses') would have agreed, and he presents here with economy a brief but very revealing and damning glimpse of numerous and various failings in Nero. Several extraordinary inversions bring out his perversity and complete unfitness to rule: instead of protecting his subjects and ensuring safety in the streets, he attacks them and makes Rome a dangerous place; he employs soldiers (and gladiators!) not in wars on Rome's enemies but against the Romans themselves when they resist his assaults, and his responsibility for Rome resembling a captured city (6–7) implies that he is a conquering, pillaging enemy of Rome.

Passage 4 Tacitus Annals *13.45.*

The tradition depicts Poppaea Sabina as a sensuous and extravagant hedonist who (according to Cassius Dio 62.28) had her mules shod in gold and bathed in the milk of 500 asses every day (he adds that after her death, her husband Nero missed her so much that he castrated a boy called Sporus who looked like her and treated him in every way as a wife). In passage 4, Tacitus halts his narrative to describe her and, unusually for the *Annals*, ushers in a personage with a detailed character sketch – all of which implies that she will be important (and also suggests that the austere historian may be despite himself rather fascinated by this femme fatale!). Tacitus does allow Poppaea good points at 4–6 (as part of her attractiveness), but he takes care to swamp them with bad points at 6ff. and negative comments at 1–3 (showing her in a poor light from the start). This picture of a seductive and corrupt woman (rivalling Agrippina) fully explains why the young Nero would have become infatuated with Poppaea. This is the beginning of Tacitus' account of the murder of Agrippina (on which, see the Introduction section 9), and it is an aptly ominous start (the very first line, Poppaea's character in itself, her interest in Nero at 11f., her first steps in his direction at 12f.).

Passage 5 Tacitus Annals *13.46.*

The remaining steps to Nero are speedily taken, as his interest is aroused; a meeting with Poppaea takes place, and she ensnares him. She is presented as an expert manipulator: at 7f. she shrewdly aims at Nero's vanity, with rapid results (8f.), and then at 9–14 she strengthens her hold on him variously (how exactly?). At 9–14 (now that she has acquired her real object all along – the emperor), she is also aiming at the removal from the scene of her nuisance of a husband, and again she promptly (14ff.) gets what she wants. (This presentation of Poppaea has real impact, although one wonders how Tacitus could know what she said and did.) As for Otho, the joke is on him either way: either he was stupid to go on and on about his wife's attractions in front of someone like Nero or his deliberate attempt to use her to increase his power backfired (thanks largely to his wife) with his transfer to Lusitania (at 2–3, Tacitus gives more weight to this second alternative, which represents Nero as even more of a puppet). There is also dark humour in Nero trying to prey on a friend's wife and promptly becoming her prey instead. This picture of Nero controlled by an attractive and ambitious woman is another link with Claudius, implying that Nero was no better than him.

Passage 6 Tacitus Annals *14.1.*

In Tacitus' original (unexcerpted) narrative, after passage 5 Poppaea was dropped for twelve chapters in the *Annals* (and Agrippina was not mentioned for even longer than that), so their sudden reappearance here is dramatic. To stress Poppaea's role as an arch-manipulator (and Nero's as a dupe), here again she easily bends him to her will, with a flurry of well-aimed points and ploys (especially in 4, 5, 8 and 9f.). As a skilled and unscrupulous speaker, she exaggerates and lies (most notably in 7), and it is particularly brazen of her to criticize Nero for being under another's control while she herself is controlling him (so she dominates the passage while he is much less in evidence). For emphasis, Nero's crime is referred to twice, at the start and close, and the fuller and more condemnatory reference is saved until the end (with *odia* as the very last word).

Passage 7 Tacitus Annals *14.2.*

With effective arrangement of his material, Tacitus takes us from everybody's desire for Agrippina's power to be broken (6.11f.) to her own desire to keep it, from one seduction of the emperor to another, and from the ploys (allowed to succeed) of one prominent and ambitious female to those of another (not allowed to succeed). The incest, which acquires a particularly nasty tinge from Nero's recent decision to murder his mother, illustrates the monstrousness of the court, where there is little real love (but rather lust and longing for power), where the natural mother–son relationship is perverted, and where Poppaea has as her rival Nero's own mother. This is one of the few cases in which Tacitus indicates disagreement among his sources. He points out that most writers agree with Cluvius and highlights his version by presenting it first, at greater length and in more detail. Presumably, Tacitus thinks that Cluvius' account is distinctly possible, if not definite. He thus includes some shocking material without actually committing himself to it and reminds us before her death that Agrippina was herself evil (at 11ff. her character is blackened, whether the incest was her idea or not).

Passage 8 Tacitus Annals *14.3.*

There is a chilling immediacy in this intimate view of the plotters coolly discussing the mechanics of the assassination of the emperor's own mother. The terse and alliterative *placuitque primo venenum* in 4 implies first thoughts eagerly grasped at, but that is followed by more careful consideration as three objections are raised (which reveal Agrippina as a canny opponent). Next, in 8 the early position of *ferrum et caedes*, outside its clause, seems to suggest a second idea blurted out, but this too is followed by objections. Then, in 11, an ex-slave comes up with an idea which has the benefits of catching Agrippina off guard and allowing her death to be passed off as an accident, and he supports it with a flurry of points at 14ff. (involving the supreme hypocrisy of 16f., where *pietati* is left to the very end). But no explanation is offered here (or presumably was by Anicetus) of just how this (rather preposterous) collapsible boat would work, and how it would manage to kill Agrippina (who could swim), and the use of winds and waves as a cover (16) would depend entirely on weather conditions. Nonetheless, the scheme will shortly be readily embraced, so that Nero seems a clown, again rather like Claudius. Do you see any other links to Claudius in passages 7 and 8?

Passage 9 Tacitus Annals *14.4.*

You may feel some sour satisfaction at Agrippina the one now being manipulated, but here she does appear in rather a better light (as a fallible and fearful victim), especially next to Nero (and any sympathy felt for her heightens one's revulsion for him). There is a powerful atmosphere of hypocrisy and deceit, as a religious festival is exploited for murderous ends and Nero plays a role intended to lure and lull Agrippina, uses various ploys (behaving in fact just as a *genuinely* loving son should), and includes (at 6f. and 11ff.) touches well aimed at a proud woman eager to recover her intimacy with her son. The condemnation is heightened by the repetition of *mater*, by *facinori* in 8 and by *ferum animum* in 15, where Tacitus allocates more words and more colour to the second alternative (which brings out the viciousness and pathos). But again, a grimly clownish element is in evidence: at 9f., shortly after Nero counted on a woman's readiness to believe the best, a suspicious Agrippina believes the worst of him and all his hard work proves futile; so too, his efforts to get back her trust at 11ff. are wasted when the boat fails to kill her.

Passage 10 Tacitus Annals *14.5.*

There is a comedy of errors from the start. The weather means that the excuses of an accident at sea or a storm won't do. But the absurd Nero still sends his mother off on the boat. In the long and initially leisurely sentence at 2–7 there is irony in the two women's relaxed state and Acerronia's cheerful reading of events immediately prior to the attempt on their lives. The grotesque misfire thanks to the couch means that the bungling plotters (who presumably put the couch there to get Agrippina under the weight) could not even manage to use enough lead to do the job properly. Still worse, 9ff. show that even the basic precaution of ensuring that most of the (supplied) crew was in on the plot had not been taken. The farcical capsizing at 10–13 is followed by the cruelly humorous death of Acerronia. The passage ends with some pointed contrasts – a deadly seriousness after all the comical antics, coolness and method after confused chaos, and an efficient lone woman after the inept men. Many readers will now feel a bit more sympathy for Agrippina (why exactly?) and some respect for her self-control and resourcefulness.

Passage 11 Tacitus Annals *14.6.*

The focus stays on Agrippina, extending the contrast with the accomplices of passage 10 and also preparing for contrast with Nero in passage 12 (where he is panicky, bankrupt of ideas, and reliant on a freedman for major assistance). Tacitus takes us inside Agrippina's mind, and with his interpretation she is cool and resourceful: she grasps the point at once, carefully reviews all of the evidence supporting her conclusion, and then briskly decides on and initiates her solution. The feigned ignorance of the plot via the message seems a shrewd enough move in a difficult situation (it might buy her time to gather support, whereas recriminations or silence or flight would probably stampede Nero into another attack), and she reinforces that with the pretence in 9 (expecting her son to have spies in her house).

Examine 6–12 for sombre irony and foreshadowing of Agrippina's death, and consider why Tacitus alludes to her avarice there.

Passage 12 Tacitus Annals *14.7.*

The focus switches to Nero, who comes across as even more of a (dangerous) clown. After the nasty shock for the poor man at 1f., there is a sly rebound in *exanimis*, as the would-be murderer is the one who is now 'dead'. At 2–5, in a grotesque parody of a naughty child afraid of mother, the emperor's imagination runs away with him (and he is quite wrong about Agrippina's immediate intentions). He can only turn to his expert advisers, who are equally ineffectual (and equally immoral, condoning matricide). There is tart humour as Seneca passes the buck to Burrus, and he passes it to Anicetus (the brief, blunt and alliterative *perpetraret Anicetus promissa* in 10f. suggests Burrus suddenly seeing a way out and blurting it out). Now (with a contrasting briskness) an ex-slave takes over as the saviour of the day (as Nero admits, apparently unabashed, in 12). At 13ff. Nero finally has an idea, an idiotic one, outrageously perverting the truth. Play-acting again (note the sneer in *scaenam*, 14), he tries to incriminate Agrippina and justify her death as suicide. How plausible is his scheme, and how does it mesh with her actual end at 13.15ff.?

Passage 13 Tacitus Annals *14.8.*

This economical narrative (restricted to details that contribute to mood and are condemnatory) employs a cinematic technique, presenting the assassination in four short scenes which take us ever closer to Agrippina and the act of murder. At 1–7, in the crowd scene, with a panoramic sweep there is a lively shifting of viewpoint and a realistic confusion (aided by the failure to explain the identity of the people and the reasons for their actions at 2–3). There is also a great show of spontaneous support for Agrippina by them (in contrast to her own son and his court), until the dramatic and menacing close at 7, which looks forward with an apt change of tone and direction. In 8–10, the focus is narrowed: fewer people figure, and we are brought to the villa, and then inside it to the door of Agrippina's bedroom. Tacitus skims details and gets to the door within a few words, suggesting a speedy, relentless advance. Then, 10–15 take us inside the bedroom and present first only two characters (females), and then just Agrippina, prior to the entry of a full three male assassins. The narrative pace slows somewhat here, as Tacitus builds atmosphere and some pathos (the dim light, Agrippina's isolation and anxious thoughts). At 15ff. there is a tight focus on the killers and their prey. In a few lines, she is quickly murdered, but her death still has impact (the brutality of the clubbing and the many blows, and the dignified defiance of Agrippina, who briskly repudiates her son and seems much braver than the assassins and Nero, who leaves the actual deed to others).

Passage 14 Tacitus Annals *14.9–10.*

Typically, this is a bleak end to the whole episode, and nobody comes out of it well. Nero appears at his worst. For example, there is the examination of Agrippina's corpse, which Tacitus does not accept as fact but still includes as it reflects so badly on Nero (in Suetonius he handles the corpse, while drinking, and praises some of her limbs, while criticizing others). Agrippina herself at 5–8 is depicted as in part to blame for her death, because of her appalling ambition (in the light of *Annals* 13.1ff. the inference to be drawn here is that she wanted her son to be emperor so that she could rule through him, and was prepared to die for that). Hypocrisy and deception (major elements in this episode generally) are here shown as not restricted to Nero but encompassing many more (at 12ff.), and one senses an increasing disgust on Tacitus' part as he depicts the rot spreading further and further. In this passage, as throughout, he engages our interest and emotions, and produces powerful implicit criticism (not moralizing openly, but getting his point across by more subtle means). Re-examine passage 14, looking for telling details, colouring, contrast, repetition of points, and effective ordering of material.

Passage 15 Tacitus Annals *14. 14–15.*

Nero was a lover of Greek culture, and in Greece chariot-racing was the sport of royalty and great athletes, while musicians were highly regarded. In Rome, however, conservative opinion disapproved of various aspects of Greek civilization (as demoralizing) and viewed racing a chariot and singing to the lyre in public as not suitable for an upper-class gentleman and unconscionable for an emperor (especially because actors and other public performers in Rome normally came from the lower social orders and were often ex-slaves). Hence Tacitus' withering onslaught here, presenting Nero as a pretentious (2–4) and undignified exhibitionist and this whole business as not simply ludicrous but positively damaging to Rome (Nero is shown as degrading not just himself but also many others, including respectable people, and at 9ff. there is a rather lurid sketch of the Juvenalia's massively deleterious effect on morals). Suetonius (*Nero* 20–2) has more scandalous stories in this connection.

Passage 16 Suetonius Nero *22–5.*

Nero's almost complete lack of sense and tact is illustrated in this passage (which also reflects broader Roman prejudice against Greeks as tricky and untrustworthy). His penchant for showmanship was united with his love of all things Greek in a single Grand Tour. He won every prize and, despite some pleas to the contrary, it seems safe to say that his victories were not entirely due to his abilities. The whole episode has an air of farce, especially the mock triumph at 29ff. (compare Caligula's similarly laughable 'triumph' at Suet. *Cal.* 47). Adding insult to injury, Nero used a chariot favoured by the great Augustus himself (Beacham 1999, 197–278). The degradation of the honoured past and the dishonourable nature of the present could not have been more clear. One incident during his tour is particularly noteworthy, and foreshadowed Nero's downfall. While in Greece, Nero summoned his most successful and popular general, Corbulo, from his command in Syria and ordered him to be executed; Corbulo anticipated this ignominious end by suicide (Cassius Dio 62(63).17.5–6). In the provinces, the emperor's military commanders, even such successful ones, were now on dangerous ground. These very men were to precipitate Nero's end.

Passage 17 Tacitus Annals *14.60.*

The many murders in the *Annals*, while usually differentiated, are often linked. The death of Octavia is part of a whole nexus of killings of family members. It has a clear connection with the murder of another female relative of Nero's – Agrippina (e.g. the part played by Poppaea and Anicetus, the crowd of well-wishers broken up by menacing troops, the lone woman slain by soldiers). But there are significant differences too: this assassination involves evil versus goodness, is more appalling and much more pathetic. As such, it is also reminiscent of the murder in passage 2 of Octavia's brother (another young, innocent, and isolated victim of Nero and his circle). Analyse the role of Poppaea in this passage and the next.

Passage 18 Tacitus Annals *14.60f.*

Of the three protagonists in this narrative, Poppaea is the prime mover. She may be largely in the wings but she does appears in three important places. She holds an aptly prominent position near the start, engineering the charge of (treasonable) adultery in 17.2f. Her major (and crucial) appearance is round about the centre, in this passage, where she is directly responsible for Nero's decision to kill Octavia. She also figures unforgettably at the end (20.14), where she views Octavia's severed head, so that one leaves this episode with Poppaea (and her quarry) uppermost in one's thoughts. Active, evil, and triumphant, she contrasts directly with Octavia, heightening sympathy for her. Examine Nero's role in passages 18 and 19.

Passage 19 Tacitus Annals *14.62.*

The second protagonist, Nero, is the tool. He is one of the villains of the story and he does emerge from it as callous and murderous, but although he issues the orders (and is very forceful with Anicetus at 5ff. here), he is in fact largely a puppet, whose strings are pulled by Poppaea in the background. She now has the cowardly and gullible emperor so much under her influence that she induces him to kill his own wife by means of the arrant nonsense at 18.9ff. Also part of the indictment of Nero and his court are the pointed barbs at 18.3 and 18.5; the effrontery of Nero and Poppaea accusing another of sexual misconduct (especially Nero's wronged and innocent wife); and the botching of both accusations of adultery (see 2f. here and 20.1f.). Investigate Octavia's role in passage 20.

Passage 20 Tacitus Annals *14.63f.*

Throughout this whole episode, the third protagonist (Octavia, the victim) is almost entirely on her own against her two powerful opponents and all their helpers, and for her things keep on going from bad to worse, so that there is a growing sense of tragic inevitability. But Tacitus does not overdo the poignancy: she is not conspicuous in the narrative until 4ff., and it is only there (shortly before she is murdered) that he starts to build up the pathos. Much of it is obvious, but note that in 4 the observers' pity for this exile (as opposed to the exiled Anicetus) encourages similar pity in readers; 8f. look like a refinement in cruelty, because (as victims of torture attest) the anticipation is often harder to bear than what is actually inflicted; and at 11ff. Tacitus invites us to picture her watching, helpless and terrified, as her veins are opened (not just one or two but veins all over her body, so that she is hurt and disfigured) and she is carried into a painfully hot bath, where she dies, a bloody mess, and then is beheaded. All this should ensure that we do not feel cloying boredom at just another murder by Nero.

Passage 21 Tacitus Annals *15.37.*

Tacitus' version of the great fire (on which, see Introduction section 9) has drama, pathos, and horror, and brings out the full extent of the disaster. He allows that Nero helped the people and rebuilt the city well, and, unlike the other ancient sources, he does not state unequivocally that Nero was behind the fire; but he clearly believed that there was a distinct possibility that he was involved to some degree (graduating now to mass-murder and wholesale devastation). So that his readers would suspect that too and infer that even if Nero was not responsible for this catastrophe, he did at least take advantage of it and came out of the whole episode badly; throughout his narrative he openly suggests the emperor's guilt and depicts his failings, and more covertly makes use of rumour, negative reactions, innuendo and dexterous arrangement of subject-matter. Here, as often in Tacitus, context is important. The orgy of Tigellinus contrasts markedly and extensively with passage 22, heightening its impact. Examine passage 22, looking for these contrasts (especially at 22.6ff.). In addition, the levity, promiscuity, and extravagance in 21 seem even more culpable in the light of what immediately follows, and Nero is here portrayed as somebody who perverts marriage, custom, decency, and his maleness (might not such a character also be capable of perverting his role as Rome's emperor and protector?).

Passage 22 Tacitus Annals *15.38.*

The very first line of Tacitus' account of the fire openly raises the possibility of Nero's responsibility for what is described as a grave disaster. Next, Tacitus starts to show how grave the disaster really was. First, at 3f., the fire breaks out (is the proximity to the Palatine suspicious?); then three lines on the strength, rapidity and extent of the conflagration in vulnerable Rome highlight the danger; at 6ff., the focus shifts to the people affected, to bring out the human face of the catastrophe, with a great sweep of victims (especially emotive ones). Suggestively, fire is present all the way through this passage, surrounding the lines on the people and in among them; 15ff. represent a sinister coda, and the suggestion (in *auctorem* and the very last word *iussu*) that the acts may have been committed by agents of Nero is especially appalling after the preceding sketch (and ensures that the whole passage is framed by intimations of Nero's culpability). How well is the nightmarish terror caught here?

Passage 23 Tacitus Annals *15.39.*

Once in Rome, in the face of the awful plight of the people (put across *again* at 2–4), Nero does take actions to help them. But *popularia* in 6 implies that he did this in a calculating way, rather than out of genuine concern. There are also two other places in this passage where Tacitus undermines Nero's relief measures. How does he do this, and where does he do it (placement is important)?

Passage 24 Tacitus Annals *15.40f.*

Reinforcing the fire's devastating effect on humans, Tacitus here dwells on the enormous material losses it caused as well. Analyse the impact of his picture of these losses, paying particular attention to the accumulation and repetition of details. Although 14ff. allow that the rebuilt Rome was beautiful, they simultaneously deflate that achievement of Nero's. More grave is the suggestion at 5–7 (in the midst of this description of desolation) that the fire may have been restarted by him, a particularly monstrous act after the conflagration had at last died down (and ascribed to a truly demented ambition).

Passage 25 Tacitus Annals *15.42f.*

After the recent stress on the great losses, the way in which Nero at 1ff. profits from the devastation of Rome to construct his extravagant Golden House must undercut his rebuilding and beautification of Rome at 3ff. (and one contrasts the much broader open spaces of the Golden House for show and luxury with the strictly utilitarian open spaces for the Roman people). Then, by way of reinforcement, there is the negative attitude at 8ff. What suggests this time that Nero may have started (or restarted) the fire? For more on the Golden House and his extravagance, see Suet. *Nero* 30f.

Passage 26 Tacitus Annals *15.44.*

The rumour of Nero's guilt resurfaces at 2f. It is followed by rejection of the Christians as culprits and dilation upon the cruelty in the persecution of large numbers of them (sick entertainment replaces formal execution; the fact that even the hated Christians aroused pity accentuates Nero's savagery; and the words *in saevitiam unius absumerentur* are emphatic by position). This further horror makes for a dismal climax and rounds off the narrative by recalling the earlier entertainment of Tigellinus (Nero in costume, and (especially pointed) flames are particular linking motifs). In what ways does this persecution support the notion that Nero could easily have been responsible for the fire and all the deaths that it entailed?

Passage 27 Tacitis Annals *16.1–3.*

One lunatic is taken in by another, because of his *vanitas* (and Nero the artist may well have been attracted by the connection of Bassus' story with Virgil's epic poem, the *Aeneid*). That connection has further significance. At *Aen.* 1.314ff. the goddess Venus tells her son Aeneas (shipwrecked near Carthage) how Dido's husband had been killed by the king of her home city and had come to her as a ghost in a dream, urging her to flee and showing her buried treasure (a mass of ancient gold and silver), and how she then had made the long journey to North Africa and had founded Carthage. Aeneas visits the queen and starts an affair with her, after she has been maddened with love, but has to leave her (and deceives her by concealing his preparations). She finds out and, mad with anguish, kills herself. In the same way, Bassus had a dream about buried treasure (a mass of ancient gold), made a long journey, was mad, was deceived (by his dream) and killed himself. The parallels are bizarre and mock-heroic (especially the absurd Bassus as the tragic Dido), and a momentous episode from lofty epic reappears here as a ludicrous little incident. There seems to be an Aeneas here too (his descendant Nero was also told about Dido and a dream of buried treasure and caused the death of a Dido-figure). This grotesque comparison accentuates Nero's faults (Aeneas was devoted to the gods, his family and people, and was a grave and noble hero, who had a close relationship with his mother).

Passage 28 Suetonius Nero *46–9.*

There is no light touch here – it is all very emphatic, dramatic and disturbing. As a biographer, Suetonius concentrates on Nero, his subject (not elaborating on the broader picture, and relating external events only as they reach and affect Nero). This tight focus means that we go through Nero's last hours right beside him. The account is full of detail and incident, including graphic and grim elements, and mundane and sordid touches from real life. As a result, it has colour and texture (giving us a clear idea of how Nero was dressed, what he said and did etc.), and it also has a suggestively bustling and even turbulent feel. There is no real pathos: Nero is depicted as fearful, irresolute, vain, preposterous at this stage, and there are also reminders of his earlier decadence. Instead, Suetonius brings out the ignominy and extent of his fall, works in some offbeat and dark humour, and gives his narrative the flavour of a nightmare (after the ominous bad dreams at the start, there is no way out for Nero, just a long series of horrors, with things becoming worse and worse, until the end, with its apt combination of the absurd and the appalling).

Examine the passage for the features alluded to above, and analyse the focus and the progressive worsening of the situation in each paragraph. One last point: scholars are left wondering about several aspects (e.g. why the stealthy entry into the villa, why the quick decision there that Nero should commit suicide, how did the cavalry find Nero so soon?) and suspecting disloyalty on the part of Nero's freedmen (trying to save their own skins by stopping him from getting well away from Rome and by ensuring his death). The fact that various things are unclear (to us, as to Nero), and the presence of murky suspicions, add to the nightmarish atmosphere.

VOCABULARY

~

[Words marked with an asterisk should be known by or intelligible to a student after two years of latin, so memorize any that you have to look up more than twice.]

*__a__ (+ abl) after, since, by, from, on the side of
*__ab__ (+ abl) by, from, at
abdo -ere -idi -itum hide, remove
*__abduco -cere -xi -ctum__ take away, remove
*__abeo -ire -i(v)i -itum__ go away, depart
*__abicio -cere -eci -ectum__ hurl, throw down
abiectus -a -um sordid, despicable
abigo -igere -egi -actum remove; **abigere partum** cause an abortion
abnuo -ere -i refuse, deny
aboleo -ere -evi -itum abolish, rescind, suppress
*__abripio -ipere -ipui -eptum__ drag away, carry off
*__abrumpo -umpere -upi -uptum__ break off, cut short
abruptus -a -um steep, precipitous
abscedo -dere -ssi -ssum go away (from)
abscessus -us (m) departure
abscido -dere -di -sum cut off
abscondo -ere -i -itum conceal
*__absens -entis__ absent
absolvo -vere -vi -utum complete, finish
abstinentia -ae (f) starving
*__abstineo -ere -ui abstentum__ abstain (from), keep away (from), restrain oneself
*__absum abesse afui__ be absent
absumo -sumere -sumpsi -sumptum squander, destroy, kill
absurdus -a -um uncouth, uncivilized, absurd, out of place
abusque all the way from (+ abl)
*__ac__ and
accedo -dere -ssi -ssum go to, be added, come
accelero -are -avi -atum accelerate, hasten
*__accendo -dere -di -sum__ ignite, inflame, kindle, enrage
accerso -ere -i(v)i -itum charge, indict
*__accido -ere -i__ happen
accido -dere -di -sum diminish, cut up
accingo -gere -xi -ctum gird, dress
accio -ire -i(v)i -itum summon, invite
*__accipio -ipere -epi -eptum__ accept, receive, acquire, welcome, entertain, agree to, take hold of, suffer, hear
accommodo -are -avi -atum apply, turn, adapt, make suitable
accurro -rrere -curri -cursum run up
*__accusator -oris__ (m) accuser
*__accuso -are -avi -atum__ accuse, prosecute
*__acer acris acre__ alert, vigorous, intense, fierce, violent, serious
acerbe rigorously, strictly
acerbus -a -um bitter, harsh, severe
acerra -ae (f) censer, casket of incense
Acerronia -ae (f) Acerronia (friend of Agrippina)
acervus -i (m) heap, pile
acetum -i (n) sour wine, vinegar
acies -iei (f) battle-line, sharp edge, point
*__acriter__ violently, forcefully, vigorously
Acte -es (f) Acte (mistress of Nero)
actus -us (m) performance, act
*__ad__ (+ acc) to, at, into, before, with a view to, for the purpose of, for, in accordance with, in response to, in addition to
adaequo -are -avi -atum make equal, liken (to), equal
adapto -are -avi -atum adapt, modify
adcingo -gere -xi -ctum gird, ready
adcursus -us (m) rushing up, attack
addico -icere -ixi -ictum sell
*__addo -ere -idi -itum__ add, assign (to), inflict (on)
addormisco -ere fall asleep

*__adduco -cere -xi -ctum__ bring
__adductus -a -um__ serious, grave
*__adeo__ to such an extent, so much so, so
*__adeo -ire -(i)i -itum__ approach, go up to, enter, accost
__adfectus -us__ (m) emotion, feeling, affection, love
*__adfero -ferre attuli allatum__ bring to, bring, report
__adficio -icere -eci -ectum__ affect, visit with, subject to (+ abl)
__adfigo -gere -xi -xum__ fix (to), fasten (on)
__adfirmo -are -avi -atum__ maintain, swear
__adflicto -are -avi -atum__ afflict, distress
__adfligo -gere -xi -ctum__ bring down, bring to the ground, strike
__adfluo -ere -xi__ come flocking
__adfundo -undere -udi -usum__ pour in
*__adgnosco -oscere -ovi -itum__ recognize, identify
__adgravo -are -avi -atum__ make worse
*__adgredior -di -ssus sum__ attack
__adhaereo -rere -si -sum__ adhere to, stay attached to
__adhaeresco -rescere -si -sum__ stick close (to)
__adhibeo -ere -ui -itum__ bring in, call upon, summon (to), bring to bear, use, apply, call in
*__adhuc__ still, as yet
__adiaceo -ere -ui__ lie nearby
__adicio -icere -ieci -iectum__ add, grant in addition
__adigo -igere -egi -actum__ plunge, inflict, impel, drive into (+ dat)
__adimo -imere -emi -emptum__ take away, take away from (+ dat)
__adipiscor -ipisci -eptus sum__ acquire, secure
*__aditus -us__ (m) access, approach, audience
__adiuro -are -avi -atum__ swear
__adiutor -oris__ (m) helper, collaborator
__adiuvo -iuvare -iuvi -iutum__ help
__adloquium -(i)i__ (n) talk, converse
*__adloquor -qui -cutus sum__ address, speak to
__Adminius -ii__ (m) Adminius (a Briton)
*__admiror -ari -atus sum__ marvel (at)
*__admitto -ittere -isi -issum__ admit, receive
*__admoneo -ere -ui -itum__ remind (of)
__admoveo -movere -movi -motum__ bring up, bring to
__adnoto -are -avi -atum__ observe, notice
__adnuo -uere -ui -utum__ nod agreement, agree to, confirm
__adoperio -ire -ui -tum__ cover over
__adopto -are -avi -atum__ adopt
__adorior -iri -tus sum__ attack
*__adorno -are -avi -atum__ decorate, equip
*__adoro -are -avi -atum__ worship
__adpello -ellere -uli -ulsum__ put in at (+ acc), bring (to shore)
__adpono -ere apposui appositum__ apply (to)
__adpropinquo -are -avi__ draw near (to)
__adquiesco -escere -evi__ find rest, be at peace
__adsector -ari -atus sum__ escort
__adsevero -are -avi -atum__ assert emphatically, declare
__adsideo -idere -edi -essum__ sit nearby
__adsigno -are -avi -atum__ ascribe
__adsimulo -are -avi -atum__ feign, counterfeit, liken (to)
__adsisto -ere adstiti__ stand by (+ dat), take up a position on
__adsoleo -ere__ be customary, be usual
__adsto -are -stiti__ stand by (+ dat), take up a position on, stand nearby, stand
__adsulto -are -avi -atum__ make an attack on (+ dat), leap, caper
*__adsum -esse -fui__ be present, be present with assistance, appear, be upon (in a hostile sense)
__adsumo -ere -psi -ptum__ enlist, acquire as a supporter, take as a companion, employ
__adsurgo -gere -rexi -rectum__ rise, extend upwards
__adtraho -here -xi -ctum__ bring in, compel to come
__adtrecto -are -avi -atum__ handle, come into contact with
__adulatio -ionis__ (f) obsequious flattery, adulation
*__adulescentia -ae__ (f) youth
*__adulter -eri__ (m) adulterer, lover
*__adultera -ae__ (f) adulteress, mistress
*__adulterium -(i)i__ (n) adultery, adulterous affair
__adultus -a -um__ adult, mature, at its height
__adveho -here -xi -ctum__ convey, bring; (passive) sail (to)
__adventus -us__ (m) arrival
__adversarius -(i)i__ (m) adversary, enemy, opponent
__adversor -ari -atus sum__ oppose, resist
__adversum -i__ (n) a point facing, trouble, calamity
__adversus__ (+ acc) in opposition to, with regard to, against
*__adversus -a -um__ unfavourable, hostile, harmful, adverse, directly in front; __res adversae__ catastrophe

adverto -tere -ti -sum inflict punishment
advocatus -i (m) advocate, lawyer
aedes -is (f) sanctuary, shrine, temple
aedificium -(i)i (n) building, shelter
***aeger -gra -grum** sick, unwell
aegre with difficulty
aemulatio -ionis (f) rivalry
aemulatus -us (m) rivalry
aemulus -i (m) rival
aequo -are -avi -atum make equal to, make level with (+ dat)
***aestas -atis** (f) summer
aestimo -are -avi -atum estimate, assess
aestus -us (m) tide
***aetas -atis** (f) age, persons of a particular age, an age group, life, generation
Afer Afri (m) Afer (Roman name)
affero -ferre attuli allatum bring news, report, cause, bestow
affirmo -are -avi -atum maintain, swear
affligo -gere -xi -ctum injure, oppress, crush, destroy, afflict
affor -ari -atus sum speak to, address
***ager agri** (m) field, land, farm, estate
Agerinus -i (m) Agerinus (a freedman)
agger -eris (m) pile of earth
aggero -are -avi -atum heap up
agito -are -avi -atum consider, discuss
***agmen -inis** (n) horde, gang, crowd, army, column
***agnosco -oscere -ovi -itum** recognize
***ago -ere egi actum** drive, ride, serve, do, act, be engaged in, perform, conduct, proceed, spend, stay, live; (in passive) occur;
ago gratias express thanks
agon -onos (m) contest
Agrippa -ae (m) Agrippa (Augustus' grandson; also a friend and general of Augustus)
Agrippina -ae (f) Agrippina (the elder Agrippina was the wife of Germanicus; the younger Agrippina was Claudius' last wife and the mother of Nero)
aio say
alacer -cris -cre lively, brisk
albens -entis white, bleached
alea -ae (f) gambling, dice; **aleam ludo** gamble, play dice
Alexander -dri (m) Alexander the Great (a famous Greek king and general)
alias at another time
alieno -are -avi -atum deprive of sanity, make to wander
alienus -a -um of a stranger, of another; (as noun) stranger
aliquamdiu for a considerable time
aliquando sometimes, occasionally
aliqui -qua -quod some, a
***aliquis -qua -quid** someone, one, something, some
aliquotiens a number of times, several times
aliter otherwise, in another way
***alius -a -ud** other, another; **alii. . .alii** some. . .others
alo -ere -ui -tum nurture, bring up
altaria -ium (n pl) altars
***alter -era -erum** another, a second, one (of two)
alteruter -tra -trum one or other (of two persons)
altitudo -inis (f) height, depth
altum -i (n) the deep, sea
***altus -a -um** tall, high, deep, penetrating
alumnus -i (m) nurseling
alveus -i (m) hull, ship, gaming-board
alvus -i (f) bowels
amatorius -a -um love-inducing
ambages -um (f pl) evasive speech, ambiguity
ambigo -ere doubt
ambiguus -a -um hybrid, uncertain
ambitus -us (m) circumference, perimeter, extent, bribery, courting
amicio -cire -xi -ctum dress
***amicitia -ae** (f) friendship, group of friends
amicula -ae (f) mistress
***amicus -i** (m) friend
amita -ae (f) aunt
amitto -ittere -isi -issum lose, give up
***amo -are -avi -atum** love
amoenus -a -um charming, attractive
***amor -oris** (m) love, passion, affection, love affair
amoveo -overe -ovi -otum remove, get rid of
amplector -cti -xus sum embrace, apply to
amplexus -us (m) embrace
amputo -are -avi -atum cut off
an really (introducing a surprised question), whether, or
ancilla -ae (f) female slave, servant, maid
ancora -ae (f) anchor
Angrivarii -iorum (m pl) the Angrivarii (a German tribe)

angustiae -arum (f pl) narrowness, narrow passage
Anicetus -i (m) Anicetus (a helper of Nero)
***anima -ae** (f) breath, soul, life
animadversio -ionis (f) punishment
animadverto -tere -ti -sum notice, execute
***animal -alis** (n) animal, creature
***animus -i** (m) mind, feelings, thoughts, senses, heart, morale, purpose, will, intention, character, spirit, temper
annales -ium (m pl) history, chronicle
***annus -i** (m) year, year of age
***ante** (+ acc) before, in front of; (adverb) beforehand, earlier, sooner, rather
***antea** formerly, up to this point
anteeo -ire -i(v)i -itum outstrip, keep ahead of
antefixus -a -um fastened in front, nailed to
Antiatinus -a -um of Antium (a town not far from Rome)
antidotum -i (n) antidote
antiquitas -atis (f) antiquity, ancient conduct
***antiquus -a -um** ancient, of old
Antium -ii (n) Antium (a town not far from Rome)
Antonia -ae (f) Antonia (mother of Claudius; also a daughter of his)
Antonius -ii (m) Antonius (a Roman name)
antrum -i (n) cave, dell
***anxie** anxiously
***anxius -a -um** anxious, worried
Apelles -is (m) Apelles (a tragic actor)
aperio -ire -ui -tum reveal, explain
apertus -a -um open
Apicata -ae (f) Apicata (wife of Sejanus)
apiscor -isci -tus sum seize, secure
Apollo -inis (m) Apollo (the god)
apparatus -a -um sumptuous, elaborate
appello -are -avi -atum call, designate, describe, address by name, make overtures to
appetens -entis greedy for (+ gen)
Appianus -a -um of Appius (stepfather of Messalina)
appono -ere apposui appositum serve
apporto -are -avi -atum bring, convey
apprehendo -dere -di -sum seize, grip
appropinquo -are -avi approach
Aprilis -is -e of April
apud (+ acc) in, at, on, in the presence of, before, with, among, in the case of, at the house of
***aqua -ae** (f) water
aquila -ae (f) eagle, the standard (colours) of a legion
ara -ae (f) altar
arbiter -tri (m) controller
arbitrium -(i)i (n) command, authority
***arbor -oris** (f) tree
arcanus -a -um secret, arcane
ardenter passionately
***ardeo -dere -si** burn, blaze, gleam
***ardesco -ere** become inflamed, become eager
***ardor -oris** (m) eagerness, desire
***arduus -a -um** difficult, arduous
area -ae (f) space, area
argentum -i (n) silver
arguo -uere -ui -utum accuse, bring an accusation against
***arma -orum** (n pl) arms, weapons
Arminius -ii (m) Arminius (a German chieftain)
***armo -are -avi -atum** arm
arripio -ere -ui arreptum seize
***ars artis** (f) skill, art, craftsmanship, guile, trick, device, work of art
arte closely
artifex -ficis (f) expert practitioner, connoisseur, artist
artus -a -um narrow, dense, thick
artus -us (m) limb; (plural) body
arvum -i (n) field, countryside
ascendo -dere -di -sum mount, board
Asia -ae (f) Asia
aspectus -us (m) watching, the action of looking, sight, view
aspernor -ari -atus sum reject, scorn
***aspicio -icere -exi -ectum** look at, see, inspect, consider
asporto -are -avi -atum carry off, remove
assero -ere -ui -tum claim
***assidue** continually
assisto -ere astiti stand by (+ dat)
asturco -onis (m) horse of Spanish breed
astus -us (m) cunning, guile
***at** but
***ater atra atrum** black
Atia -ae (f) Atia (Augustus' mother)
***atque** and
atratus -a -um wearing black
atrocitas -atis (f) dreadfulness, savageness, enormity
***atrox -ocis** terrible, alarming, fierce, ruthless
attempto -are -avi -atum attack, assault

attigo -ere touch
attineo -ere -ui attentum hold, confine, detain, keep
attingo -tingere -tigi -tactum have contact with, have to do with
auctor -oris (m) author, source, giver, instigator, one who gives authority
auctoritas -atis (f) authority, standing, impressiveness
***audacia -ae** (f) daring, boldness, audacious action
***audax -acis** bold, daring, reckless
***audeo -dere -sus sum** intend, dare, dare to do
***audio -ire -i(v)i -itum** hear, hear of, listen, listen to, listen properly
***augeo -gere -xi -ctum** increase, multiply, heighten, raise (the voice), make much of, elaborate, aggravate
auguratus -us (m) office of augur (a priest)
Augustiani -orum (m pl) the Augustiani (Nero's claque)
Augustus -i (m) Augustus (the first Roman emperor)
aureus -a -um golden
aureus -i (m) gold coin
auricula -ae (f) ear
auriga -ae (m) charioteer
aurigo -are -avi -atum drive a chariot
auris -is (f) ear
***aurum -i** (n) gold
auspex -icis (m) diviner (one who took the omens at a wedding)
auster -tri (m) the south wind
***aut** or; **aut. . .aut** either. . .or
***autem** but, and
***autumnus -i** (m) autumn, fall
auxilium -(i)i (n) a supporting force, auxiliaries, support, help
aversus -a -um rear
averto -tere -ti -sum avert, distract
avia -ae (f) grandmother
***avis -is** (f) bird
avitus -a -um belonging to one's grandfather, ancestral
avunculus -i (m) great-uncle
avus -i (m) grandfather, ancestor

Baccha -ae (f) a Bacchante (female worshipper of the wine god Bacchus)
bacchor -ari -atus sum rave, rage
baculum -i (n) sceptre
Baiae -arum (f pl) Baiae (a seaside resort near Naples)
balineum -i (n) bath
ballista -ae (f) ballista (military equipment that hurled stones etc.)
balneae -arum (f pl) bathing
balneum -ei (n) bath
barba -ae (f) beard
***barbarus -a -um** barbaric
basilica -ae (f) basilica (hall used as law-court and exchange)
Bassus -i (m) Bassus (a lunatic from Carthage)
Batavi -orum (m pl) the Batavi (a German people)
Bauli -orum (m pl) Bauli (name of a villa belonging to Agrippina)
bellaria -orum (n pl) sweets, candies, dainties
***bellum -i** (n) war
belua -ae (f) beast
***bene** well, fairly, thoroughly
benignitas -atis (f) kindness, benevolence
bestia -ae (f) beast of prey (used in the arena)
biduum -i (n) a period of two days
blandimentum -i (n) cajolery, flattery
blanditia -ae (f) endearment, flattery
boletus -i (m) mushroom
bonum -i (n) possession, effects
***bonus -a -um** good, fair, beautiful
***bracchium -(i)i** (n) arm
***brevis -is -e** brief, short
Britanni -orum (m pl) the British
Britannia -ae (f) Britain
Britannicus -i (m) Britannicus (son of Claudius and Messalina)
Brundisium -(i)i (n) Brundisium (a port on the east coast of Italy)
Brutus -i (m) Brutus (assassin of Caesar and enemy of Augustus)
Burrus -i (m) Burrus (commander of the praetorian guard)

C. abbreviation for Gaius
cachinnus -i (m) guffaw, laugh
***cadaver -eris** (n) corpse
***cado -ere cecidi casum** fall, die, turn out
Caecina -ae (m) Caecina (a companion of Claudius)
caedes -is (f) murder, killing, slaughter
caedo -dere -si -sum kill, sacrifice, flog
caelebs -ibis without a wife
caelestis -is -e divine

Caelius -a -um Caelian (name of a hill in Rome)
***caelum -i** (n) sky, heaven, climatic conditions
Caesar -aris (m) Julius Caesar, a Caesar (member of the imperial family)
caesim with a slashing blow
Caesonia -ae (f) Caesonia (a wife of Caligula)
Caesoninus -i (m) Caesoninus
caespes -itis (m) sod, piece of turf, turf
Calabria -ae (f) Calabria (region in south Italy)
calamitas -atis (f) disaster
calidus -a -um hot
Callistus -i (m) Callistus (freedman of Claudius)
Calpurnia -ae (f) Calpurnia (a mistress of Claudius)
Calpurnianus -i (m) Calpurnianus
calumnior -ari -atus sum bring false accusations
camelus -i (m) camel
Campania -ae (f) Campania (an area of Italy south of Rome)
***campus -i** (m) plain, field, open space
***canis -is** (m) dog
***cano -ere cecini** sing, sing of, play (+ abl)
canorus -a -um tuneful, melodious
canto -are -avi -atum sing, play (a musical instrument)
cantus -us (m) song, music
canus -a -um grey-haired
capax -acis capable (of), capable of the production of
capesso -ere -i(v)i see to, attend to, engage in, seize
capillamentum -i (n) wig
***capillus -i** (m) hair
***capio -ere cepi captum** capture, captivate, enter on, get
capital -lis (n) a capital offence, a crime punishable by death
Capitolinus -a -um Capitoline, of the Capitoline Hill
Capitolium -(i)i (n) the Capitoline Hill at Rome together with the temple of Jupiter there
capra -ae (f) she-goat
Capreae -arum (f pl) Capri
captivitas -atis (f) captivity
***captivus -i** (m) captive
capto -are -avi -atum try to win over
***caput -itis** (n) head
carcer -eris (m) prison, custody
caritas -atis (f) love, affection
carnifex -ficis (m) executioner
carpo -ere -si -tum criticize
Carthago -inis (f) Carthage (city in North Africa)
Cassius Cassi (m) Cassius (name of various Romans, including the assassins of Julius Caesar and Caligula)
caste in a state of ceremonial purity
Castor -oris (m) Castor (a minor god)
***castra -orum** (n pl) camp
castus -a -um pure, chaste
***casus -us** (m) accident, fortune, misfortune, danger, chance, situation
catadromus -i (m) tightrope
catena -ae (f) chain
caupona -ae (f) tavern, drinking-place
causa -ae (f) cause, reason, case; (in ablative) for the sake of, as a result of; **causam dicere** plead one's case
causor -ari -atus sum plead as an excuse, allege
***cautus -a -um** cautious, wary
cavea -ae (f) cage
caveo -ere cavi cautum (+ **a**) be on one's guard against
caverna -ae (f) hole
cedo -dere -ssi -ssum go; (+ **in**) pass into the possession of
celeber -bris -bre distinguished, celebrated
celebro -are -avi -atum praise, attend (in large numbers), celebrate, carry out, perform
***celer celeris celere** quick
***celero -are -avi -atum** act quickly, be quick
cella -ae (f) store, larder, pantry, small room (belonging to a slave)
***celo -are -avi -atum** conceal, disguise
cena -ae (f) dinner
ceno -are -avi -atum dine
censeo -ere -ui -um decide, decree
centum (indeclinable) a hundred
centurio -ionis (m) centurion (a captain in the army or fleet)
cerebrum -i (n) brain
cerno -ere crevi cretum see
certamen -inis (n) contest, point of contention, competition, rivalry
certatim with rivalry, in competition
***certe** without doubt, definitely, certainly, at any rate
certo -are -avi -atum compete
certus -a -um knowing, determined, certain, evident, definite, determined on (+ gen); **certior fio** be informed
cervix -icis (f) neck, head

cetera in other respects, in other areas
ceterum but, moreover
*__ceterus -a -um__ the rest (of), the other
Chaerea -ae (m) Chaerea (assassin of Caligula)
Chaldaeus -i (m) a Chaldaean (from Assyria), an astrologer
Charicles -is (m) Charicles (a doctor)
Chauci -orum (m pl) the Chauci (a German tribe)
Cherusci -orum (m pl) the Cherusci (a German tribe)
chlamys -ydis (f) cloak
chorus -i (m) chorus, band, group of worshippers
Christiani -orum (m pl) Christians
*__cibus -i__ (m) food, a meal
cicatrix -icis (f) scar
cieo ciere civi citum summon, stir up
cinis -eris (m) ashes
*__circa__ (+ acc) in connection with, around
circensis -is -e in the circus (in Nero's gardens)
*__circum__ round about; (as preposition + acc) around
circumdo -are -edi -atum place someone (acc) around someone (dat), post nearby (to), surround, contribute
*__circumfero -ferre -tuli -latum__ carry around
*__circumiaceo -ere__ lie around, surround
circumicio -icere -ici -iectum place around
circumsedeo -edere -edi -essum sit around, surround
circumsisto -ere stand around, surround
circumstrepo -ere -ui -itum make a noise round about, shout around (a person)
circumvenio -enire -eni -entum enclose, outflank
Circus -i (m) the Circus Maximus (place in Rome where games were held)
cithara -ae (f) lyre (a stringed musical instrument)
citharoedicus -a -um of a lyre player
citharoedus -i (m) lyre player (a musician who sang to his own accompaniment on the lyre)
cito quickly
civilis -is -e civil, involving fellow-citizens, legal
*__civitas -atis__ (f) state, city, citizenship
*__clades -is__ (f) disaster
*__clam__ secretly
clamito -are -avi -atum shout repeatedly
*__clamor -oris__ (m) shout, shouting
clare clearly, out loud
claresco -escere -ui become bright, be illuminated
claritudo -inis (f) distinction, renown
classiarius -a -um in charge of marines
classis -is (f) fleet
Claudius -a -um Claudian (belonging to an ancient Roman family); (as noun) a member of the Claudian family
Claudius -i (m) Claudius (the emperor)
claudo -dere -si -sum close (off), block, shut, enclose, confine
claudus -a -um lame, crippled
clementia -ae (f) leniency, mercy
Cleopatra -ae (f) Cleopatra (a mistress of Claudius)
*__cliens -entis__ (m) client, dependant
clientela -ae (f) body of clients
Clitumnus -i (m) the Clitumnus (an Italian river)
cludo -dere -si -sum close
Cluvius -(i)i (m) Cluvius (a historian)
coaxo -are croak
codicilli -orum (m pl) a set of writing-tablets, document, letter
∗**coepi -isse -tum** begin
∗**coerceo -ere -ui -itum** restrain, keep in order, control, restrict, regulate, shut up
coetus -us (m) gathering, gang
cognomentum -i (n) name, sobriquet
cognosco -oscere -ovi -itum find out, get to know; (perfect) know
∗**cogo -ere coegi coactum** bring together, force
cohibeo -ere -ui -itum restrain, prevent
∗**cohors -ortis** (f) cohort (tenth part of a legion)
colligo -igere -egi -ectum collect, pick up, recover
collis -is (m) hill
colloco -are -avi -atum place, locate
collum -i (n) neck
colonia -ae (f) colony, settlement, town
∗**color -oris** (m) colour, complexion
∗**comes -itis** (m) companion
comis -is -e affable, elegant, cultured
comitas -atis (f) friendliness, courtesy, elegance
comitatus -us (m) retinue, escort (of attendants), company, attendance (on somebody)
comiter courteously, pleasantly
comitialis -is -e epileptic, of epilepsy
comitor -ari -atus sum accompany
commeatus -us (m) supplies

commendo -are -avi -atum entrust
commeo -eare -eavi -eatum travel, be conveyed
comminiscor -inisci -entus sum think up, devise, invent
∗**committo -ittere -isi -issum** commit, perpetrate, cause to compete, match
commode properly, appropriately
∗**commoveo -overe -ovi -otum** move, touch
communico -are -avi -atum share, frame together
∗**communis -is -e** joint, belonging to two people
como -ere -psi -ptum adorn, dress up, comb
compareo -ere -ui be seen, be able to be found
comparo -are -avi -atum procure, obtain
comperio -ire -i -tum discover
compertus -a -um ascertained
complano -are -avi -atum reduce to ground level
∗**complector -cti -xus sum** embrace, grasp
compleo -ere -evi -etum fill
∗**complexus -us** (m) embrace
complures -es -ia several, many
compono -onere -osui -ositum calm, compose, modify, write about, fabricate, construct, arrange
compos -otis in possession of; **voti compos** having been granted one's prayer
compositus -a -um calm, contrived
comprimo -imere -essi -essum rape
comptus -a -um adorned, dressed up
concaco -are -avi -atum mess, make a mess of, soil
concavus -a -um hollow, sunken
concedo -dere -ssi -ssum grant, hand over, withdraw, retire
concerto -are -avi -atum race
concha -ae (f) sea shell
concido -ere -i collapse, be brought to ruin
concipio -ipere -epi -eptum produce, form, adopt, conceive, plan
concors -dis in agreement with (+ dat)
concubitus -us (m) sexual intercourse
concupisco -iscere -i(v)i -itum long for, desire ardently
concursus -us (m) crowd
condemno -are -avi -atum condemn
∗**condicio -ionis** (f) condition, state, love affair, liaison, circumstances, status
∗**condo -ere -idi -itum** bury, inter, found, establish, sheathe
∗**conduco -cere -xi -ctum** bring together, be conducive (to)
confero -rre contuli collatum carry, convey; (passive, reflexive) go
confessio -ionis (f) confession, admission of guilt
confestim immediately
∗**conficio -icere -eci -ectum** finish, finish off, kill
confingo -ngere -nxi -ctum pretend
∗**confirmo -are -avi -atum** confirm, corroborate, strengthen, reassure
confiteor -fiteri -fessus sum confess
conflicto -are -avi -atum trouble, torment
confodio -odere -odi -ossum run through, wound fatally
confrico -are -atum rub
confugio -ugere -ugi flee for refuge
confundo -undere -udi -usum upset, ruin
confusus -a -um inarticulate
congero -rere -ssi -stum heap up
congredior -di -ssus sum approach, join battle, meet
congressus -us (m) meeting, encounter, companionship
coniectus -us (m) throwing
conitor -ti -sus sum clamber
coniugalis -is -e connected with marriage, belonging to a husband/wife
∗**coniugium -(i)i** (n) marriage, wife
coniungo -gere -xi -ctum join together, unite, join in marriage
∗**coniunx -iugis** (m + f) husband, wife
coniurati -orum (m pl) conspirators
conlabor -bi -psus sum collapse
∗**conlaudo -are -avi -atum** praise, commend
conloco -are -avi -atum give in marriage
conloquium -ii (n) discussion, conference
conluvies -ei (f) scum (of a gang of disreputable people)
∗**conor conari conatus sum** try
conquiro -rere -si(v)i -situm search out, look for, collect, bring together
consaluto -are -avi -atum greet as, hail as
conscientia -ae (f) complicity, guilty conscience
∗**conscius -a -um** sharing knowledge, privy; (as noun) accomplice
conscribo -bere -psi -ptum enrol, enlist
conscriptus -i (m) senator
consecro -are -avi -atum deify, declare to be a god
consensus -us (m) agreement, combined action
consido -sidere -sedi take up a position

*consilium -(i)i (n) plan, plot, scheme, measure, discussion, diplomacy, council of state
consisto -sistere -stiti take up a position, stand
consocio -are -avi -atum share, communicate
consono -are -ui sound together, resound
consortium -(i)i (n) sharing, partnership
conspectus -us (m) sight
conspergo -gere -si -sum sprinkle (with water)
constanter steadfastly, faithfully
constantia -ae (f) constancy, loyalty, firmness, fearlessness
consterno -ernere -ravi -ratum cover, strew
consterno -are -avi -atum frighten
*__constituo -uere -ui -utum__ decide, set up, establish
consto -are -iti stand together; **constat** it is known
constupro -are -avi -atum rape
consuesco -escere -evi -etum become accustomed; (perfect) be in the habit, be accustomed to
*__consuetudo -inis__ (f) habitual practice, habit, sexual intercourse
*__consul -ulis__ (m) consul (a high-ranking Roman magistrate)
consularis -is -e belonging to a consul, of consular rank (i.e. an ex-consul)
consulatus -us (m) consulship, office of consul
*__consulo -ere -ui -tum__ consult, see to, pay attention to the safety of (+ dat), look out for (+ dat)
consulto -are -avi -atum deliberate, discuss, seek advice
consultum -i (n) decree
*__consumo -ere -psi -ptum__ destroy, use up, exhaust, squander
*__consurgo -rgere -rrexi -rrectum__ rise
contaminatus -a -um filthy, degenerate
contego -gere -xi -ctum cover
*__contemno -nere -psi -ptum__ regard with contempt, disregard
*__conterreo -rere -rui -ritum__ terrify
contiguus -a -um adjacent (to)
continens -entis (f) mainland
continentia -ae (f) restraint, holding oneself in
contineo -inere -inui -entum contain, enclose
contingo -ingere -igi -actum touch
continuus -a -um continuous, uninterrupted, lasting, successive
contio -onis (f) speech, meeting
contionor -ari -atus sum deliver a speech
*__contra__ (+ acc) facing, against, in opposition to; (adverb) on the other side, opposite, on the other hand, in opposition
contraho -ahere -axi -actum draw/bring together, collect
contrecto -are -avi -atum touch, feel
contrucido -are -avi -atum slaughter in large numbers, butcher
contubernium -(i)i (n) cohabitation, relationship, concubinage
contumelia -ae (f) insult, indignity
contus -i (m) pole
convello -ellere -elli -ulsum convulse, shatter
*__convenio -enire -eni -entum__ come together, muster, be united
conventiculum -i (n) place for an assignation
converto -tere -ti -sum turn, resort
convicior -ari -atus sum utter abuse, revile
convictus -us (m) banquet
convinco -incere -ici -ictum expose, convict
conviva -ae (m + f) guest
convivium -(i)i (n) dinner-party, banquet, guests
coprea -ae (m) jester
*__coram__ (adverb) openly, in public, in front of one; (preposition + abl) in front of
Corcyra -ae (f) Corcyra (modern Corfu, an island off the west coast of Greece)
Cordus -i (m) Cordus (name of a Roman historian)
corona -ae (f) garland, wreath, crown (as a prize)
corono -are -avi -atum award the crown (of victory)
*__corpus -oris__ (n) body, corpse, constitution
corrigo -igere -exi -ectum put right
*__corripio -ipere -ipui -eptum__ seize, criticize
*__corrumpo -umpere -upi -uptum__ spoil, seduce, corrupt, bribe
corruptus -a -um depraved
cothurnus -i (m) high boot
cotidie every day
*__creber -bra -brum__ placed at frequent intervals, numerous, frequent, persistent
crebro frequently
*__credibilis -is -e__ credible, plausible
*__credo -dere -didi -ditum__ believe, imagine, suppose
credulitas -atis (f) credulity
cremo -are -avi -atum burn, cremate
Cremutius -(i)i (m) Cremutius (a Roman historian)

Crepereius -i (m) Crepereius (friend of Agrippina)
crepido -inis (f) quay
crepitus -us (m) short and sharp sound, succession of such sounds
***crimen -inis** (n) charge, crime
criminatio -ionis (f) reproach, accusation
criminator -oris (m) accuser, slanderer
criminose abusively, slanderously
criminosus -a -um constituting a criminal offence, criminal
***crinis -is** (m) hair
crocum -i (n) saffron perfume
***crudelis -is -e** cruel
***cruentus -a -um** involving bloodshed
***cruor -oris** (m) blood
***crus cruris** (n) leg
crux crucis (f) cross
crypta -ae (f) covered passage
cubiculum -i (n) bedroom
cubito -are -avi -atum lie down, rest
cubo -are -ui -itum lie down, sleep, recline (at dinner)
culcita -ae (f) mattress
culleus -i (m) a leather sack
***culpa -ae** (f) fault, wrongdoing
cultus -us (m) luxury, adornment, habitation, style, elegance, clothes, finery, refinement
***cum** (conjunction) when, since, although; **cum primum** as soon as; (preposition + abl) with, along with
cunae -arum (f pl) cradle
cunctatio -ionis (f) hesitation, delay
cunctor -ari -atus sum delay, hang back, hesitate
***cunctus -a -um** all
cupide eagerly
cupiditas -atis (f) passionate desire, lust
***cupido -inis** (m) desire, longing
***cupio -ere -i(v)i -itum** desire
***cur** why, on account of which
***cura -ae** (f) care, carefulness, attention, attentiveness, devotion, eagerness, supervision
curator -oris (m) manager, superintendent
curia -ae (f) senate house
***curiosus -a -um** inquisitive, nosey
curriculum -i (n) chariot
***currus -us** (m) chariot
cursor -oris (m) courier
cursus -us (m) course, voyage
***custodia -ae** (f) guard, watchman, bodyguard, supervision
***custos -odis** (m) guard, guardian, sentry, caretaker

damnatio -ionis (f) condemnation
damno -are -avi -atum condemn, find guilty of (+ gen)
damnum -i (n) loss
***de** (+ abl) about, concerning, with regard to, down from, from, for
***dea -ae** (f) goddess
***debeo -ere -ui -itum** ought, should
decedo -dere -ssi -ssum depart, leave, go away, disappear
***decem** ten
decerno -ernere -revi -retum decree, award
decet -ere -uit it suits, it is becoming
decimus -a -um tenth
decocta -ae (f) decoction (a special drink)
decoquo -quere -xi -ctum brew, concoct by boiling
decor -oris (m) good looks, beauty, elegance
decorus -a -um handsome, fine, glorious
Decrius -i (m) Decrius
decumbo -mbere -bui lie down
***decurro -rrere -(cu)rri -rsum** run down, travel down
decursus -us (m) finish
decus -oris (n) glory, distinction, dignity, decorum, splendour
dedecus -oris (n) disgrace
dedico -are -avi -atum dedicate
deditio -ionis (f) surrender
deduco -cere -xi -ctum lead, escort, bring as a bride
defectio -ionis (f) weakness, decline
***defendo -dere -di -sum** ward off, combat
***defensio -ionis** (f) defence
defero -ferre -tuli -latum report, send, grant
***defessus -a -um** exhausted
deficio -icere -eci -ectum fail, wane, die, be lacking
defigo -gere -xi -xum fix, lower, root to the spot
***deformis -is -e** ugly, offensive, horrible, indecent
deformitas -atis (f) hideousness, disgrace
deformiter in an ugly fashion, shamefully
***deformo -are -avi -atum** disfigure, disgrace
defunctus -a -um dead
defungor -gi -ctus sum die

dego -ere spend one's time, live
dehinc from that point on, then
dehonesto -are -avi -atum discredit, disfigure, disgrace
deicio -icere -ieci -iectum throw down, bring down, depose, debar (from)
deiero -are -avi -atum swear, take an oath
*__dein__ then
*__deinde__ then, subsequently
delabor -bi -psus sum glide down
delatio -ionis (f) act of informing, laying a charge
delectabilis -is -e delicious
delego -are -avi -atum order
delenio -ire -ii -itum soothe, soften
delibero -are -avi -atum think carefully
delicate luxuriously, comfortably, without exertion
delicatus -a -um luxurious, giving comfort, delicate
delictum -i (n) offence, slip
deligo -igere -egi -ectum choose, select (for)
delinquo -inquere -iqui -ictum commit (an offence)
delubrum -i (n) temple, shrine
deminutio -ionis (f) diminution, loss
demitto -mittere -misi -missum put down, insert
demo -ere -psi -ptum remove, cut (off)
*__demonstro -are -avi -atum__ point out, show
demoror -ari -atus sum detain
demoveo -overe -ovi -otum remove, banish
*__demum__ at last, only
*__denique__ finally, and also, in short
denoto -are -avi -atum disparage, censure
*__densus -a -um__ dense, closely packed
denubo -bere -psi -ptum (of a woman) get married (to)
*__denudo -are -avi -atum__ strip
denuntio -are -avi -atum order (+ dat)
*__depello -ellere -uli -ulsum__ drive off, expel, get rid of, force to withdraw from, stop (from)
deposco -scere -posci demand, ask for
deprecor -ari -atus sum intercede, beg mercy
deprehendo -dere -di -sum catch in the act, detect, discover
derigo -igere -exi -ectum form up, draw up
*__desero -ere -ui -tum__ abandon, leave
desidero -are -avi -atum desire, request, need
designatus -a -um designate (appointed but not yet installed)
desilio -ire -ui jump down
*__desino -inere -(i)i -itum__ stop
*__desisto -istere -titi__ leave off, stop, give up
despectus -a -um despicable
destinatum -i (n) design; **ex destinato** according to a plan
destino -are -avi -atum make up one's mind (to), intend, earmark
destituo -uere -ui -utum fail to support
destringo -ngere -nxi -ctum unsheathe, draw
*__desum -esse -fui__ be lacking
detego -gere -xi -ctum uncover, expose
detergeo -gere -si -sum wipe away
deterior -ior -ius worse
detestor -ari -atus sum pray to avert
detineo -inere -inui -entum detain, keep
detrudo -dere -si -sum drive off
*__deus dei__ (m) god
deverticulum -i (n) tavern, wine-shop
devincio -cire -xi -ctum bind, subjugate, seduce
devotio -ionis (f) incantation, curse
*__dexter -tra -trum__ right
*__dextera -ae__ (f) right hand
*__dico -ere dixi dictum__ say, tell, relate, call, plead
dictito -are -avi -atum say repeatedly
Dido -onis (f) Dido (queen of Carthage)
diduco -cere -xi -ctum pull open
*__dies diei__ (m + f) day, daylight; **in dies** day by day
differo -ferre distuli dilatum defame, slander, postpone
diffugio -ugere -ugi scatter, run away in different directions
*__digitus -i__ (m) finger
dignatio -ionis (f) esteem, respect
dignitas -atis (f) dignity, distinction, grandeur
dignor -ari -atus sum consider worthy of (+ abl)
*__dignus -a -um__ worthy of (+ abl)
*__digredior -di -ssus sum__ depart, separate
dilabor -bi -psus sum slip away, disperse
dilanio -are -avi -atum tear to pieces
dilectus -us (m) levy, recruitment of troops
*__diligenter__ carefully
diligentia -ae (f) diligence, carefulness
diligo -igere -exi -ectum love, feel affection for
diluo -uere -ui -utum refute, rebut
*__dimitto -ittere -isi -issum__ send away
diripio -ipere -ipui -eptum steal
discerno -ernere -revi -retum distinguish between
discerpo -pere -psi -ptum tear apart

discidium -(i)i (n) divorce
discido -dere -di -sum split, flay, beat severely
*__disco -ere didici__ learn
*__discrimen -inis__ (n) decisive stage, danger
discumbo -mbere -bui -bitum recline (at table, to eat)
disicio -icere -ieci -iectum break up and scatter, scatter, end
dispergo -gere -si -sum scatter, disperse
*__displiceo -ere -ui -itum__ displease
dispono -onere -osui -ositum place in position
disseco -are -ui -tum cut apart
dissimulatio -ionis (f) dissimulation, concealment, powers of concealment
dissimulo -are -avi -atum conceal, pretend not to know (of)
dissolutio -ionis (f) breaking up
distendo -dere -di -tum stuff, fill to capacity
distineo -inere -inui -entum distract
distinguo -guere -xi -ctum distinguish, set apart, specify, adorn, spangle
disto -are differ
*__diu__ for a long time
diutius for long, for any considerable time
*__divello -ellere -elli -olsum__ tear, tear apart
*__diversus -a -um__ contradictory, different, opposite, distant, separated
*__dives -itis__ rich
*__divido -idere -isi -isum__ divide
*__divinus -a -um__ divine, to do with/proper to the gods; **res divina** ceremony
*__do dare dedi datum__ give, assign, consign, administer, provide, grant, allow, make, impart
*__doceo -ere -ui -tum__ tell, point out
dolor -oris (m) grief, indignation
*__dolus -i__ (m) trick, stratagem, plot, treachery
domesticus -a -um private, in one's home; (as noun) member of the household
*__domina -ae__ (f) mistress
dominatio -ionis (f) dominion, position of supreme power
dominor -ari -atus sum be in control, be empress
*__dominus -i__ (m) master, lord
*__domus -us__ (f) house, palace, household, family
donativum -i (n) gift (money given to troops by the emperor)
*__donec__ until
*__dono -are -avi -atum__ present with (+ abl)
*__dormio -ire -i(v)i -itum__ sleep
dormito -are -avi drowse, feel sleepy
dos dotis (f) dowry
draco -onis (m) snake
Drusilla -ae (f) Drusilla (sister or daughter of Caligula)
Drusus -i (m) Drusus (son of Tiberius)
*__dubito -are -avi -atum__ doubt, waver
*__dubius -a -um__ doubtful, uncertain;
sine dubio without doubt, certainly
*__duco -ere duxi ductum__ lead, take, prolong
*__dum__ while, until, provided that
*__duo duae duo__ two
duplex -icis folded over, double, twofold
duro -are -avi -atum last, continue, harden, steel
*__durus -a -um__ hard
*__dux ducis__ (m) general, leader

*__e__ (+ abl) from, out of, of
ebur -oris (n) ivory
eburneus -a -um of ivory
ecquid whether
edictum -i (n) edict, decree, proclamation
editus -a -um high
edo edere edidi editum publish, put on (of games and shows), utter, emit
educator -oris (m) tutor (one who brings up a child)
*__educo -are -avi -atum__ nurture, rear
effeminatus -a -um unmanly, effeminate
*__effero -rre extuli elatum__ carry out, bring out, carry out for burial
effero -are -avi -atum make beast-like, make ferocious
*__efficio -icere -eci -ectum__ render, make, produce, bring about, achieve
effigies -ei (f) representation, statue, image
efflo -are -avi -atum breathe out
effodio -odere -odi -ossum gouge out, dig up/out
*__effugio -ugere -ugi__ escape
effugium -ii (n) means of escape, escape
effundo -undere -udi -usum pour out, eject, tip out; (passive) break out (into)
effuse extravagantly, with extravagant applause
*__egeo -ere -ui__ lack (+ gen), be in need, lack money
*__ego mei__ I
*__egredior -edi -essus sum__ come/go out, leave, disembark, go away
egregius -a -um distinguished, outstanding

egressus -us (m) the action of going out, emergence
eicio eicere eieci eiectum drive ashore, cast up
elabor -bi -psus sum escape, be dropped
elegantia -ae (f) refinement, elegance
Elephantis -idis (f) Elephantis (a Greek erotic author)
elephantus -i (m) elephant
elicio -ere -ui -itum lure, coax
elido -dere -si -sum eject
eludo -dere -si -sum render ineffectual, foil, trick, fool
emercor -ari -atus sum procure by bribery
emetior -tiri -nsus sum cover, cross
emico -are -ui -atum shine out, flash out, appear briefly
∗**eminens -entis** outstanding, very tall
emineo -ere -ui project, jut
∗**emitto -ittere -isi -issum** let go, emit, publish, send out
eneco -are -avi -atum kill
∗**enim** for
enimvero however, and what is more
enitor -ti -xus sum give birth
enormis -is -e unshapely
∗**eo** to that place, to that point, to such a point, to such a degree, therefore
∗**eo ire i(v)i itum** go, resort
eodem to the same place
Epaphroditus -i (m) Epaphroditus (Nero's private secretary)
∗**epistula -ae** (f) letter
∗**epulae -arum** (f pl) banquet
epulor -ari -atus sum dine sumptuously, feast, banquet
∗**eques -itis** (m) a member of the equestrian order, cavalryman, rider
equile -is (n) stable
equitatus -us (m) cavalry
∗**equus -i** (m) horse
erga (+ acc) towards, for
ergo therefore, so then
erigo -igere -exi -ectum build (up), rouse, stimulate, revive, restore
∗**eripio -ipere -ipui -eptum** snatch away from (+ dat), snatch away, rescue
erumpo -umpere -upi -uptum burst out, break out from hiding
essedum -i (n) carriage
∗**et** and, also, even; **et. . .et** both. . .and
∗**etiam** also, even, actually; **sed etiam** but also
∗**etsi** although
Euodus -i (m) Euodus (a freedman of Claudius)
evado -dere -si -sum escape, pass, emerge
∗**evenio -enire -eni -entum** come about, happen
eventus -us (m) success
evidens -entis clear, obvious
evinco -incere -ici -ictum overcome, win over, reduce
evolo -are -avi -atum fly away
evomo -ere -ui -itum vomit
∗**ex** (+ abl) since, from, out of, of, made out of, as a result of, by (indicating parentage), to the extent of, in accordance with
exactor -oris (m) supervisor
exanimis -is -e dead, faint, frightened out of one's wits
exanimo -are -avi -atum kill
exardesco -descere -si burn, be inflamed with desire
∗**exaudio -ire -i(v)i -itum** hear
excedo -dere -ssi -ssum depart, die, exceed, surpass
excidium -ii (n) destruction
excido -dere -di -sum excavate, tunnel through
excindo -ndere -di -ssum exterminate, destroy
excio -ire -i(v)i -itum summon, call out
excipio -ipere -epi -eptum gather, remove, greet, receive
excito -are -avi -atum rouse, excite, stimulate, wake up, erect
∗**exclamo -are -avi -atum** cry out, shout
excogitatus -a -um elaborate, carefully thought up
∗**excogito -are -avi -atum** devise, invent
excolo -olere -olui -ultum improve, adorn
excubiae -arum (f pl) the keeping of watch, guard
∗**excuso -are -avi -atum** excuse, plead in excuse
excutio -tere -ssi -ssum knock out, throw out
∗**exemplar -aris** (n) model, illustration
∗**exemplum -i** (n) example, precedent
∗**exerceo -ere -ui -itum** practise, train, carry on, carry out, do
∗**exercitus -us** (m) army
exhaurio -rire -si -stum bail out, deprive of possessions, impoverish
exhibeo -ere -ui -itum show, display
exigo -igere -egi -actum remove, demand
exiguus -a -um small
exilium -(i)i (n) exile
exim then, next

eximo -imere -emi -emptum remove, banish, remove from (+ dat)
***existimo -are -avi -atum** consider
exitiabilis -is -e fatal
exitialis -is -e fatal, bringing death
***exitium -(i)i** (n) destruction, disaster, death
exitus -us (m) exit, end
exoletus -i (m) male prostitute, boyfriend
exonero -are -avi -atum relieve (of a burden)
exoptatus -a -um longed for, much desired
exordior -diri -sus sum begin (a speech)
exorior -iri -tus sum come into view, rise
exoro -are -avi -atum win over, persuade
exortus -us (m) rising, sunrise
exosculor -ari atus sum kiss fondly
expallidus -a -um very pale
***expecto -are -avi -atum** expect, await, long for
expedio -ire -i(v)i -itum make ready, prepare
expeditio -onis (f) military operation, raid, expedition
expergefacio -facere -feci -factum wake up
***experientia -ae** (f) experience
expers -ertis lacking experience (of)
expeto -ere -i(v)i -itum ask for, beg
expleo -ere -evi -etum reach the end of, complete, put the final touch to
explico -are -avi -atum unfold, spread out
exploro -are -avi -atum test, investigate
expono -onere -osui -ositum expose (for sale), display
exprobro -are -avi -atum criticize, condemn, reproach
expromo -ere -psi -ptum reveal
exquiro -rere -sivi -situm ask, inquire into, find out
exquisitus -a -um carefully selected, recondite
exscreo -are -avi -atum cough
exsequiae -arum (f pl) funeral rites, funeral ceremony
exsequor -qui -cutus sum carry out
exsolvo -vere -vi -utum pay, loosen, relax, open
***exspecto -are -avi -atum** expect
exsto -are exstiti be conspicuous, exist, bulge
exstruo -ere -xi -ctum heap up, raise, construct
***exsul -ulis** (m + f) banished person, exile
exsultatio -ionis (f) elation, roar of delight
***exsurgo -gere -rexi** get to one's feet, stand up
exter -era -erum foreign
***externus -a -um** foreign
***exterreo -ere -ui -itum** terrify, frighten off
***extinguo -guere -xi -ctum** extinguish; (passive) die
***extollo -ere** praise, extol
extorqueo -quere -si -tum wrench away from (+ dat)
extremum -i (n) final stage, desperate situation
***extremus -a -um** final, extreme, desperate
extructio -ionis (f) construction
extrudo -dere -si -sum drive out
exturbo -are -avi -atum throw out, drive out, make homeless
***exul -ulis** (m + f) banished person, exile
exuro -rere -ssi -stum destroy by fire, burn completely

Fabius -ii (m) Fabius (a Roman name)
fabrico -are -avi -atum construct, build; (also deponent **fabricor -ari -atus sum** with the same senses)
fabulor -ari -atus sum talk, chat
fabulosus -a -um incredible
facetia -ae (f) joke, amusing remark
***facies -iei** (f) face, appearance, beauty, form
***facile** easily
***facilis -is -e** easy, ready
facilitas -atis (f) ease, pliancy
facilius more easily
***facinus -oris** (n) crime
***facio facere feci factum** make, do, bring about, engage in
factito -are -avi -atum do frequently
***factum -i** (n) deed, action, crime
facultas -atis (f) opportunity, chance
***fallax -acis** treacherous, deceptive
***fallo -ere fefelli falsum** deceive, escape notice
***falsus -a -um** false, untrue, fictitious
***fama -ae** (f) report, popularity, rumour, tradition, public opinion, reputation
fames -is (f) hunger, starvation
***familia -ae** (f) family, a household's troop of slaves
familiaris -is -e closely associated, private; (as noun) friend
familiaritas -atis (f) close friendship, intimacy
fastidium -(i)i (n) boredom, weariness
fastigium -(i)i (n) elevation, eminence
fatalis -is -e fatal, for death
fateor -eri fassus sum confess, admit
***fatum -i** (n) fate, death
fauces -ium (f pl) throat, neck
faustus -a -um of good omen, favourable

*faveo -ere favi fautum** support
fax facis (f) torch
*****Februarius -a -um** of February
fecunditas -atis (f) fertility, fecundity
felicitas -atis (f) happiness
*****femina -ae** (f) woman, wife
fera -ae (f) wild animal
feralis -is -e associated with the dead, funerary
fere more or less, almost, almost always
ferinus -a -um belonging to a wild animal
*****ferio -ire** strike, wound
feritas -atis (f) ferocity, brutality
ferme approximately
*****fero ferre tuli latum** bear, carry, tolerate, say, relate, raise up, elevate, lead; (passive) move
*****ferocia -ae** (f) fierceness, fighting spirit
*****ferrum -i** (n) sword, dagger
ferula -ae (f) rod, cane
ferus -a -um brutal, barbarous, ferocious, cruel
fervor -oris (m) heat
*****fessus -a -um** tired, weary
festinanter hurriedly, hastily
*****festino -are -avi -atum** hurry through, perform with haste
*****festus -a -um** festal; **festus dies** festival
*****fides -ei** (f) trust, credibility, fidelity; **habeo fidem** (+ dat) put trust in
fidicula -ae (f) rack (instrument of torture)
fido -ere fisus sum have confidence in, trust, trust in (+ dat)
fiducia -ae (f) confidence, courage
figo -gere -xi -xum pierce, transfix, shoot, strike rigid
figura -ae (f) figure, posture
*****filia -ae** (f) daughter
filiola -ae (f) little daughter
*****filius -(i)i** (m) son, child
fingo -ngere -nxi -ctum pretend to be, make up, fabricate
*****finio -ire -i(v)i -itum** finish, end, die
*****finis -is** (m) end
*****fio fieri** become, be made, be dug
firmitudo -inis (f) firmness, steadfastness
firmo -are -avi -atum affirm, assure, ensure the support of, encourage
*****firmus -a -um** strong, firm, reliable
flagellum -i (n) whip
flagitium -(i)i (n) outrage, disgraceful sexual misconduct, disgrace, scandal
flagito -are -avi -atum demand, insist
flagrans -antis warm, burning, passionate, in the ascendant, outrageous
flagro -are -avi be on fire, burn
flagrum -i (n) whip
flammeum -i (n) bride's veil
*****flammo -are -avi -atum** set on fire
flatus -us (m) wind
fleo -ere -evi -etum weep
flexus -a -um winding
floreo -ere -ui be at the height of one's power, fame etc.
*****flos floris** (m) flower
*****fluctus -us** (m) wave
fluito -are -avi float, be carried along
*****flumen -inis** (n) river
fluo -ere -xi -xum flow, overflow
fluxus -a -um streaming
foedo -are -avi -atum defile, degrade
foedus -a -um foul, loathsome, monstrous, disgraceful
fomentum -i (n) soothing application, poultice, dressing
for fari fatus sum speak, talk
foris -is (f) door, one of the leaves of a double door; (plural) door
foris outside
*****forma -ae** (f) form, shape, appearance, handsomeness, beauty
formica -ae (f) ant
formido -inis (f) terror, dread, dreadfulness, reason for alarm
formidolosus -a -um fearful
*****formo -are -avi -atum** form, shape
fors fortis (f) chance
*****forte** by chance, accidentally
*****fortis -is -e** strong, manly
fortuitus -a -um chance; (neuter as noun) accident, misfortune
*****fortuna -ae** (f) fortune, high position, fate, good fortune, misfortune, circumstances; (plural) possessions, wealth; **Fortuna** goddess of fortune
*****forum -i** (n) forum (public square used for political and legal business etc.)
fossa -ae (f) ditch, moat
fossura -ae (f) excavation
fragmen -inis (n) fragment
*****frango -ere fregi fractum** break
*****frater fratris** (m) brother
fraus fraudis (f) treachery, deception

fremitus -us (m) neighing
fremo -ere -ui -itum growl, complain
frequento -are -avi -atum observe, celebrate
*__frigidus -a -um__ cold
frons frontis (f) brow, forehead, front
fruges -um (f pl) crops, produce
frumentarius -a -um of corn; **res frumentaria** the corn supply
frumentum -i (n) corn
fruor frui fructus sum enjoy, delight in (+ abl)
*__frustra__ ineffectually
fruticetum -i (n) thicket, mass of bushes
*__fuga -ae__ (f) flight, running away
*__fugio -ere fugi__ flee
fulgens -entis shining, radiant
fulgur -uris (n) flash of lightning
fundo -ere fudi fusum pour; (passive) be stretched out
funebris -is -e of a funeral, funerary
funus -eris (n) funeral, funeral procession, corpse, death; **funere efferre** carry out for burial
furca -ae (f) forked frame
*__furor -oris__ (m) madness, insanity
*__furtim__ secretly, stealthily
fustis -is (m) club, cudgel
futurum -i (n) the future, a future event
*__futurus -a -um__ future, coming

Gaius -(i)i (m) Gaius (the emperor Caligula)
Galba -ae (m) Galba (Roman governor who revolted from Nero)
galea -ae (f) helmet
Gallicus -a -um Gallic, from Gaul
Gallius -ii (m) Gallius (a Roman name)
Gallus -i (m) Gallus (friend of Agrippina)
ganea -ae (f) common eating house
*__gaudium -(i)i__ (n) joy
gemitus -us (m) groan, moaning
*__gemma -ae__ (f) precious stone, jewel
gemmatus -a -um set with precious stones, jewelled
Gemoniae -arum (f pl) the Gemonian steps (down which bodies of criminals were dragged to the Tiber)
genialis -is -e of a marriage; **genialis torus** marriage-bed
*__gens gentis__ (f) race
genu -us (n) knee
*__genus -eris__ (n) type, kind, species, race, way, birth, origin

Germanicus -i (m) Germanicus (a Roman general)
Germanicus -a -um German, to Germany
Germanus -i (m) a German
*__gero -rere -ssi -stum__ perform, wear, have; **res gestae** exploits
gestamen -inis (n) carriage, conveyance
gestatio -ionis (f) driving (in a carriage)
gesto -are -avi -atum carry
gestus -us (m) gesture, posture
Geta -ae (m) Geta (a friend of Claudius)
gigno -ere genui genitum create, father, give birth to, produce
*__gladiator -oris__ (m) gladiator
*__gladius -(i)i__ (m) sword
glisco -ere grow, increase
globus -i (m) mass, gang, band
*__gloria -ae__ (f) glory, honour, distinction
glorior -ari -atus sum boast
gnarus -a -um knowing, having knowledge (of), known
gracilitas -atis (f) thinness, slenderness
*__Graecia -ae__ (f) Greece
*__Graecus -a -um__ Greek; (as noun) a Greek
grandis -is -e much, lots of
grando -inis (f) hail
graphium -(i)i (n) stylus (sharp-pointed instrument for writing on wax tablets)
grassatura -ae (f) highway robbery
grassor -ari -atus sum prowl, roam in search of victims, advance, run riot
grate gratefully, delightedly
*__gratia -ae__ (f) favour, influence, kindness, gratitude, thanks; (abl) for the sake of; **gratias ago** express thanks
grator -ari -atus sum congratulate
*__gratus -a -um__ welcome, appreciated, handsome
gravesco -ere worsen
*__gravis -is -e__ heavy, stern, oppressive, grievous, obnoxious, painful, serious, weighty
*__graviter__ violently, with force
gremium -ii (n) lap
grex gregis (m) group, gang
gubernaculum -i (n) tiller, helm
gusto -are -avi -atum taste
gustus -us (m) tasting

habeo -ere -ui -itum have, retain, observe, regard, treat, employ, keep, involve; **habeo fidem** (+ dat) put trust in

habilis -is -e fit
habitus -us (m) condition, state, dress, get up
hactenus to this extent, on this question only
*__haereo -rere -si -sum__ cling
Halotus -i (m) Halotus (Claudius' food-taster)
*__haud__ not
haurio -rire -si -stum swallow up, engulf, scoop up
hebes -etis dull-witted, stupid
hebeto -are -avi -atum dull, make torpid, impair
hedera -ae (f) ivy
Hercules -is (m) Hercules (Greek hero)
*__heres -edis__ (m + f) heir
hiatus -us (m) splitting open, fissure
hiberna -orum (n pl) winter quarters
*__hibernus -a -um__ wintry
*__hic__ here
*__hic haec hoc__ this, this man
*__hiem(p)s -mis__ (f) winter
hieronica -ae (m) victor in the games
hilaritas -atis (f) cheerfulness, gaiety
*__hinc__ from here, next, as a result of this, on this side
hinnitus -us (m) whinny, neigh
hio -are -avi gape, have one's mouth wide open
*__hirsutus -a -um__ hairy
histrio -ionis (m) actor
*__homo -inis__ (m) human, person, man
*__honestus -a -um__ honourable, decent
*__honos -oris__ (m) honour, respect
*__hora -ae__ (f) hour, appointed time
*__horridus -a -um__ grim, dreadful, horrible
*__horror -oris__ (m) trembling, dread, horror, a cause of horror
hortor -ari -atus sum encourage, urge
hortus -i (m) garden
hospitium -(i)i (n) guest accommodation, lodgings, home
hostia -ae (f) sacrificial animal
*__hostilis -is -e__ hostile, enemy
*__hostis -is__ (m) enemy
*__huc__ to this place, to this side, in this direction, this way
*__humanus -a -um__ human, characteristic of a human being
humilis -is -e shallow
*__humus -i__ (f) earth, ground; **humi** on the ground
hypocrita -ae (m) actor

*__iaceo -ere -ui -itum__ lie, lie on the ground
*__iacio -ere ieci iactum__ throw, hurl, toss, throw off (remarks)
iacto -are -avi -atum say forcefully, assert
iactus -us (m) throwing
*__iam__ now, already, by this point, further, besides; **iam iamque** at any moment; **non iam** no longer
*__ianua -ae__ (f) door
Ianus -i (m) Janus; **ianus Quirinus** a temple of Janus in the forum
*__ibi__ there
iconicus -a -um giving an exact image, looking exactly like
ictus -us (m) stroke, blow (of a weapon), wound
*__idem eadem idem__ the same
identidem repeatedly, again and again
ideo for that reason
idoneus -a -um suitable
*__Idus -uum (f pl)__ the Ides (15th or 13th day of the month)
*__igitur__ therefore, and so
*__ignarus -a -um__ unaware, off guard, ignorant
ignavia -ae (f) cowardice
*__ignis -is__ (m) fire
ignobilis -is -e unknown, unimportant
*__ignominia -ae__ (f) disgrace
*__ignotus -a -um__ unknown
ilico immediately
illa by that route
*__ille illa illud__ that, the famous; he, she, it
*__illic__ there
illido -dere -si -sum dash against (+ dat)
*__illuc__ to that place, to there, in that direction, that way
illudo -dere -si -sum to use someone (in dat) for sexual pleasure
Illyricum -i (n) Illyria
imago -inis (f) mental picture, memory, appearance, likeness, bust, statue, vision
imber -bris (m) rain, shower, rainstorm
immanis -is -e savage, frightful
immanitas -atis (f) monstrousness, barbarity
*__immensus -a -um__ vast, immeasurable
*__immerito__ unjustly, wrongly, without cause
*__immineo -ere__ impend, be imminent, threaten
*__immitto -ittere -isi -issum__ send in
immo rather, no rather
immolo -are -avi -atum sacrifice
immuto -are -avi -atum modify
impar -aris not a match (for), unequal (to)

impatiens -entis not tolerant of, not tolerating (+ gen)
*__impedio -ire -i(v)i -itum__ obstruct, impede
impello -ellere -uli -ulsum strike, drive off, dislodge, push down, impel, urge on; (passive) strike against (+ dat)
impendeo -dere -sum threaten, impend
*__imperator -oris__ (m) general, emperor
imperito -are -avi -atum be in command, rule, be emperor
*__imperium -(i)i__ (n) order, command, supreme power, the emperor's power, government, dominion, empire
*__impero -are -avi -atum__ order, command, prescribe, be emperor, enjoin something (acc) on somebody (dat)
*__impetus -us__ (m) violent onward movement, impetus, charge, attack, vigorous effort, impulse
impono -onere -osui -ositum put in command of (+ dat), place in, place on
imprecor -ari -atus sum wish on, call down something on (+ dat)
improvisus -a -um unexpected
*__imprudens -entis__ ignorant, unaware (of what is happening)
*__imprudentia -ae__ (f) ignorance, imprudence
impudicitia -ae (f) immorality, sexual impurity
impudicus -a -um immoral
imputo -are -avi -atum claim something as a credit, take credit for doing something
in (+ abl) in, on, into, on to, to, during, in the course of, among, in the case of; (+ acc) into, in, on, to, on to, towards, in accordance with, against, for, with regard to, with a view to, in order to cause
inanis -is -e illusory, vain, futile
inauditus -a -um unheard of
incalesco -escere -ui become heated, become excited
incautus -a -um incautious, unguarded, indiscreet
incedo -dere -ssi advance, arise, enter (+ acc), arrive, come on
*__incendium -(i)i__ (n) conflagration, fire
*__incendo -dere -di -sum__ inflame
*__incertus -a -um__ uncertain, mysterious, restless, fluctuating
incesso -ere -(iv)i attack, pelt
incessus -us (m) gait, way of walking
incesto -are -avi -atum defile, pollute
*__incestum -i__ (n) incest
*__incestus -a -um__ incestuous
incido -ere -i incasum fall, collapse
*__incipio -ipere -epi -eptum__ begin
Incitatus -i (m) Incitatus (Caligula's horse)
incito -are -avi -atum provoke, trouble
inclinatio -ionis (f) inclination, trend, tendency
*__inclino -are -avi -atum__ incline, lean, throw one's weight
*__incognitus -a -um__ unknown, strange
incoho -are -avi -atum begin
incolumis -is -e safe and sound, still living, with power unimpaired
incolumitas -atis (f) safety
incomptus -a -um untidy, dishevelled
inconditus -a -um disorderly, disorganized
*__incredibilis -is -e__ incredible, unbelievable
increpo -are -ui -itum criticize, reproach, complain about
incumbo -umbere -ubui bear down on, fling oneself at (+ dat)
incurvus -a -um bent, stooping
incuso -are -avi -atum criticize, condemn, accuse, charge
*__inde__ from that place, then, as a result, on that side
indecens -entis unseemly, unattractive
indefensus -a -um undefended
index -dicis (m) informant, revealer (of)
*__indicium -(i)i__ (n) sign, indication, disclosure, information, memorial, evidence
indico -cere -xi -ctum impose (as punishment), proclaim
indigeo -ere -ui need, lack (+ gen)
*__indignus -a -um__ undeserved, unseemly
indo -ere -idi -itum insert, put on, put in, bestow, attach
indoles -is (f) natural excellence, good qualities
indolesco -escere -ui grieve, be distressed
induco -cere -xi -ctum put on, bring into the arena
*__industria -ae__ (f) diligence, industry; **de/ex industria** deliberately
inedia -ae (f) starvation
*__ineo -ire -i(v)i -itum__ enter, go on, go into
inermus -a -um unarmed
*__infamia -ae__ (f) infamy, notoriety, stigma, scandal, disgraceful conduct
*__infamis -is -e__ notorious, disreputable
infamo -are -avi -atum slander, blacken
*__infans -antis__ (m + f) infant, little child

*__infantia -ae__ (f) infancy
*__infelix -icis__ unlucky, unhappy
__infensus -a -um__ aggressive, hostile, furious
__inferior -ior -ius__ lower
__infero -ferre intuli illatum__ bring forward, bring in, put in, inter, inflict, inflict on (+ dat); take to (+ dat); (passive) attack, charge
__infestus -a -um__ dangerous, hostile (to), aggressive
__infringo -ingere -egi -actum__ break, crush
__infulcio -cire -si -tum__ push in, cram in
__infundo -undere -udi -usum__ pour on
*__ingenium -(i)i__ (n) natural disposition, person of genius, ingenuity, genius, skill, talent, intellect, wit, clever scheme
*__ingens -entis__ very great, huge
__ingenuus -i__ (m) free-born boy
__ingero -rere -ssi -stum__ shower on
*__ingredior -gredi -gressus sum__ enter, begin, walk
__ingruo -uere -ui__ advance threateningly, bear down, fall on
__Inguiomerus -i__ (m) Inguiomerus (a German chieftain)
__inhibeo -ere -ui -itum__ restrain, check
__inhorresco -escere -ui__ shudder, shake with fear
__inicio -icere -ieci -iectum__ throw (at), place on (+ dat)
__iniectus -us__ (m) the action of placing on top, laying on
*__inimicus -i__ (m) enemy
*__iniquus -a -um__ unfair, harsh, prejudiced
*__initium -(i)i__ (n) beginning, first phase
*__iniuria -ae__ (f) wrong, injustice, attack
__inlacrimo -are -avi -atum__ shed tears, weep, weep over (+ dat)
__inlecebra -ae__ (f) allurement, enticement
__inlicitus -a -um__ unlawful, immoral
__inlido -dere -si -sum__ dash against (+ dat)
__inlino -inere -evi -itum__ smear, coat
__inludo -dere -si -sum__ (+ dat) mock, make sport of
__inlustris -is -e__ distinguished, famous, shining, bright
__inmemor -oris__ forgetting
__inmisceo -scere -scui -xtum__ involve in (+ dat)
*__innocens -entis__ innocent (of)
__innoxius -a -um__ harmless, innocent
__inops -opis__ devoid (of), poor, destitute
__inpedio -ire -i(v)i -itum__ obstruct, impede
*__inpotentia -ae__ (f) lack of self-restraint, imperiousness
__inprecor -ari -atus sum__ invoke for, call down on (+ dat)
__inprovisus -a -um__ unexpected; __ex inproviso__ unexpectedly, suddenly
*__inquam inquis inquit (irregular verb)__ say
__inquies -etis__ restless, in turmoil
__inquieto -are -avi -atum__ disturb
__inrepo -pere -psi__ creep in, penetrate, insinuate oneself
__inritamentum -i__ (n) stimulus, incentive
__inritus -a -um__ useless; __in inritum cadere__ turn out to have no effect
__inrumpo -umpere -upi -uptum__ rush in, force a way in, invade
*__insanio -ire -i(v)i -itum__ rave, be mad
__inscendo -dere -di -sum__ mount
__insector -ari -atus sum__ pursue, harry
__insepultus -a -um__ unburied
__insequor -sequi -secutus sum__ pursue
__insero -erere -evi -itum__ implant, ingrain
__insero -ere -ui -tum__ insert in (+ dat)
__insidiae -arum__ (f pl) ambush, treachery, plot, snare
__insidior -ari -atus sum__ plot, attack treacherously
__insigne -is__ (n) honour, decoration, outward trappings
__insignio -ire -i(v)i -itum__ distinguish
__insignis -is -e__ conspicuous, striking, outstanding, very handsome/beautiful, distinguished
__insisto -ere institi__ set foot on, stand in
__insolitus -a -um__ extraordinary
__insomnium -(i)i__ (n) sleeplessness, insomnia
__inspicio -icere -exi -ectum__ watch, inspect
__instar__ (n) equivalent
__instauro -are -avi -atum__ start afresh, prolong
__instituo -uere -ui -utum__ establish, set up, institute, adopt a practice of (doing something expressed by the infinitive), appoint, instruct
__insto -are -iti__ press (to), be insistent, threaten, be at hand
__instruo -ere -xi -ctum__ equip, furnish, fit out, provide
__insuesco -escere -evi -etum__ become accustomed
*__insula -ae__ (f) island, apartment block
*__insum -esse -fui__ be in
__insumo -ere -psi -ptum__ expend, employ

insuo -uere -ui -utum sew up in
insusurro -are -avi -atum whisper (in someone's ear)
intectus -a -um open, free-spoken
integer -gra -grum intact, undamaged, unchanged, youthful
∗**intellectus -us** (m) comprehension, understanding
∗**intellego -gere -xi -ctum** realize, deduce, understand, have understanding (of), perceive, recognize as existing
intemperans -antis over the top, going too far
intempestive at the wrong time
intendo -dere -di -tum stretch out, intensify, make stronger, set about, decide, point/level (a weapon)
intento -are -avi -atum threaten
intentus -a -um intent (on), attentive, energetic, on the alert (for)
∗**inter** (+acc) among, during, between
intercipio -ipere -epi -eptum kill
intercludo -dere -si -sum block, interrupt
interdiu in the daytime
interdum sometimes, from time to time
∗**interea** meanwhile
∗**intereo -ire -ii -itum** die
∗**interficio -ficere -feci -fectum** kill
intericio -icere -ieci -iactum insert, add
∗**interim** meanwhile
interimo -imere -emi -emptum kill
interior -ior -ius further, more remote
intermitto -ittere -isi -issum discontinue, interrupt
internuntius -(i)i (m) messenger, intermediary
∗**interpono -ponere -posui -positum** interpose, insert, introduce, invite
∗**interrogo -are -avi -atum** ask, interrogate
interstinguo -guere -xi -ctum patch
intersum -esse -fui be present at, attend as an onlooker (+ dat)
∗**intestina -orum** (n pl) intestines, insides
∗**intimus -a -um** intimate, closest
∗**intra** within (+ acc)
intrepidus -a -um undaunted, unperturbed
∗**intro -are -avi -atum** enter, start on
introeo -ire -i(v)i -itum go in, enter
introrsus inland, into the interior
introspicio -icere -exi -ectum look into, understand properly
intueor -eri -itus sum inspect, stare at
intus inside, inwardly
inultus -a -um unpunished, acting with impunity
inundatio -onis (f) flooding
∗**invado -dere -si -sum** come upon, take hold of, attack
invalidus -a -um weak, infirm
∗**invenio -enire -eni -entum** find, discover
invicem mutually, reciprocally, in turn
∗**invictus -a -um** undefeated, invincible
∗**invidia -ae** (f) indignation
invisus -a -um hateful, odious (to), hated
invito -are -avi -atum invite
invoco -are -avi -atum summon, invoke
∗**iocus -i** (m) joke, joking
∗**ipse ipsa ipsum** he himself, she herself, it itself, the actual, the very, in person
∗**ira irae** (f) anger
∗**iracundia -ae** (f) irascibility, anger
irrepo -pere -psi to glide (to/into)
irrumpo -umpere -upi -uptum burst in, rush in
∗**is ea id** this, he, she, it
∗**ita** so, thus, in such a way, in this way, on the condition (that), to such an extent
∗**Italia -ae** (f) Italy
∗**itaque** and so, therefore
item similarly, also
∗**iter itineris** (n) journey, road, street
iterum again, for a second time
iubar -aris (n) radiance, light
∗**iubeo -bere -ssi -ssum** order
iudex -icis (m) judge
iudico -are -avi -atum pronounce, declare
iugulo -are -avi -atum kill (by cutting the throat), slaughter
iugulum -i (n) throat
iugum -i (n) ridge, upper slope
Iulius -ii (m) Julius
iumentum -i (n) pack-animal, animal for carrying baggage
Iuncus -i (m) Juncus
∗**iungo -gere -xi -ctum** join, make to succeed to
Iunius -a -um member of the Junian family
∗**Iuppiter Iovis** (m) Jupiter (king of the gods)
iure with good reason, deservedly
iurgium -(i)i (n) quarrel, abuse
∗**ius iuris** (n) judicial decision, control; **ius dicere** give a decision on a point of law, administer justice
∗**iussum -i** (n) command, order
∗**iussus -us** (m) command; **iussu** on orders, on the command

iustitium -(i)i (n) cessation of public business (at a time of a national calamity)
***iustus -a -um** deserved, lawful, just, justified
Iuvenalia -ium (n pl) Juvenalia (Youth Games)
***iuvenilis -is -e** young, youthful
iuvenis -is -e young
***iuvenis -is** (m) young man
***iuventa -ae** (f) youth
***iuventus -utis** (f) youth, men of military age
iuvo -are iuvi iutum help
***iuxta** (+ acc) near, beside; (adverb) nearby

kalendae -arum (f pl) the Calends (the first day of the month)

L. abbreviation for Lucius (a Roman name)
labefacio -facere -feci -factum cause to totter/collapse
***labo -are -avi** falter, be on the point of collapse
labor -oris (m) labour, work, toil
labor labi lapsus sum drop, collapse, slip away, flow
lacer -era -erum mangled, badly damaged
***lacero -are -avi -atum** mangle, lacerate, rend
***lacrima -ae** (f) tear
lacuna -ae (f) pool, pond
***lacus -us** (m) vat, lake
***laedo -dere -si -sum** injure, hurt
***laetitia -ae** (f) joy, pleasure
***laetor -ari -atus sum** rejoice, be delighted, be fond of (+ abl)
***laetus -a -um** cheerful, happy, pleasurable, successful
***lamenta -orum** (n pl) wailing, groans, laments
***lamentor -ari -atus sum** wail, lament
Lamianus -a -um Lamian (belonging to the Lamiae family)
languesco -escere -i calm down, decline
laniatus -us (m) rending, tearing
laqueus -i (m) noose, loop of rope for strangling
largior -iri -itus sum lavish, give generously
largitio -ionis (f) largess, generosity, bribery, bribe
Largus -i (m) Largus (a Roman name)
***lascivia -ae** (f) playfulness, immorality, wantonness
lascivio -ire -ii -itum be undisciplined, be demoralized
***lascivus -a -um** lascivious, indecent
late over a broad area, extensively
latebra -ae (f) hiding-place
Lateranus -i (m) Lateranus
latericius -a -um built of brick
***Latinus -a -um** Latin
latrina -ae (f) latrine, public lavatory
***latus -eris** (n) side, flank
***latus -a -um** broad, wide, extensive
***laudo -are -avi -atum** praise
***laus laudis** (f) praise
laute sumptuously, elegantly
lavo -are lavi lautum wash, bathe; (reflexive passive) bathe
laxitas -atis (f) spaciousness
lectica -ae (f) litter
lecticarius -(i)i (m) litter-bearer
lectus -i (m) couch, bed
legatio -ionis (f) deputation
legatus -i (m) assistant to general, staff-officer, governor (of a province), envoy, representative
***legio -ionis** (f) legion (a unit of 4,200–6,000 infantry, plus cavalry)
lego -ere legi lectum gather, collect, read
lemniscus -i (m) ribbon (attached to a garland as a sign of honour)
lenio -ire -i(v)i -itum appease, placate
lenis -is -e mild, gentle
lenitas -atis (f) clemency, leniency
leniter gently
lentus -a -um slow
lenunculus -i (m) small boat
Lepida -ae (f) Lepida (Messalina's mother)
***levis -is -e** light, slight, insignificant, modest, thin
levo -are -avi -atum lighten
***lex legis** (f) law, rules
libellus -i (m) note, petition (document containing a request)
***liber libri** (m) book
***liber -era -erum** free
liberalitas -atis (f) generosity, magnanimity
libere frankly, boldly
***liberi -orum** (m pl) children
***liberta -ae** (f) freedwoman (ex-slave)
libertas -atis (f) freedom
***libertus -i** (m) freedman (ex-slave)
***libido -inis** (f) lust, sexual appetite or desire, longing, debauchery, depravity
libo -are -avi -atum sip, reduce slightly
Liburnica -ae (f) Liburnian galley (a fast warship)
licenter without restraint, freely, boldly

*licentia -ae (f) freedom to act as one pleases, lack of restraint, wantonness, licence
liceor -eri -itus sum bid
licet -ere -uit or **-itum est** it is permitted, be allowed
licitatio -ionis (f) bidding, bid
licitus -a -um lawful, legitimate
*__lingua -ae__ (f) tongue, language
liquefacio -facere -feci -factum dissolve
litigator -oris (m) litigant, someone engaged in a lawsuit
littera -ae (f) letter; (plural) letter
*__litus -oris__ (n) shore, coast
Livia -ae (f) Livia (Augustus' wife)
Livilla -ae (f) Livilla (wife of Drusus or sister of Claudius)
Livius -i (m) Livy (Roman historian)
locum -i (n) place, spot, location
*__locus -i__ (m) place, room, location, opportunity, footing
Locusta -ae (f) Locusta (a poisoner)
Lollianus -a -um connected with Lollius
*__longe__ far off
*__longinquus -a -um__ far away
Longinus -i (m) Longinus (husband of Drusilla)
*__longus -a -um__ long, lengthy
*__loquor loqui locutus sum__ speak
Lucrinus -a -um Lucrine (name of a lake near Baiae)
luctuosus -a -um causing grief, unhappy
luctus -us (m) grief
Lucullianus -a -um Lucullan (once belonging to Lucullus)
lucus -i (m) grove
ludibrium -(i)i (n) derision, mockery, an outrage
ludicer -cra -crum theatrical
ludicrum -i (n) show, entertainment
*__ludo -dere -si -sum__ play
*__ludus -i__ (m) sport, jest, school, gladiatorial school; **ludi** games, festival
lugeo -ere luxi luctum mourn
*__lumen -inis__ (n) light, torch
*__Luna -ae__ (f) Moon
lupanar -aris (n) brothel
Lusitania -ae (f) Lusitania (a province, in modern Portugal)
Lusius -i (m) Lusius (a friend of Claudius)
lusus -us (m) playing, game
*__lux lucis__ (f) light, morning light, day
*__luxuria -ae__ (f) extravagance, licentiousness
luxus -us (m) extravagance, luxury, excess, opulence, debauchery
Lygdus -i (m) Lygdus (a slave of Drusus)

machina -ae (f) siege equipment (for hurling boulders etc.), crane, scaffolding
machinamentum -i (n) device, machinery
Macro -onis (m) Macro (a commander of the praetorian guard)
macto -are -avi -atum sacrifice, kill
macula -ae (f) mark
madeo -ere be drunk
maereo -ere be sad, mourn
*__maeror -oris__ (m) sorrow
*__maestus -a -um__ sad, dismal, grim
*__magis__ rather, more
magisterium -(i)i (n) office, post
*__magistratus -us__ (m) a state official, magistrate
*__magnificus -a -um__ magnificent, splendid, grand, lordly, boastful
*__magnitudo -inis__ (f) magnitude, greatness, gravity
*__magnus -a -um__ great, large, important, loud
*__maiestas -atis__ (f) majesty, grandeur, high treason
*__maior -or -us__ greater, louder, rather loud, more intense
maiores -um (m pl) ancestors
mala -ae (f) jaws
male scarcely
maledictum -i (n) insult, taunt
*__malignus -a -um__ spiteful, unkind
*__malo malle malui__ prefer, wish rather
*__malum -i__ (n) trouble, damage, disaster, evil
mancipium -(i)i (n) slave
mando -are -avi -atum send as a message, order
*__maneo -ere -si -sum__ survive, remain
mango -onis (m) slave-dealer
*__manifestus -a -um__ obvious
mano -are -avi leak
mansuetudo -inis (f) clemency
mansuetus -a -um tame, domesticated
*__manus -us__ (f) hand, handiwork, violence, band
marceo -ere be enfeebled, be weak
Marcus -i (m) Marcus (a Roman name)
*__mare -is__ (n) sea
margarita -ae (f) pearl
margaritum -i (n) pearl
maritus -i (m) husband
marmoreus -a -um made of marble

∗**Mars Martis** (m) Mars (god of war)
mas maris (m) male
∗**mater -tris** (f) mother; **mater familias** matron, woman in charge of a household
materia -ae (f) topic, material, occasion
materies -iei (f) reason, grounds
∗**maternus -a -um** of a mother
∗**matrimonium -(i)i** (n) marriage, wife
∗**matrona -ae** (f) matron, married woman
∗**maturus -a -um** mature
Mausoleum -i (n) the Mausoleum (of Augustus)
maxilla -ae (f) jaw
∗**maxime** very much, most, in particular
∗**maximus -a -um** greatest, very great, chief, extreme
Maximus -i (m) Maximus (a Roman name)
∗**medicamen -inis** (n) a healing substance applied to the body, salve, cosmetic, drug
∗**medicamentum -i** (n) medication, remedy, drug, potion
∗**medicus -i** (m) doctor
meditatio -ionis (f) devising, planning
meditor -ari -atus sum contemplate, have in mind, rehearse
∗**medium -ii** (n) the middle (of a period of time)
∗**medius -a -um** middle (of), in the middle
∗**melior -ior -ius** better
∗**membrum -i** (n) limb, organ
∗**memini -inisse** remember (+ gen), recollect, bear in mind, mention
memor -oris mindful of (+gen), remembering
memoria -ae (f) memory, recollection, period, repute
memoro -are -avi -atum state, say, relate, talk about
∗**mens mentis** (f) mind, wits, attitude
mensa -ae (f) table
mensis -is (m) month
meridies -ei (m) midday
meritum -i (n) meritorious action, service
Messalina -ae (f) Messalina (a wife of Claudius)
-met a particle attached to pronouns for emphasis
metallum -i (n) mine, quarry
∗**metuens -entis** apprehensive
∗**metuo -ere -i metutum** fear
∗**metus -us** (m) fear, a source of dread, ground for alarm, threat
∗**meus mea meum** my
mico -are -ui to play mora
∗**miles -itis** (m) soldier
∗**militaris -is -e** military, connected with the army, belonging to a soldier or soldiers
militia -ae (f) military service, fighting
∗**mille** (plural milia) a thousand; **mille passuum** a Roman mile
mimus -i (m) mime, farce
minae -arum (f pl) threats
minax -acis threatening, menacing
∗**Minerva -ae** (f) Minerva (a goddess)
minister -tri (m) servant, assistant, accomplice, agent, one who administers
minitor -ari -atus sum threaten (+ dat)
∗**minor -ari -atus sum** threaten
∗**minor -or -us** smaller, less
minuo -uere -ui -utum reduce
minus less, not very, not properly
minutus -a -um small, slight
∗**miraculum -i** (n) miracle, marvel, wonder, amazement
∗**mirus -a -um** marvellous, astonishing, extraordinary
Misenum -i (n) Misenum (Italian port)
∗**miser -era -erum** poor, wretched
miseratio -ionis (f) pity, compassion
misericordia -ae (f) pity
miseror -ari -atus sum feel sorry, pity
missicius -a -um retired, discharged
missile -is (n) token (for gifts, thrown to the crowd)
mitis -is -e gentle, mild, clement
∗**mitto -ere misi missum** send, send orders that
Mnester -eris (m) Mnester (an actor)
moderor -ari -atus sum use with moderation
∗**modestia -ae** (f) modesty, decency
∗**modestus -a -um** modest, respectable
modicus -a -um moderate, slight, modest, common, mediocre, dim
modo only, recently, now, at one time; **modo. . .modo** at one moment. . .at another moment; **non modo** not only
∗**modus -i** (m) manner, method, way; **in modum** in a manner, after the fashion of
∗**moenia -ium** (n pl) walls
moles -is (f) mass, vast undertaking, heavy responsibility, embankment, piling
molior -iri -itus sum engineer, set in motion, labour at, attempt
molitor -oris (m) contriver
mollio -ire -i(v)i -itum soften, enervate, weaken, tame
mollis -is -e soft, effeminate, homosexual

***moneo -ere -ui -itum** suggest, warn of, warn, caution, advise, tell
monile -is (n) collar
***mons montis** (m) hill, mountain
***monstrum -i** (n) monster
Montanus -i (m) Montanus
monumentum -i (n) record, document
mora -ae (f) delay, stay, postponement
morbus -i (m) illness, disease
***morior mori mortuus sum** die
***mors mortis** (f) death
***mortalis -is** (m) mortal, human
mortalitas -atis (f) mortal existence
mos moris (m) custom, manner; **more** in the manner of, according to the custom of; **mores** morals, character
motus -us (m) movement
moveo -ere movi motum move, wag, go
***mox** soon, next, later on
***muliebris -is -e** female, of a woman; **muliebria** (n pl) private parts
***mulier -eris** (f) woman
***multitudo -inis** (f) crowd, multitude, large numbers
multo by much, much
***multum** much
***multus -a -um** many, large, much
munia (n pl) duties, functions
municipalis -is -e belonging to a small town
municipium -(i)i (n) municipality, town
munificentia -ae (f) generosity, munificence
munimentum -i (n) fortification
munio -ire -i(v)i -itum fortify, protect
***munus -eris** (n) gift, tribute, function, task, gladiatorial show
murmillo -onis (m) gladiator
***murmur -uris** (n) murmur, rumble
***murus -i** (m) wall
***musicus -a -um** musical
***muto -are -avi -atum** change, alter
mutuo to each other
***mutuus -a -um** mutual, reciprocated, felt by both alike

***nam** for
***namque** for
Narcissus -i (m) Narcissus (freedman of Claudius)
naris -is (f) nostril, nose
***narro -are -avi -atum** describe, tell of
***nascor nasci natus sum** be born
natalis -is -e of one's birth, birthday
***natio -ionis** (f) tribe, people, nation
***nativus -a -um** natural
natrix -icis (f) water-snake
***natura -ae** (f) nature, character
naufragium -(i)i (n) shipwreck
***nauta -ae** (m) sailor
***navalis -is -e** belonging to a ship, nautical
navigatio -ionis (f) sailing
navigium -(i)i (n) ship
***navigo -are -avi -atum** sail
***navis -is** (f) ship
***ne** in order that not, that not, for fear that, that
***-ne** particle denoting a question, whether
ne. . .quidem not even
Neapolis -is (f) Naples
***nec** and not, but not, not even; **nec. . .nec** neither. . .nor
necdum and not yet
***necessario** of necessity
***necessarius -a -um** essential, unavoidable
***necessitas -atis** (f) necessity, need, difficulty, straits
neco -are -avi -atum kill, execute
nedum let alone, still more, still less
nefastus -a -um unfit for public business
***nego -are -avi -atum** deny, say not, refuse
negotium -(i)i (n) business, annoyance, activity; **dare negotium** give a commission, issue an order
***nemo -inis** (m) nobody
nemus -oris (n) wood, grove
nepos -otis (m) grandchild
***neque** and not, nor, neither, but not, not even; **neque. . .neque** neither. . .nor
nequeo -ire -i(v)i be unable
Nero -onis (m) Nero (the emperor)
***nescio -ire -i(v)i -itum** not to know
nescioquis -quis -quid someone/something or other
***nescius -a -um** ignorant, unaware
nex necis (f) death, murder
ni if not, unless
***nihil** nothing; (adverbial) in no way, not at all
***nihilum -i** (n) nothing, no amount
***nimius -a -um** excessive
***nisi** if not, unless, except
nisus -us (m) strong muscular effort, advance
nitor niti nisus sum struggle, climb with difficulty, lean, incline
no nare navi swim

∗**nobilis -is -e** of noble birth
∗**nobilitas -atis** (f) nobility of birth, illustriousness, heroism
∗**nocturnus -a -um** nocturnal, of a night, done by night, at night
Nola -ae (f) Nola (a town in Italy)
∗**nomen -inis** (n) name, authority, title
nomenculator -oris (m) page (slave who informed his master of the names of people he met, or announced courses at a feast)
∗**nomino -are -avi -atum** name, mention
∗**non** not
nonagies ninety times
nondum not yet
nonnullus -a -um some
nonnumquam sometimes
∗**nos nostrum/nostri** we, us
∗**nosco -ere novi notum** know, recognize, find out about
∗**noster -tra -trum** our
nota -ae (f) mark
∗**notus -a -um** known, well known, familiar; **notum facio** (+ **dat**) make it known (to someone)
noverca -ae (f) stepmother
novies nine times
novissime finally
novissimus -a -um last, worst, most extreme
∗**novitas -atis** (f) novelty
∗**novus -a -um** new, young, novel, renewed, extraordinary, strange
∗**nox noctis** (f) night
nubes -is (f) cloud
nubo -bere -psi -ptum get married (to), marry
∗**nudus -a -um** naked, bare, devoid of (+ abl)
∗**nullus -a -um** not any, none, no; **(as a noun)** nobody
∗**num** surely not (introduces a question expecting the answer no), whether
Numa -ae (m) Numa (early king of Rome)
numen -inis (n) godhead, divinity, god
numerus -i (m) number, numbers, company
Numida -ae (m) a Numidian
∗**numquam** never
∗**nunc** now, as it is/was; **nunc. . .nunc** at one point. . .at another
nuntio -are -avi -atum announce, report, instruct
nuntius -(i)i (m) message, messenger
nuper recently
nuptiae -arum (f pl) marriage, wedding
nuptialis -is -e nuptial, of marriage, marriage
nurus -us (f) daughter-in-law
nuto -are -avi -atum nod
nutricula -ae (f) nurse
nutrimenta -orum (n pl) upbringing, nurture
nutus -us (m) nod (of command)
∗**Nympha -ae** (f) a Nymph (minor goddess of the countryside)

∗**o** oh
∗**ob** (+ acc) on account of
obdormio -ire -i(v)i -itum fall asleep
obdormisco -ere fall asleep
obeo -ire -i(v)i -itum visit, attend, die
obicio -icere -ieci -iectum throw (to), present (to), expose (to), bring (upon), occasion, charge (with), accuse, put in the way, throw in someone's face, bring something (in acc) as a charge against someone (in dat)
obiectus -us (m) barrier
obiurgo -are -avi -atum reprimand, censure
oblido -dere -si -sum squeeze
oblino -inere -evi -itum smear, cover
∗**oblivio -ionis** (f) forgetfulness
∗**obliviscor -visci -tus sum** forget (+ gen)
obnoxius -a -um subject (to), subservient (to), vulnerable (to)
oboedio -ire -i(v)i -itum (+ dat) be under the control of, obey
obruo -ere -i -tum bury, crush
∗**obsc(a)enus -a -um** indecent, obscene; **obscaena** (n pl) the private parts
∗**obsequium -ii** (n) deference, servility, subservience
observo -are -avi -atum note, pay attention to, show respect to
obses -idis (m) hostage
obsigno -are -avi -atum sign, seal up
obsoletus -a -um faded, dingy
obsonium -(i)i (n) food
obstrepo -ere -ui -itum make a loud noise, shout down
obstringo -ngere -nxi -ctum bind, attach, pledge
obtegens -entis secretive about (+ gen)
obtestor -ari -atus sum assert, insist
obtineo -inere -inui -entum occupy
obversor -ari -atus sum be in front of one's eyes
obviam in the way of, so as to meet
obvius -a -um in the path/way, met, positioned so as to meet
occasio -ionis (f) right moment, opportunity

occido -dere -di -sum kill
occulo -ere -ui -tum conceal
***occulto -are -avi -atum** hide
***occultus -a -um** hidden, concealed, secret
occumbo -mbere -bui meet with (death)
occurro -rrere -rri -rsum meet, oppose, check (+dat)
occursus -us (m) meeting
Oceanus -i (m) Oceanus (the river or sea that flowed around the land masses of the earth, sometimes viewed as a god), sea
octaphoron -i (n) a litter carried by eight bearers
Octavia -ae (f) Octavia (daughter of Claudius and Messalina)
Octavius -i (m) Octavius (father of Augustus)
octavus -a -um eighth
October -bris -bre of October
***oculus -i** (m) eye
***odi -isse osum** hate
***odium -(i)i** (n) hate, hatred
***odor -oris** (m) perfume, spice, smell
offendo -dere -di -sum offend, displease
offero -rre optuli/obtuli oblatum offer, volunteer, provide, put in the way of (+dat), bring forward
officio -icere -eci -ectum be an obstacle to, spoil (+ dat)
officium -(i)i (n) service, act of respect, visit, function, work, duty
offundo -undere -udi -usum fill, overwhelm
olea -ae (f) olive
***olim** for a long time, long ago, formerly
Olympia -ae (f) Olympia (shrine of Jupiter in Greece)
Olympia -orum (n pl) Olympic Games
Olympiacus -a -um Olympic, from the Olympic Games
***omen -inis** (n) omen
ominor -ari -atus sum predict
omitto -ittere -isi -issum let slip
***omnino** altogether, in all, just, at all, in any circumstances
***omnis -is -e** all, entire, every, every conceivable, all possible
***onus -eris** (n) load, mass, bulk, burden
opera -ae (f) job, assistance, effort
operio -ire -ui -tum cover, overwhelm, conceal
opifex -icis (m) workman
opinio -onis (f) opinion, belief
opinor -ari -atus sum believe, imagine
opperior -iri -(i)tus sum wait, wait for, await the outcome of
oppeto -ere -i(v)i -itum die
***oppidum -i** (n) town
oppleo -ere -evi -etum fill up, cover completely
oppono -onere -osui -ositum place in the way of (+ dat)
opportunus -a -um suitable, strategic
opprimo -imere -essi -essum smother, suffocate, destroy
oppugnatio -ionis (f) attack
ops opis (f) wealth
optendo -dere -di -tum spread out, hold out
***optime** very well
***opto -are -avi -atum** desire, pray for
***opus -eris** (n) work; **opus est** (+ abl) there is need of
ora -ae (f) coast
***oratio -onis** (f) speech
***orator -oris** (m) orator, public speaker
***orbis -is** (m) ring; **orbis terrarum** world
orbus -a -um without a child
ordior -diri -sus sum begin
ordo -inis (m) rank
***origo -inis** (f) birth
***orior oriri ortus sum** arise
***ornatus -a -um** richly adorned, magnificent, equipped
***orno -are -avi -atum**, adorn, equip
***oro -are -avi -atum** ask, beg, beg pardon of
***os oris** (n) mouth, face, head, features
***os ossis** (n) bone, stone
osculor -ari -atus sum kiss
osculum -i (n) kiss
ostendo -dere -di -tum show
***ostentatio -ionis** (f) display, exhibition
ostento -are -avi -atum display, testify to, hold out (a prospect)
Ostia -ae (f) Ostia (Rome's port)
Ostiensis -is -e to Ostia
Otho -onis (m) Otho (a friend of Nero)
***otium -(i)i** (n) leisure, holiday

paelex -icis (f) mistress, rival to a wife
***paene** almost
paenitentia -ae (f) regret, change of mind
paenula -ae (f) cloak
palam openly, outwardly
Palatinus -a -um Palatine (name of a hill in Rome)
***palatium -(i)i** (n) palace

Palatium -(i)i (n) the Palatine Hill at Rome, the emperor's residence on the Palatine Hill
Pallas -antis (m) Pallas (freedman of Claudius)
palmula -ae (f) date
Pandataria -iae (f) Pandataria (a small island off the west coast of Italy)
Pandateria -iae (f) same island as Pandataria above
panis -is (m) bread, loaf
Paniscus -i (m) a little Pan (a god of the countryside)
par paris equal, equal to (+ dat), similar
***paratus -a -um** ready (for)
paratus -us (m) furniture, trappings, paraphernalia
***parco -ere peperci** spare, show consideration to, refrain from harming (+ dat)
parcus -a -um frugal, moderate
***parens -entis** (m + f) parent
paries -etis (m) side, wall
pario -ere peperi partum give birth, bring about
pariter alike, at the same time
***paro -are -avi -atum** prepare, prearrange
parricidium -(i)i (n) parricide, matricide, murder of a close relative
***pars partis** (f) part, some, extent, place, role
partus -us (m) foetus; **abigere partum** cause an abortion
parum not enough, not
***passim** all over the place, indiscriminately, in all directions
passus -us (m) step; **mille passuum** a Roman mile
patefacio -facere -feci -factum open; passive = **patefio**
patefio passive of patefacio above
pateo -ere -ui be open, be available, be visible
***pater patris** (m) father, senator
***paternus -a -um** paternal, of a father
patibulum -i (n) gibbet (to which people were fastened)
patientia -ae (f) endurance, hardiness, patience
***patior pati passus sum** endure, submit to
patrator -oris (m) perpetrator
patria -ae (f) fatherland
patro -are -avi -atum bring to completion, finish off, accomplish
patruus -i (m) uncle
patulus -a -um open, not cramped
***paucus -a -um** few
paulatim gradually, little by little
paulo by a little, a little
paulum narrowly
pavefacio -facere -feci -factum terrify, alarm
***paveo -ere** be afraid, be terrified
***pavidus -a -um** frightened, alarmed, fearful
pavo -onis (m) peacock
***pavor -oris** (m) sudden fear, terror, dread
***pax pacis** (f) peace
pectus -oris (n) chest, breast
***pecunia -ae** (f) money, wealth
pedester -tris -tre consisting of infantry
pelagus -i (n) sea, deep sea
pellicio -icere -exi -ectum win over, seduce
pellis -is (f) hide, skin
***pello -ere pepuli pulsum** defeat, repulse, drive away, force open, exile
pelta -ae (f) light shield
penates -ium (m pl) household gods, house
penes in the possession of, among (+ acc)
penetro -are -avi -atum penetrate, get to
penso -are -avi -atum counterbalance, make up for (with)
penuarius -a -um used for the storage of food
***per** (+ acc) through, throughout, over, all over, along, by means of, with, in, on account of, during, according to, by
perago -agere -egi -actum complete
peragro -are -avi -atum travel along
peramoenus -a -um very delightful
percontor -ari -atus sum ask, question
percussor -oris (m) assassin, killer
percutio -tere -ssi -ssum strike, hit
perditus -a -um reckless, abandoned, depraved
***perdo -dere -didi -ditum** lose, destroy
perduro -are -avi -atum hold out, carry on
***pereo -ire -i(v)i -itum** perish, die
pererro -are -avi -atum wander through/over, roam
perfero -ferre -tuli -latum deliver (a message), bring
perficio -icere -eci -ectum accomplish, complete, carry out
perfuga -ae (m) deserter
pergo -gere -rexi -rectum advance, proceed
periclitor -ari -atus sum be in danger
***periculum -i** (n) danger
perinde as much, to an equal degree
peritus -a -um having knowledge
permisceo -scere -scui -xtum bring into association, mingle with, mix with (+ dat)

*__permitto -ittere -isi -issum__ permit, allow, cede
permodicus -a -um very small
permoveo -overe -ovi -otum move violently, stir, incline
perniciabilis -is -e ruinous
pernicies -ei (f) destruction, death
pernotesco -escere -ui become generally known
perodi -odisse -osus sum loathe, detest
perpello -ellere -uli -ulsum induce
perpetro -are -avi -atum bring to completion, fulfil, carry out
*__perpetuo__ for all time, indefinitely
*__perpetuus -a -um__ constant
perrumpo -umpere -upi -uptum penetrate
*__persevero -are -avi -atum__ persist, continue resolutely
persono -are -ui -atum make a loud, continuous noise
perspicio -icere -exi -ectum inspect thoroughly, perceive, recognize
persto -are -iti -atum continue, persist, stand firm
pertinaciter determinedly, stubbornly
*__perturbatus -a -um__ confused, jumbled, alarmed
*__perturbo -are -avi -atum__ confuse, alarm
*__pervado -dere -si -sum__ get through, spread through, make one's way, spread
pervagor -ari -atus sum range over, spread through
perveho -here -xi -ctum carry, convey
pervinco -incere -ici -ictum prevail upon, persuade, gain (an objective)
pervulgo -are -avi -atum make widely known
*__pes pedis__ (m) foot
*__pestilentia -ae__ (f) plague, pestilence
*__peto -ere -i(v)i or -i -itum__ ask for, seek, make for, attack, procure
Phaethon -ontis (m) Phaethon (son of the Sun)
Phaon -ontis (m) Phaon (a freedman of Nero's)
Pharos -i (f) an island off Alexandria, the lighthouse on it
phasiana -ae (f) pheasant
Philippensis -is -e of Philippi (a town in north Greece)
Phoebe -es (f) Phoebe (a freedwoman)
phoenicopterus -i (m) flamingo
piaculum -i (n) means of appeasing, rite of expiation
pictus -a -um coloured
pietas -atis (f) dutiful respect
Pinarius -i (m) Pinarius (a Roman)
pingo -ngere -nxi -ctum paint
pinna -ae (f) feather
pinnatus -a -um winged
placamentum -i (n) appeasement, method of placating
*__placeo -ere -ui/placitus sum__ be pleasing, seem good, be chosen, be decided
*__placidus -a -um__ calm, peaceful
placo -are -avi -atum soothe, appease
Planasia -ae (f) Planasia (an island near Elba)
planctus -us (m) lamentation
plane clearly, quite, absolutely
plango -gere -xi -ctum beat one's breast, mourn
planus -a -um that is on ground level, level
plausor -oris (m) one who applauds, member of a claque
plausus -us (m) applause
Plautii -orum (m pl) men like Plautius (a lover of Messalina)
Plautius -i (m) Plautius
*__plebes -bei__ (f) the people, masses
*__plebs plebis__ (f) the people, masses
plenus -a -um full, well-stocked
plerumque often, generally, largely
plerusque -aque -umque most; (in plural) most, very many
ploratus -us (m) wailing, crying
plumbum -i (n) lead
*__plures -es -a__ more, most
plurifariam in many places, extensively
*__plurimus -a -um__ most, very many
*__plus pluris__ (n) a greater amount, more
*__plus__ (adverb) more
*__poculum -i__ (n) wine-cup, drink
*__poena -ae__ (f) punishment
Poenus -a -um Carthaginian
pollex -icis (m) big toe
polliceor -eri -itus sum promise
polluo -uere -ui -utum defile, violate
Pollux -ucis (m) Pollux (a minor god)
pomifer -era -erum fruit-bearing
pompa -ae (f) procession, array
Pompeianus -a -um a supporter of Pompey
Pompeius -i (m) Pompey (a Roman statesman and soldier), Pompeius (associate of Messalina)
pomum -i (n) fruit
*__pono ponere posui positum__ place, set down, set out, set up, lay aside
*__pons pontis__ (m) bridge

pontifex -icis (m) priest; **pontifex maximus** head priest
poples -itis (m) knee
Poppaea -ae (f) Poppaea (Nero's mistress and later second wife)
popularis -is -e intended to win the support of the people
populor -ari -atus sum plunder, devastate
*__populus -i__ (m) people, nation
porrigo -igere -exi -ectum hold out, offer
*__porta -ae__ (f) gate
portendo -dere -di -tum foreshadow, reveal
portentosus -a -um strange, abnormal, fantastic
*__portentum -i__ (n) monster, portent (= something abnormal foreshadowing some momentous event)
*__porticus -us__ (f) portico, colonnade
*__porto -are -avi -atum__ carry, bring
*__portus -us__ (m) harbour
*__posco -ere poposci__ demand
*__possessor -oris__ (m) owner
*__possum posse potui__ be able
*__post__ (adverb) later, afterwards; (preposition + acc) after
*__postea__ later, subsequently
*__posterior -ior -ius__ hind, rear
*__posteritas -atis__ (f) posterity, descendants
posterus -a -um following, next, future; **in posterum** for the future; (as masculine noun) descendant
postquam after, since, now that
postremo finally
postremum last of all
postremus -a -um last, rear; **ad postremum** finally
*__postulo -are -avi -atum__ ask, ask for, prosecute
Postumus -i (m) Postumus
*__potens -entis__ in control (of), powerful
*__potentia -ae__ (f) power
potio -ionis (f) drink
potionatus -a -um doped
potior -iri -itus sum (+ acc or gen or abl) be/make oneself master of, seize, win sexually, possess
potissimus -a -um chief, foremost
potius rather
poto -are -avi -um drink
potus -us (m) drink
prae (+ abl) under the pressure of, because of
praealtus -a -um very tall
praebeo -ere -ui -itum present, provide, produce
praecalidus -a -um very hot
praecello -ere be superior, be pre-eminent
praeceps -ipitis having an instant effect, instant
praeceptum -i (n) command
praecipio -ipere -epi -eptum order
praecipito -are -avi -atum hurl down, throw to death, throw overboard
praecipue especially
praecipuus -a -um special, exceptional
praeclarus -a -um outstanding, famous
praeco -onis (m) auctioneer
*__praeda -ae__ (f) loot, booty, prize
praedico -are -avi -atum proclaim, declare (as), appoint
praeditus -a -um endowed, invested (with)
praedium -ii (n) estate, landed property
praedulcis -is -e very sweet
praeeo -ire -i(v)i go in front
praefectura -ae (f) command of the praetorian guard
praefectus -i (m) controller, head, commander, officer
*__praefero -ferre -tuli -latum__ carry in front of oneself, exhibit, present
praefervidus -a -um exceedingly hot, burning
praeficio -icere -eci -ectum put in charge of (+ dat)
praegracilis -is -e exceptionally slender
praegravis -is -e extremely troublesome, intolerable
praegredior -di -ssus sum go ahead
praematurus -a -um very early, too early
*__praemitto -ittere -isi -issum__ send on ahead
*__praemium -(i)i__ (n) reward
*__praemoneo -ere -ui -itum__ warn in advance
praemunio -ire -ivi -itum protect in advance
praenuntius -a -um giving advance notice (of), heralding
*__praeparo -are -avi -atum__ prepare, rehearse
praeripio -ipere -ipui -eptum seize first
praesagium -(i)i (n) presentiment, premonition
praescius -a -um aware in advance
praescriptum -i (n) precept, principles
*__praesens -entis__ present, contemporary; **praesentia** (n pl) the present; **ad praesens** for the present
praesepe -is (n) manger, feeding-stall
praesumo -ere -(p)si -ptum consume beforehand
praeter (+acc) apart from, in addition to
praetereo -ire -i(v)i -itum overlook, ignore

praeteritum -i (n) the past
praetextatus -a -um wearing the toga praetexta (i.e. being a boy)
∗**praetor -oris** (m) praetor (a high-ranking Roman magistrate)
∗**praetorianus -a -um** belonging to the praetorian troops (the emperor's bodyguard); (as noun) member of the praetorian guard
∗**praetorium -(i)i** (n) the praetorian guard, large mansion, palace
∗**praetorius -a -um** praetorian, belonging to the emperor's bodyguard, ex-praetor
praevaleo -ere -ui have the upper hand, have superior influence
praevenio -enire -eni -entum anticipate, forestall
prandeo -dere -di -sum eat lunch
prandium -(i)i (n) lunch
∗**precor -ari -atus sum** pray, ask, beg
prelum -i (n) wine-press (apparatus for crushing grapes)
∗**premo -ere pressi pressum** press, crush, repress, hide, arrest the movement of
prenso -are -avi -atum grasp, clasp
∗**pretiosus -a -um** expensive
∗**pretium -(i)i** (n) payment, reward, price
∗**prex precis** (f) prayer, begging letter
pridianus -a -um of the day before
pridie on the day before
∗**primo** at first, first
primordium -(i)i (n) beginning
∗**primum** first, for the first time; **quam primum** as soon as possible
∗**primus -a -um** first, earliest, leading
princeps -ipis first, eminent, distinguished; (as noun) emperor, leader
principatus -us (m) principate, government
prior -ior -ius earlier, first
prius beforehand, earlier, first, sooner
priusquam before
privatus -a -um private; (as noun) a private citizen
∗**pro** (+ abl) on behalf of, for, on, as being, in accordance with
probo -are -avi -atum approve of, commend
probrosus -a -um disgraceful
probrum -i (n) offence, insult
procax -acis wild, lively, frivolous
procedo -dere -ssi -ssum proceed, advance
procella -ae (f) gale
proceres -um (m pl) leading men (of a country)
proceritas -atis (f) tallness
procido -ere -i collapse
proclamo -are -avi -atum declare loudly
∗**proconsul -ulis** (m) proconsul, governor
∗**procul** far off; (as preposition) far from (+ abl)
Proculus -i (m) Proculus
procurator -oris (m) superintendent
procurro -currere -(cu)curri -cursum run out
∗**prodigium -ii** (n) prodigy (an unnatural event portending a disaster etc.)
prodigus -a -um unrestrained, prodigal, extravagant
proditor -oris (m) traitor, informer
prodo -dere -didi -ditum reveal, betray, record
∗**proelior -ari -atus sum** fight
∗**proelium -(i)i** (n) battle, fight
profanus -a -um defiled, sacrilegious
profectio -ionis (f) departure
∗**proficiscor -icisci -ectus sum** set out
profiteor -fiteri -fessus sum claim, declare
profluo -uere -uxi drift, be carried
profugus -a -um fugitive
profundum -i (n) sea
profundus -a -um deep
profusus -a -um immoderate, excessive
progenies -iei (f) offspring, child
progredior -di -ssus sum advance
∗**prohibeo -ere -ui -itum** keep off, exclude, prevent
prolato -are extend, prolong
proloquor -qui -cutus sum declare
∗**prominens -entis** projecting, jutting out
promiscus -a -um public, open to the public
∗**promissum -i** (n) promise
∗**promitto -ittere -isi -issum** promise
promo -mere -mpsi -mptum set forth, point to
promoveo -overe -ovi -otum move forward, extend
promptus -a -um readily inclined (to), eager (for), practical, prompt, quick, easy
pronus -a -um favourable, well-disposed, inclined
propalam openly
prope near, almost, all but
∗**propere** quickly, without delay
∗**propero -are -avi -atum** hasten, cause quickly, inflict hurriedly
∗**properus -a -um** hasty, quick, quick to grasp hold of

propinquo -are -avi come near (to)
propinquus -a -um near, neighbouring, imminent; (as noun) relative
propior -ior -ius nearer
proprius -a -um private, personal, one's own, special (to)
∗**propter** (+ acc) on account of
proripio -ipere -ipui -eptum hurl forth, move rapidly
prorsus thoroughly, absolutely
prorumpo -umpere -upi -uptum rush out, break out
proruo -ere -i -tum overturn, fell, knock over or down
prosequor -qui -cutus sum escort
prosilio -ire -ui leap, rush
∗**prospecto -are -avi -atum** look out on, give a view of
∗**prospectus -us** (m) the ability to see, view, prospect
∗**prosperus -a -um** successful, favourable
∗**prospicio -icere -exi -ectum** look out
prosterno -ernere -ravi -ratum debase, prostitute
prosto -are -iti -itum stand for hire (as a prostitute)
protego -gere -xi -ctum protect
protendo -dere -di -tum stretch out, hold out, present
proturbo -are -avi -atum drive away, dismiss
proveho -here -xi -ctum carry forward
provenio -enire -eni -entum be fruitful
provideo -idere -idi -isum see to, foresee, secure in advance
∗**provincia -ae** (f) province
∗**provincialis -is** (m) inhabitant of a province, a provincial
provoco -are -avi -atum provoke, rouse
provolvo -vere -vi -utum roll forward; (passive) fall down, prostrate oneself
proximus -a -um next, adjacent, nearest; (as noun) close relative or companion
prudens -entis clever, skilled
pubes -is (f) the adult population
∗**publicum -i** (n) the open, public
∗**publicus -a -um** public
pudicitia -ae (f) sexual purity, chastity
pudor -oris (m) shame, source of shame, modesty, decency, restraint
∗**puella -ae** (f) girl
∗**puer -eri** (m) boy
∗**puerilis -is -e** childish, normally inflicted on children
∗**pueritia -ae** (f) boyhood
pugio -onis (m) dagger
∗**pugna -ae** (f) battle
∗**pulcher -chra -chrum** beautiful, handsome, glorious
∗**pulchritudo -inis** (f) beauty
pullus -i (m) chick (as a pet name for a child or young man)
pulsus -us (m) pulse
pulvinar -aris (n) couch for statues of gods, shrine
pulvis -eris (m) dust
∗**punio -ire -i(v)i -itum** punish
pupillus -i (m) ward, a minor under a guardian's care
puppis -is (f) stern
pupus -i (m) boy, child
purgamentum -i (n) rubbish, garbage
purifico -are -avi -atum purify
∗**purpureus -a -um** purple
∗**puto -are -avi -atum** think
∗**putrefacio -acere -eci -actum** cause to rot or decay

quadraginta forty
quadriga -ae (f) chariot-team, group of (four) animals drawing a chariot
quadripes -edis moving on all fours, on all fours
∗**quaero -rere -si(v)i -situm** search for, seek, aim, aim at, obtain, acquire by effort, inquire
quaesitus -a -um elaborate, exquisite
quaestio -ionis (f) examination, interrogation
∗**quaestor -oris** (m) quaestor (a Roman magistrate)
∗**quaestorius -a -um** belonging to a quaestor (Roman magistrate)
∗**qualis -is -e** such as, of such a type that, what a great, what
∗**quam** than, as, how, as much as; **quam primum** as soon as possible
∗**quamquam** although
quamvis although, however much
quando since
quandoque some day
∗**quantus -a -um** how much, as much, how great
quare and so, therefore
quasi as if, as though, on the grounds that, that
quatio -tere -ssum brandish

*quattuor four
*quattuordecim fourteen
*-que and
queo quire qui(v)i be able
querela -ae (f) complaint
queror queri questus sum complain, complain of
questus -us (m) complaint, protest
*qui quae quod who, which, what, what kind of, any
*quia because, on the pretext that
quicumque quaecumque quodcumque any, whoever, whatever
quidam quaedam quoddam a certain, some, a kind of
quidam quaedam quiddam a certain person, someone, a certain thing, something
quidem really, it is true; ne...quidem not even
quidnam why
*quies -etis (f) tranquillity, privacy, quiet, sleep, rest
*quiesco -ere quievi quietum lie down, sleep
*quietus -a -um peaceful, serene
quilibet quaelibet quodlibet any, any at all
quin (adverb) furthermore; (conjunction) so as not to, so as to prevent
quinam quaenam quodnam which, what
Quinquatrus -uum (f pl) the Quinquatrus (a festival of Minerva held in March)
quinquennium -(i)i (n) a period of five years
Quintilius -i (m) Quintilius (a Roman name)
quintus -a -um fifth
Quintus -i (m) Quintus (a Roman name)
quippe for, in fact
quis quis quid anyone, anything, who, what
quisnam quaenam quidnam just who, just what; (neuter) why
quisquam quisquam quicquam anyone
quisque quaeque quidque each, each person, every
quisquis quisquis quidquid whoever, whatever
quivis quaevis quodvis anyone/anything at all
quo to which place, in order that, whereby
quoad until
*quod the fact that, that, because, on the grounds that
quominus so as to prevent
quondam once
quoniam since, because
*quoque also, even
quoquo to any place
*quot how many
*quotiens whenever

Raeti -orum (m pl) the Raeti (a people who lived in the Alps)
ramus -i (m) branch
rana -ae (f) frog
*rapide quickly
*rapidus -a -um fast-working
rapina -ae (f) plunder, pillage
*rapio -ere -ui- tum snatch, seize, carry off, snatch away
raptim hurriedly
raptus -us (m) looting, plunder
*raro rarely, occasionally
rarus -a -um sparse, few, occasional
ratio -ionis (f) reasoning, policy
ratis -is (m) raft
ratus -a -um fulfilled, come true
rea -ae (f) defendant, female on trial
*recedo -dere -ssi -ssum withdraw, retire
*recens -entis recent
recipero -are -avi -atum recover, get back
recipio -ipere -epi -eptum accept, allow, receive, admit, take in
recito -are -avi -atum read out
reclinis -is -e lying back, reclining
reconciliatio -ionis (f) reconciliation
*reddo -ere -idi -itum give back, restore, return
*redeo -ire -ii -itum return
redimo -imere -emi -emptum recover by purchase, ransom
reduco -cere -xi -ctum bring back, lead back
refero -rre rettuli relatum recall, report, tell, mention, count (among), ascribe
reficio -icere -eci -ectum repair
refringo -ingere -egi -actum break open
regia -ae (f) imperial court, palace
regimen -inis (n) steering, control (of a ship)
regio -onis (f) region, district
*regius -a -um royal, done by royalty
*regnum -i (n) monarchy, dominion, political control
*rego -gere -xi -ctum guide, drive, steer
regredior -di -ssus sum return
regulus -i (m) minor king, chieftain
relabor -bi -psus sum flow back, ebb
relego -are -avi -atum banish
religio -onis (f) taboo, impediment due to awe, religious fear, sanctity

∗**relinquo -inquere -iqui -ictum** leave, leave behind, leave untried
∗**reliquiae -arum** (f pl) remains
∗**reliquum -i** (n) remainder
∗**reliquus -a -um** remaining, left, surviving
∗**remedium -(i)i** (n) antidote, remedy, means of counteracting, countermeasure
remex -igis (m) rower
remigium -(i)i (n) oarage, oars, rowing
reminiscor -i remember (+ gen)
remisse light-heartedly, at play
remissus -a -um slack, remiss
∗**remitto -ittere -isi -issum** send back, remit, forgo
remus -i (m) oar
renuntio -are -avi -atum report, reply
∗**reor reri ratus sum** think, deem
∗**reparo -are -avi -atum** replace, restore
repello -ere reppuli repulsum drive back, repulse
rependo -dere -di -sum give as a due, give in payment
repente suddenly
repentinus -a -um acting suddenly, sudden
reperio -ire repperi repertum find, discover, think up
repeto -ere -i(v)i -itum resume, recover
repono -onere -osui -ositus put down, place, put back in, restore
reposco -ere demand back
reprehendo -dere -di -sum catch
reputo -are -avi -atum bear in mind, reflect on, reflect
requiro -rere -si(v)i -situm look for
∗**res rei** (f) thing, situation, activity, state; plural = affairs (of state), state, the world; **res frumentaria** the corn supply; **res publica** the state, Rome, affairs of state
resideo -ere resedi sit (on)
∗**resisto -istere -titi** stop, resist, make a stand, remain in one's place
respecto -are keep on looking round
respergo -gere -si -sum splash, spatter
respicio -icere -exi -ectum look round (at), look around and see
∗**respondeo -dere -di -sum** reply, say in reply
restinguo -guere -xi -ctum extinguish, put out
restringo -ngere -nxi -ctum bind, tie up
resumo -mere -mpsi -mptum pick up again
∗**resurgo -rgere -rrexi -rrectum** rise again, be restored
∗**reticeo -ere -ui** keep silent about (+ acc)
retineo -ere -ui retentum retain, keep, give pause to, catch at
reus rei (m) the person responsible for (+ gen), defendant, culprit
reveho -here -xi -ctum bring back; (passive) ride back
reverto -tere -ti return
revertor -ti -sus sum return
revoco -are -avi -atum recall, restrain
revolvo -vere -vi -utum roll back; (passive) revert, relapse
∗**rex regis** (m) king
Rhenus -i (m) the Rhine (a German river)
rictus -us (m) open mouth
∗**rideo -dere -si -sum** laugh (at)
rigeo -ere be fixed, stare
rigor -oris (m) unbending quality, sternness
ripa -ae (f) river-bank
∗**risus -us** (m) laugh, laughter
rixa -ae (f) brawl, fight
robur -oris (n) strength, might
rogito -are -avi -atum ask frequently
∗**rogo -are -avi -atum** ask, beg
rogus -i (m) funeral pyre
∗**Roma -ae** (f) Rome
∗**Romanus -a -um** Roman; (as noun) a Roman
rubens -entis red
rudis -is -e tender, inexperienced
Rufus -i (m) Rufus
ruina -ae (f) collapse, ruin, ruinous condition
∗**rumor -oris** (m) gossip, rumour, report
∗**rumpo -ere rupi ruptum** break through, break, cancel
∗**ruo -ere -i** rush, collapse
rupes -is (f) cliff, crag
∗**rursum** again
∗**rursus** back, again, a second time, in addition, on the other hand, at other points
Rusticus -i (m) Rusticus (a historian)

Sabina -ae (f) Sabina (a name)
Sabinus -i (m) Sabinus (an assassin of Caligula)
∗**sacer -cra -crum** holy, sacred
sacerdos -otis (m) priest
sacerdotium -ii (n) priesthood
sacrificium -(i)i (n) sacrifice
∗**sacrifico -are -avi -atum** perform a sacrifice
∗**sacrum -i** (n) rite, ceremony
∗**saepe** often
saepio -ire -si -tum surround, flank

*saevio -ire -ii -itum behave savagely
*saevitia -ae (f) savagery, cruelty
*saevus -a -um savage, severe, cruel
sagax -acis perceptive, sharp
sagittarius -(i)i (m) archer
salubritas -atis (f) good health
salutatio -ionis (f) a formal morning call
saluto -are -avi -atum greet
sancio -cire -xi -ctum enact
sanctitas -atis (f) purity, virtue
sane admittedly, really
*sanguis -inis (m) blood, descendant
sarcina -ae (f) baggage
Sardinia -ae (f) Sardinia (an island off Italy)
satio -are -avi -atum satisfy, content
*satis enough, sufficiently, well enough
Saturninus -i (m) Saturninus
saucius -a -um wounded
Saufeius -i (m) Saufeius
*saxum -i (n) rock, cliff, reef
scaena -ae (f) stage, pretence
scando -ere climb, scale
scapha -ae (f) light boat, skiff
*scelus -eris (n) crime, sin
schema ae (f) sexual position
*sciens -entis aware, having knowledge
*scientia -ae (f) knowledge
scilicet of course, doubtless
*scio scire sci(v)i scitum know, know how to (+ infin)
sciscitor -ari -atus sum ask
scopulus -i (m) projecting rock, cliff
scortum -i (n) prostitute
*scribo -bere -psi -ptum write
*scriptor -oris (m) writer, author
*scriptum -i (n) letter
scrobis -is (f) pit, grave
scrutor -ari -atus sum search
*se sui himself, herself, itself, themselves
secessus -us (m) place of retirement
*secreto secretly, in private
*secretum -i (n) seclusion, a private interview
*secretus -a -um secret, private, secluded
secundo -are be favourable
securitas -atis (f) peace of mind, freedom from danger, safety, complacent negligence
*sed but; sed et and what's more
*sedeo -ere sedi sessum sit
*sedes -is (f) centre, seat
seduco -ducere -duxi -ductum take aside
segniter slowly, without energy, without enthusiasm
segnities -ei (f) inertia, inactivity
Seianus -i (m) Sejanus (commander of the praetorian guard under Tiberius)
sella -ae (f) litter
semel once
*semen -inis (n) seed, parentage
semiambustus -a -um half-cremated, charred
semianimis -is -e half-dead, half-alive
semirutus -a -um half-demolished
*semper always
semustus -a -um half-burnt
*senator -oris (m) senator
*senatorius -a -um of senators, senatorial
*senatus -us (m) senate
Seneca -ae (m) Seneca (a chief minister of Nero)
senecta -ae (f) old age
*senectus -utis (f) old age
*senex -is (m) old man
senior -ior -ius older
*sensus -us (m) sensation, sense, consciousness
*sententia -ae (f) decision
*sentio -tire -si -sum perceive, discern, feel
sentis -is (m) thorny bush
sepelio -elire -eli(v)i -ultum bury, inter
*septem seven
septimus -a -um seventh
septuagesimus -a -um seventieth
*sequor -qui -cutus sum follow, ensue
*serio seriously, in earnest
*serius -a -um important, serious
*sermo -onis (m) speech, word(s), conversation
sero too late
serra -ae (f) saw
*servilis -is -e involving slaves, typical of a slave, with a slave, of a slave, ignoble
*servio -ire -i(v)i -itum serve, be a slave to (+ dat)
servitium -(i)i (n) slave
*servus -i (m) slave
*sese himself, herself, itself, themselves
sestertium -ii (n) a hundred thousand sesterces
set but
setius to a lesser degree
seu whether, either, or, or else; seu. . .seu whether. . .or, either. . .or
sexaginta sixty
sextus -a -um sixth
*sexus -us (m) sex, members of one sex or another

∗**si** if
∗**sic** in this way
sicubi if anywhere
sidus -eris (n) star
sigillum -i (n) statuette
signum -i (n) sign, indication, signal, watchword, (military) standard
Silana -ae (f) Silana (wife of Silius)
∗**silentium -(i)i** (n) silence
∗**sileo -ere -ui** be silent
silex -icis (m) flint, hard rock
Silius -ii (m) Silius (a lover of Messalina)
silva -ae (f) forest, wood
simia -ae (f) monkey, ape
∗**similis -is -e** like, similar, similar to (+ dat)
∗**simul** together, at the same time, as well
simulac as soon as
simulacrum -i (n) likeness, mock-up, statue
∗**simulatio -ionis** (f) pretence, play-acting
∗**simulo -are -avi -atum** pretend, feign, make up
∗**sine** (+ abl) without; **sine dubio** without doubt, certainly
singuli -ae -a (plural adjective) each one, individual
sino sinere si(v)i situm leave alone, allow
sinus -us (m) bosom, breast, bay
siquidem since
sisto -ere stiti statum check, stop
situs -a -um situated
sive or, either; **sive. . .sive** whether. . .or, either. . .or
soccus -i (m) slipper
socer -eri (m) father-in-law
socia -ae (f) sharer, associate
societas -atis (f) partnership, complicity
socio -are -avi -atum win over
∗**socius -(i)i** (m) sharer, partner, ally
socordia -ae (f) dullness, lack of alertness
∗**sol solis** (m) sun
∗**solacium -(i)i** (n) consolation, solace
∗**soleo -ere -itus sum** be accustomed
∗**solitudo -inis** (f) solitude, isolation
∗**solitus -a -um** customary, usual, accustomed, normal
solium -(i)i (n) throne
sollemne -is (n) religious ceremony, ritual offering, formality
∗**sollemnis -is -e** solemn, ceremonial, traditional
sollertia -ae (f) cleverness, resourcefulness
solum -i (n) ground, earth
∗**solum** only; **non solum. . .sed etiam** not only. . .but also
∗**solus -a -um** only, alone
solutus -a -um unrestrained, careless, relaxed
solvo -vere -vi -utum perform, relax, loosen, dislodge
∗**somnio -are -avi -atum** dream
∗**somnium -(i)i** (n) dream
∗**somnus -i** (m) sleep
∗**sonitus -us** (m) sound
∗**sonus -i** (m) sound, noise
sorbeo -ere -ui -itum drink up
∗**sordidus -a -um** filthy, shabby, vulgar, degrading
∗**soror -oris** (f) sister
sors sortis (f) lot, fate
sortior -iri -itus sum draw lots, acquire
spado -onis (m) eunuch
spargo -gere -si -sum scatter, sprinkle, strew
spatior -ari -atus sum walk about
spatium -ii (n) interval, period, breadth, width, area, racecourse
species -iei (f) show, semblance, likeness, pretext, pretence
specimen -inis (n) embodiment
∗**spectaculum -i** (n) sight, performance, show, game, entertainment, viewing
spectatus -a -um of known merit, distinguished
∗**specto -are -avi -atum** watch, view, inspect, examine
speculator -oris (m) spy, scout
speculum -i (n) mirror
specus -us (m) cave
∗**sperno -ere sprevi spretum** spurn, reject
∗**spero -are -avi -atum** hope (for)
∗**spes spei** (f) hope, prospect, ambition, promise
Spiculus -i (m) Spiculus (a gladiator)
spiritus -us (m) life, breath, consciousness
spiro -are -avi -atum breathe, be alive
∗**splendidus -a -um** illustrious, distinguished
∗**spolium -ii** (n) spoil, booty
sponte of one's/its/their own accord
Sporus -i (m) Sporus (a boy loved by Nero)
spumo -are -avi -atum froth, slobber
stagnum -i (n) pool, lake
∗**statim** immediately, directly afterwards
statio -ionis (f) body of men, guard
Stator -oris (m) the Stayer (one who halts flight)
∗**statua -ae** (f) statue
statuo -uere -ui -utum decide, set (up)
statura -ae (f) stature, height

stella -ae (f) star
***sterilis -is -e** infertile, barren
***sterilitas -atis** (f) infertility
sterno -ere stravi stratum strew; (passive) throw oneself down
sterto -ere snore
stigma -atis (n) mark of infamy (tattooed with a hot needle on criminals)
***sto stare steti statum** stand, stand to solicit custom (as a prostitute)
***stomachus -i** (m) stomach
strages -is (f) mass, slaughter
stragulum -i (n) blanket, bedclothes
***strangulo -are -avi -atum** strangle
stratum -i (n) bedclothes
strepitus -us (m) noise, uproar, turmoil
strepo -ere -ui -itum yell, howl
***studiosus -a -um** eager, devoted
***studium -(i)i** (n) eagerness, enthusiasm, support, ambition, pursuit, study
***stultus -a -um** stupid
stuprum -i (n) illicit sexual intercourse, rape, incest
***suadeo -dere -si -sum** urge, advise
***sub** (+ acc) just before, at about; (+ abl) under, under cover of
subdo -ere -idi -itum fraudulently introduce/substitute
subeo -ire -i(v)i -itum go under, come over, take on (a task etc.)
subicio -icere -ieci -iectum place at the foot of (+ dat)
subinde repeatedly
subitarius -a -um hastily erected, emergency
***subito** suddenly
***subitus -a -um** sudden
sublevo -are -avi -atum relieve, alleviate
submergo -gere -si -sum sink, capsize
suborno -are -avi -atum instruct, prepare
subscribo -bere -psi -ptum note down
subsellium -(i)i (n) bench
subsidium -(i)i (n) help, support
suburbanum -i (n) place in the country (near Rome)
subveho -here -xi -ctum bring in
subvenio -enire -eni -entum help, give help (to)
subverto -tere -ti -sum topple, take down
succedo -dere -ssi -ssum approach
***successor -oris** (m) successor
***successus -us** (m) success
succlamatio -ionis (f) shout of approval
succumbo -mbere -bui -bitum collapse, break down in health
sudarium -(i)i (n) handkerchief
sudor -oris (m) sweat
suetus -a -um customary, usual
sufficio -icere -eci -ectum be equal to, match (+ dat)
suggredior -gredi -gressus sum approach
Suillius -i (m) Suillius
Sulpicius -i (m) Sulpicius
***sum esse fui** be, exist
summa -ae (f) overall control, completion
summitto -ittere -isi -issum allow to grow long
summoveo -overe -ovi -otum remove, disqualify
***summus -a -um** topmost, highest, upper, crucial, supreme; **summa res** critical situation
***sumo -mere -mpsi -mptum** take, procure, have recourse to, embrace, take up
sumptus -us (m) extravagant expenditure
supellex -ectilis (f) furniture
super (+ acc) over, above, right after, on top of; (+ abl) concerning
superabilis -is -e able to be conquered
superbia -ae (f) arrogance, haughtiness
supergredior -gredi -gressus sum surpass
superinduo -uere -ui -utum put on (over one's other clothes)
***superior -ior -ius** higher
supero -are -avi -atum surpass
superpono -onere -osui -ositum set on top of, put aboard (+ dat)
supersideo -idere -edi -essum sit on (+ dat)
superstes -itis surviving
supersum -esse -fui remain to be done, be a sequel, survive, be additional to the requirements of (+ dat)
supervacuus -a -um superfluous, unnecessary
supervenio -enire -eni -entum turn up, come along as well
***supinus -a -um** lying on one's back
suppleo -ere -evi -etum make up, raise to the full
supplicatio -ionis (f) thanksgiving
supplicium -(i)i (n) punishment, execution
supra (+ acc) more than
***supremus -a -um** final, desperate, critical; (n pl) funeral rites, end of life
***surgo -rgere -rrexi -rrectum** rise, get up
suscipio -ipere -epi -eptum take on, accept
***suspecto -are -avi -atum** suspect

*__suspectus -a -um__ suspected, viewed with mistrust
suspendium -(i)i (n) hanging
suspendo -dere -di -sum hang, suspend, place in a raised position
suspensus -a -um vague, inconclusive
*__suspicio -ionis__ (f) suspicion
*__suspicor -ari -atus sum__ suspect
sustento -are -avi -atum maintain, keep going
*__suus sua suum__ belonging to him(self), her(self), it(self), them(selves); (m pl as noun) a person's dear ones, relatives
symphonia -ae (f) band

tabella -ae (f) a writing-tablet, picture
tabernaculum -i (n) tent
*__tabula -ae__ (f) writing-tablet, panel of wood (used for a painting); (plural) contract, agreement
taeda -ae (f) torch, firebrand
taedium -(i)i (n) weariness, boredom, disgust
taeter -tra -trum horrible, repulsive
*__talis -is -e__ of such a kind, such, the following
*__tam__ so much, so, as much
*__tamen__ however, nevertheless
tamquam as if, that, on the grounds that
*__tandem__ finally
tantopere so much, to such a great degree
tantum -i (n) so much; (as adverb) only
*__tantus -a -um__ so serious, so great, so many
tarde slowly, sluggishly
tardo -are -avi -atum slow down, restrain
taurus -i (m) bull
tectum -i (n) roof, building
Tedius -i (m) Tedius (Roman name)
tego -gere -xi -ctum cover, hide, bury
tegumentum -i (n) blanket
*__telum -i__ (n) weapon
temere recklessly, without due care, without good cause, readily
temperies -iei (f) climate
tempestas -atis (f) storm
tempestivus -a -um early
templum -i (n) temple, shrine
*__tempto -are -avi -atum__ test, attempt, try for, work on, suborn
*__tempus -oris__ (n) time, period, circumstances
*__tempus -oris__ (n) side of the head, temple
temulentus -a -um drunk
*__tenax -acis__ persistent, obstinate
tenebrae -arum (f pl) darkness
*__teneo -ere -ui -tum__ hold, possess, occupy
tenus as far as (+ abl)
ter three times
tergum -i (n) back, skin, hide; **a tergo** from behind; **in tergum** to the rear, behind
*__terra -ae__ (f) land, country, earth
*__terreo -ere -ui -itum__ terrify
*__terrestris -is -e__ living on land, on land
*__terror -oris__ (m) intimidation, terror, something causing terror
tertius -a -um third
*__testamentum -i__ (n) will
testor -ari -atus sum demonstrate, display, declare, affirm
*__theatrum -i__ (n) theatre
thermae -arum (f pl) hot baths
thyrsus -i (m) a thyrsus (rod carried by Bacchantes)
Tiberis -is (m) the Tiber (Rome's river)
Tiberius -(i)i (m) Tiberius (Augustus' successor as emperor)
tibicen -inis (m) pipe-player
Tigellinus -i (m) Tigellinus (a commander of the praetorian guard)
*__timeo -ere -ui__ fear, be afraid of
*__timiditas -atis__ (f) fear, timidity
Titius -i (m) Titius
titubantia -ae (f) stumbling, stammering
titulus -i (m) inscription
*__tolerans -antis__ tolerant (of)
tolero -are -avi -atum support, feed, endure, tolerate
Toranius -ii (m) Toranius (a slave-dealer)
tormentum -i (n) torture
torqueo -quere -si -tum torture
torus -i (m) bed
torvus -a -um grim
*__tot__ so many
totidem as many, the same number
*__totus -a -um__ all, entire
trabeatus -a -um wearing the trabea (dress uniform)
tractus -us (m) dragging, towing
*__trado -dere -didi -ditum__ hand down information, relate, report, hand in, hand over, surrender
*__tragicus -a -um__ of a tragedy
*__tragoedus -i__ (m) actor of tragedy
*__traho -here -xi -ctum__ draw, assign, transform, drag, drag off, drag along, tow, derive, acquire, prolong, take

traicio -icere -ieci -iactum transfix, transport, convey across
tramitto -mittere -misi -missum transfer, hand over, cause to pass through
trano -are -avi -atum swim across
***trans** (+ acc) across
transeo -ire -i(v)i -itum pass, pass by, come to an end
***transfero -ferre -tuli -latum** transfer
***transfiguro -are -avi -atum** change, transform
transfugio -ugere -ugi desert
transgredior -gredi -gressus sum cross, pass
transigo -igere -egi -actum play, act to the end, run through, transfix, pass
transmitto -ittere -isi -issum send across, extend across, pass over in silence, disregard
Traulus -i (m) Traulus
tredecim thirteen
***tremor -oris** (m) tremor, quake
***tremulus -a -um** shaking, tossing
***trepidatio -ionis** (f) confused alarm, perturbation
***trepide** fearfully
***trepido -are -avi -atum** fear, be nervous, be anxious
***tres trium** three
tribunal -alis (n) platform (for addressing troops, passing judgment etc.)
***tribunus -i** (m) tribune (senior army officer)
tribuo -uere -ui -utum grant
triclinium -(i)i (n) dining-room
trierarchus -i (m) captain of a trireme (a ship)
triginta thirty
triremis -is (f) trireme (ship with three banks of oars)
tristitia -ae (f) sadness
***triumphalis -is -e** who won a triumph
***triumpho -are -avi -atum** celebrate a triumph
***triumphus -i** (m) triumph (a victory-parade)
triumviralis -is -e capital
Trogus -i (m) Trogus
Troianus -a -um of Troy
trucido -are -avi -atum slaughter, massacre
***truncus -i** (m) trunk
trux trucis harsh, savage, pitiless
***tu tui** you
tuba -ae (f) trumpet
tueor -eri tuitus sum speak in support of, maintain
***tum** then
tumultuarius -a -um improvised, makeshift
tumultuose with confusion, with alarm
***tumultus -us** (m) fuss, disturbance, uprising, riot
tumulus -i (m) burial-mound, grave, mausoleum, tomb
***tunc** then, at that time
***tunicatus -a -um** wearing a tunic
***turba -ae** (f) crowd
turbidus -a -um wild, stormy, disturbed, disordered
turbo -inis (m) tornado, whirlpool
***turbo -are -avi -atum** disturb, disrupt, throw into confusion
turpis -is -e disgraceful, ignominious, offensive, repulsive
turpiter in an ugly/vulgar way, shamefully
Turranius -i (m) Turranius (a friend of Claudius)
turris -is (f) tower
tuto securely
***tuus -a -um** your

ubertas -atis (f) fertility
***ubi** where, when; **ubi primum** as soon as
ubicumque wherever
ubique everywhere
***ulcerosus -a -um** full of ulcers, covered in sores
***ullus -a -um** any
***ultimus -a -um** last, final
ultio -ionis (f) revenge
ultra any more, longer; (preposition + acc) beyond
ultro unprovoked
umbra -ae (f) ghost
umeo -ere be wet, run
***umerus -i** (m) shoulder
***umquam** ever
una together, at the same time
uncus -i (m) hook
***unda -ae** (f) wave, sea water
***unde** from where, from whom, as a result of which
undevicensimus -a -um nineteenth
***undique** from all sides, from all quarters
unguentum -i (n) perfume
***unicus -a -um** peerless, sole
***universus -a -um** whole, entire; (plural) all without exception
***unus -a -um** one, alone
***urbanus -a -um** of the city, Roman
Urbicus -i (m) Urbicus

∗**urbs urbis** (f) city, Rome
urgeo -ere ursi urge, press, work vigorously
urna -ae (f) urn
usquam anywhere
usque all the way, right up (to), up to the point (of)
∗**usus -us** (m) use, experience, function, purpose
∗**ut** that, with the result that, in order that, as, as if, how, like, when; **ut. . .ita** although. . .yet, like. . .so; **ut qui** as being one who
utensilia -ium (n pl) necessities, food
uter utra utrum which (of two)
uterque utraque utrumque each (of two)
uterus -i (m) womb, uterus
∗**utilitas -atis** (f) advantage, usefulness, interest
∗**utinam** would that! if only! (introducing a wish)
∗**utor uti usus sum** (+ abl) use, employ, wear, exploit, follow, practise
utrimque on both sides
∗**uxor -oris** (f) wife
∗**uxorius -a -um** of a wife

vacuus -a -um unattached, free
vado -ere advance, go
vadum -i (n) a shallow piece of water, a shallow, shoal
vae alas (+ acc = alas for. . .)
vaecordia -ae (f) delusion
vagus -a -um wandering, roaming
Valens -entis (m) Valens (a lover of Messalina)
∗**valeo -ere -ui -itum** be well, have force, be effective; **vale** = farewell, goodbye
valesco -ere establish one's ascendancy, become powerful
valetudo -inis (f) health, illness
valide forcefully, vigorously
validus -a -um strong, in a good state
∗**vallis -is** (f) valley
vallum -i (n) rampart, earthwork with stakes
vanesco -ere fade, vanish
vanitas -atis (f) foolishness, credulity
vapor -oris (m) steam, heat
Varianus -a -um connected with Varus
∗**varietas -atis** (f) variety
∗**varius -a -um** various, of different kinds, variable
Varus -i (m) Varus (a Roman general)
∗**vastus -a -um** huge, desolate, awe-inspiring
vates -is (m) poet
Vaticanus -a -um Vatican (by the Vatican Hill in Rome)
∗**-ve** or
vectigal -alis (n) tax
vehiculum -i (n) vehicle, cart
∗**veho -here -xi -ctum** convey; (passive) sail, be conveyed
∗**vel** or, even
velo -are -avi -atum cover, veil
∗**velocitas -atis** (f) speed
velum -i (n) sail
∗**velut** as if, like
∗**veluti** as if
∗**vena -ae** (f) vein
venatio -ionis (f) animal-hunt (in the arena)
venditio -ionis (f) sale
vendo -ere -idi -itum sell
venefica -ae (f) poisoner
veneficium -(i)i (n) poisoning
venenum -i (n) poison, poisoning
Venerius -a -um sacred to Venus, connected with sex
∗**veneror -ari -atus sum** worship, revere
venia -ae (f) permission, leave (with defining genitive), pardon
∗**venio venire veni ventum** come, arrive
veno for sale
venter -tris (m) bowels, belly
ventito -are -avi -atum go frequently
∗**ventus -i** (m) wind
vepris -is (m) thorn-bush
verber -eris (n) blow, beating, flogging, whip
verbero -are -avi -atum strike, beat
∗**verbum -i** (n) word; **verba facio** speak words
Vergilianus -i (m) Vergilianus
vergo -ere decline, draw to an end
verro -ere versum sweep clean, brush
versicolor -oris of changing colour, iridescent
versus -us (m) verse, line of poetry
vertex -icis (m) head, crown of the head
∗**verto -tere -ti -sum** pass through its cycle, turn, move, subvert, rebound, change course
verum but
∗**verus -a -um** true, consistent with fact, sound, genuine, honest
vescor -i eat, dine
vespere in the evening
Vestalis -is -e of Vesta
vestibulum -i (n) entrance hall, forecourt
vestigium -(i)i (n) trace
∗**vestis -is** (f) clothing, bedclothes, robe

Vettii -orum (m pl) men like Vettius (a lover of Messalina)
Vettius -i (m) Vettius (a lover of Messalina)
***vetus -eris** old, old-time, existing in the past, long-standing
vetustas -atis (f) age, the condition of being old
***vetustus -a -um** long-established, old, ancient
***via ae** (f) street, road, line, way, method
Vibidia -ae (f) Vibidia (a priestess)
vicesimus -a -um twentieth
vicinitas -atis (f) neighbourhood, neighbours
vicinus -a -um nearby, local
***victima -ae** (f) animal offered in sacrifice
***victoria -ae** (f) victory
vicus -i (m) street
***video videre visi visum** see, witness, view; **videor** seem, be deemed, seem good
viduus -a -um without a husband
vigil -ilis (m) member of the watch at Rome
***vigilantia -ae** (f) doing without sleep, vigilance
***vigilia -ae** (f) watch, wakefulness (during the hours of sleep)
***vigilo -are -avi -atum** be awake
vilis -is -e of little importance, cheap, contemptible, inferior, humble
***villa -ae** (f) place in the country, villa
***vincio -cire -xi -ctum** bind, wreath
***vinco -ere vici victum** overcome, prevail upon
***vinc(u)lum -i** (n) chain, rope, bond, tie
Vindelici -orum (m pl) the Vindelici (a people living near the Danube)
vindemia -ae (f) vintage, grape-harvest
vindicta -ae (f) revenge, punishment
vinolentia -ae (f) drunkenness
***vinum -i** (n) wine
***violentia -ae** (f) violence, destructive force
***violentus -a -um** violent, wild
***vir viri** (m) man, husband, soldier
virga -ae (f) rod, stick
***virgo -inis** (f) virgin
***virtus -utis** (f) bravery, virtue, merit
virus -i (n) poison
***vis vis** (f) strength, vigour, force, violence, power, effect, potency, quantity; (plural) **vires** strength
viscus -eris (n) flesh, bowels, entrails
***viso -ere -i** visit, look, view; (passive) be on view
Visurgis -is (m) Visurgis (a river in north Germany)
***visus -us** (m) appearance, aspect, power of sight, gaze
***vita -ae** (f) life
Vitellius -i (m) Vitellius (companion of Claudius)
vitio -are -avi -atum deflower
vitis -is (f) vine
vitium -(i)i (n) vice, failing
vito -are -avi -atum avoid, keep clear of, evade
***vivo -ere vixi victum** be alive, live, live on
***vivus -a -um** alive
***vix** scarcely, with difficulty
vixdum scarcely yet, only just
vocabulum -i (n) name, term, designation
vociferor -ari -atus sum shout, announce loudly
***voco -are -avi -atum** summon, invite, designate, call
***volo velle volui** want, intend
***volucris -is** (f) bird
***voluntarius -a -um** voluntary
***voluptas -atis** (f) pleasure
voluto -are -avi -atum roll; (reflexive passive) roll about, wallow
***vos vestrum/vestri** you (plural)
votum -i (n) wish, desire, vow, prayer
***vox vocis** (f) voice, utterance, words
vulgo -are -avi -atum spread, spread a report, make widely known
***vulgus -i** (n + m) common people, general public, mob
***vulnus -eris** (n) wound, blow
***vultus -us** (m) expression, face, look

Xenophon -ontis (m) Xenophon (Claudius' doctor)